Mexican American Baseball in South Texas

Against the Odds

How times have changed—it's much different now than what it was,
But memories remain, memories of the struggles, memories of the games.
The Hidalgo County Colt League All Stars of 16 players comprised,
Eight players were Mexican Americans and the other eight were white.

They started playing as rivals, as members of opposing teams;
But ended up together, attaining what others only dream.
Most boys were small—all played with heart,
They played the game as if it was an art.

Against the Odds, the team would take the field,
Against other favorite teams they would not yield.
Their hustle, their defense, their quickness and their speed,
Became their trademark, their style of play in time of need.

Finally the time arrived, the World Series began,
For the 16 boys led by the three young men.
To win the Series, four teams aspired,
Defeating all others would be required.

Against the Odds and supported by the hometown crowd,
They gave it all to make their families and hometowns proud.
It would take five games to beat them all,
To win the 1962 World Series of Colt League Baseball.

—Roberto Zamora

A tribute to the team that set aside all differences and together beat the odds.

Front Cover: Francisco "Frank" Maldonado is pictured at the plate playing college baseball at the University of Colorado in 1949. After playing baseball in Brownsville, Maldonado served in World War II. Upon his return to the states in 1946, Maldonado had a tryout with the New York Giants major league baseball team. (Courtesy of Francisco "Frank" Maldonado.)

Cover Background: The 1962 Hidalgo County Colt World Series champions are pictured here. This all-star team comprised of 15 and 16 year olds from Hidalgo County, Texas, won the 1962 Colt World Series in Shawnee, Oklahoma. The boys were a true Cinderella story as they overcame great odds to win it all. (Courtesy of Reynaldo Valadez and Roberto Zamora.)

Back Cover: Pictured is the 1965 Brownsville High School Golden Eagles baseball team. The Golden Eagles were within a hand's reach of the state 4A title but fell short by just one game, making them state finalists. Led by coach Joe Rodríguez, the Golden Eagles were loaded with talent, and several players went on to play college and professional ball. (Courtesy of Charlie Vaughan.)

MEXICAN AMERICAN BASEBALL IN SOUTH TEXAS

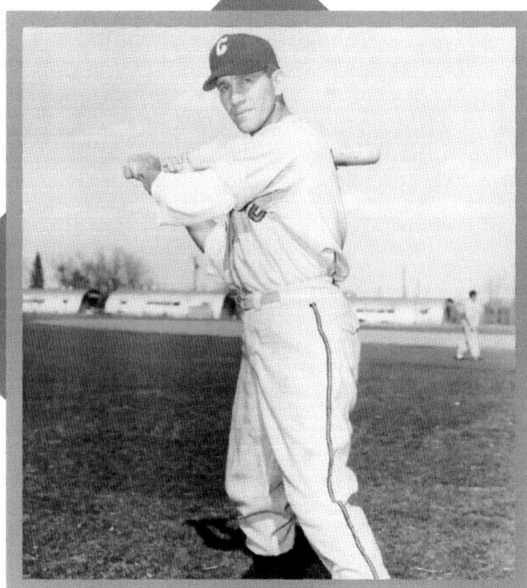

Richard A. Santillán, Gregory Garrett,
Juan D. Coronado, Jorge Iber, and Roberto Zamora
Foreword by Emilio Zamora

ARCADIA PUBLISHING

ISBN 978-1-4671-1664-0

Published by Arcadia Publishing
Charleston, South Carolina

Printed in the United States of America

Library of Congress Control Number: 2016937028

For all general information, please contact Arcadia Publishing:
Telephone 843-853-2070
Fax 843-853-0044
E-mail sales@arcadiapublishing.com
For customer service and orders:
Toll-Free 1-888-313-2665

Visit us on the Internet at www.arcadiapublishing.com

To my three grandchildren, Alec, Román, and Rhiannon, who all played ball, and to my wife, Teresa, who has been the best teammate in my life.
—Richard

To my best friend and love of my life, Kimberly Kelley; babe, without you there is no me. Also to the baseball gods who have chosen me as a vessel.
—Gregory

Para mis padres, David and Joséfina S. Coronado; para mi hermana Yesenia Coronado y su esposo, Leonel Pulido Jr.; and especially for my wife, Ana V. Satterfield, who patiently endured throughout all the baseball meetings; and finally, for all the ballplayers, who dreamed on the diamond in the Rio Grande Valley.
—Juan

To Raquel and Matthew, who are always on my team, even when studying baseball (and other sports) distracts me from what really matters in life, thank you both for your love and support. Also, to three great mentors, colleagues, and dear friends, Dr. Sam Regalado, Dr. Arnoldo De León, and Dr. Richard A. Santillán, thank you for your help and guidance over the years.
—Jorge

To my wife, Angélica, for instilling God's love in our family, and to my children and grandchildren for being a daily reminder of the many blessings the Lord provides us.
—Roberto

CONTENTS

FOREWORD

Although my father would tell me of excelling in sprint races in Matamoros in the late 1930s, I had never seen him participate in organized sports until around 1960, when young and middle aged men would gather on Sundays to play *beisbol* in a deserted meadow that they converted into a playing field. I remember that my dad, a well-respected member of our community—La Feria—loved the game and received the most applause when he approached the batter's box, although he would only occasionally hit the hardball past the infield. I will always associate baseball with my father, especially his enthusiasm for the game, and the approbation that he received from his community (in large part because our small store, Zamora's Meat and Market, co-sponsored the games).

My early exposure to community baseball also involved games with teams from other parts of the Rio Grande Valley. Consequently, I learned early on that baseball in the spring brought Mexican Americans together from all over town and other places who would not otherwise congregate and enjoy each other's company. Baseball, in other words, reflected and reinforced community and its long welcoming reach inside and beyond my small town.

The game had a prior history and also continued past the 1960s, as the present volume demonstrates. It had become the community's favorite pastime by the end of the Second World War. Baseball also went beyond an informal community activity; it took more serious turns, as when some teams assumed semi-professional and professional status. By the late 1980s and early 1990s, Mexican Americans had made sufficient strides in the social and political realms of South Texas that they could devote more time to the home-grown activity and the baseball city leagues that they established. Like our store, Mexican American businesses continued sponsoring most of the teams while older, experienced, and able players assumed the responsibility of training and coaching the teams.

Clearly, baseball gave expression and meaning to our communities. For me, this meaningful pastime also continues as memory, especially in my wonderful remembrance of my father and my community in some of their happiest moments. I can now also understand how the joy of playing and seeing the game served as a welcome respite from the daily burden of discrimination and inequality. As such, this book is a fitting tribute to the generations that played and viewed the game and a sensitive contribution to an important part of the Mexican American historical experience. I commend the authors for their important work.

Professor Emilio Zamora
Department of History
University of Texas at Austin

ACKNOWLEDGMENTS

The foundation of this project to publicize the rich history of Mexican American baseball and softball in South Texas is due to the remarkable work of the Latino Baseball History Project at California State University, San Bernardino (CSUSB). Others who supported this effort include the following individuals and staff at the CSUSB's John M. Pfau Library: Dean Cesar Caballero and Sue Caballero, Jill Vassilakos-Long (head of archives and special collections), Iwona Contreras, Ericka Saucedo, Amina Romero, Carrie Lowe, Manny Veron, Brandy Montoya, Hayley Parke, John Baumann, and Stacy Magtedanz.

The authors are indebted to the players and families who provided the treasures of photographs and extraordinary oral histories. These dedicated individuals and groups include coach Francisco "Cisco" Estévis and his brother Vicente Estévis, Charlie Vaughan, Pikey Rodríguez, Jim Caldwell, Gary West, Francisco "Frank" Maldonado, coach Joe Rodríguez, Jack Bloomfield, coach Al Ogletree, Manuel Hinojosa, Mo Molina, Eddie Martínez, Jesse Alañiz, Bert Lozono, José Mario Cavazos, the Valadez family, Gloria Guerra Ayala, Evangelina Garza, Rene Torres, Fred Ramos, Juan de la Rosa, José Omar Rivera, Fidencio López Jr., Humberto Barrera, Dr. Rumaldo Z. Juárez, Cruz C. Torres, Darcy Meyer, Ray Loya, Bobby Recendez, the Salazar family, Rod Martínez, Maggie Salazar Guzmán, Ron González, Gabriel and Jody López, Phyllis Pérez, Isabel Ramírez, Andy Gutiérrez, Gene Chávez, Tony Solíz, Rick Salas, Michael D. Innis-Jiménez, Frank Jacinto, Christine Marín, Pete López, the Molina family, José Garza, Pedro Seañez, Greg Seañez, Richard Seañez, Alfonso Aguilar, Hank Carrillo, Gil Terrones, Bob Lagunas, Jess Badillo Jr., Carlos and Mike Salazar, Gabe Peña, Patricia Castro, Fred Martínez, Dr. Rubén Martínez, Elida Garza Alañiz, the Julian Samora Research Institute at Michigan State University, the Leo Najo Oldtimers Baseball Committee, Rio Grande Valley Sports Hall of Fame, Lower Rio Valley Collection at the University of Texas–Pan American, Southwest Chicago Project, Las Señoras of Yesteryear, the Robstown Area Historical Museum, and all the military veterans who contributed to our fourth chapter and our freedom. Thanks to all of you for your service.

We recognize again our in-house editor Elisa Grajeda-Urmston for her extraordinary and professional work, and our utmost gratitude goes to our technical consultant Monse Segura. Last but not least, our heartfelt appreciation to Arcadia Publishing and to our remarkable and patient editors, Jeff Ruetsche and Jim Kempert.

INTRODUCTION

Sitting on the southernmost tip of Texas and bordering the state of Tamaulipas, México, is the Rio Grande Valley. Comprising the valley are Cameron, Willacy, Hidalgo, and Starr Counties, with Hidalgo and Cameron being more densely populated. At the time of the Texas Revolution in 1836, the region was disputed by both the Republic of Texas and Mexico. After military occupation, the Mexican-American War, and finally the Treaty of Guadalupe Hidalgo, the territory officially became part of the United States. For the next several decades, South Texas had a strong military presence especially during and after the Civil War. Generally recognized as the last battle of the American Civil War, the Battle of Palmito Ranch was fought east of Brownsville, Texas, between the Union army and the Confederate army.

It was long believed that Gen. Abner Doubleday invented baseball during the Mexican-American War while he was stationed at Fort Brown in what has become the present-day city of Brownsville. Today, baseball historians and experts have come to the realization that the Doubleday theory is a myth, and that he did not invent the game. Whether baseball was introduced to South Texas during the Mexican-American War is debatable. Local historians and sportswriters Rene Torres and Pikey Rodríguez have spent countless hours researching and piecing together that lost history.

The earliest written evidence that could be found of baseball in South Texas comes from an 1868 Christmas Day match between the Rio Grande Club of Brownsville and their neighboring team from across the river, Union Club de Matamoros. On a box score that reads more like the results of a football game, the Mexican squad defeated the Texans 49-32. The lineups that day included names such as García, Medrano, Cavazos, Evans, Mason, and Schreck. Interestingly, it was the Mexican club whose lineup included both Anglo and Spanish surnames.

This would not be the last of these types of matchups. For the next hundred years, baseball expanded throughout the region, and baseball clubs from either side of the border traveled across the river for challenging outings that often turned into friendly rivalries. Hence, baseball in the Rio Grande Valley became one of the first social activities to bridge the cultural divide and temporarily blur ethnic barriers. The sport became, in many ways, a focal point and a fundamental component of the social fabric that influenced the development of South Texas. Baseball transcended physical and geographical borders that divided the two nations and two cultures. Yet, much like the evolution of the game itself, culture and society in South Texas uniquely developed as it fused into a bicultural Rio Grande Valley identity.

1

UPPER VALLEY

Being primarily an agricultural region, the large majority of the Mexican American population in South Texas was historically employed as laborers in ranching, farming, or both. After long days of intense labor, young children, adolescents, and adults found time to partake in America's pastime. At the time, baseball was the most popular sport in the country, and players from South Texas dreamed of making it to the Major Leagues. Few Mexican Americans played in the Major Leagues then; hence, the road to the top had its challenges. Whether they played ball in an actual ballpark or on an imaginary diamond laid out in the unscathed rural sector (or as many Mexican Americans say, "*En el a labor*"), South Texans played with passion—they played for the love of the game.

By the 1950s, baseball grew tremendously in the Rio Grande Valley. Local ballparks were inundated with enthusiastic fans cheering for their favorite teams. Among the most loyal aficionados were family members and friends, who attended games from Little League all the way to the semiprofessional level

The impact of the great Leonardo "Leo Najo" Alanis, who was drafted by the Chicago White Sox in 1925, resounded not only in his hometown of Mission, Texas, but also in the surrounding communities of McAllen, Pharr, Edinburg, Donna, Weslaco, Harlingen, Brownsville, Mercedes, Edcouch-Elsa, Peñitas, Abram, and Los Ebanos. Semiprofessional baseball had a cult following, as Sunday matinees were regularly enjoyed and youngsters dreamed of one day representing their local teams. Others, of course, dreamed of following in Leo Najo's footsteps, and they did, as a number of young men were offered Major League contracts.

In Mission, Leo Najo, along with Bernardo Peña, José Carreon Garza, and other ballplayers, founded the Mission 30-30 Rifles; Edinburg had the Merchants, which then became the Joe Davis Ginners; McAllen had the Palms; the Merchants represented Pharr; the Donna Cardinals were very popular. The small communities outside of Mission also had teams, such as the Madero Valley Brickers and the Granjeno Lions. In Edinburg, Ramón Cantu, after serving in World War II, began to organize sandlot baseball. He recognized the tremendous talent that existed throughout the entire Rio Grande Valley and organized semiprofessional baseball. Cantu, along with others such as Pánfilo Ávila, Pete Lerma, Leo Najo, and Bernardo Peña, served as promoters of the sport in their respective communities.

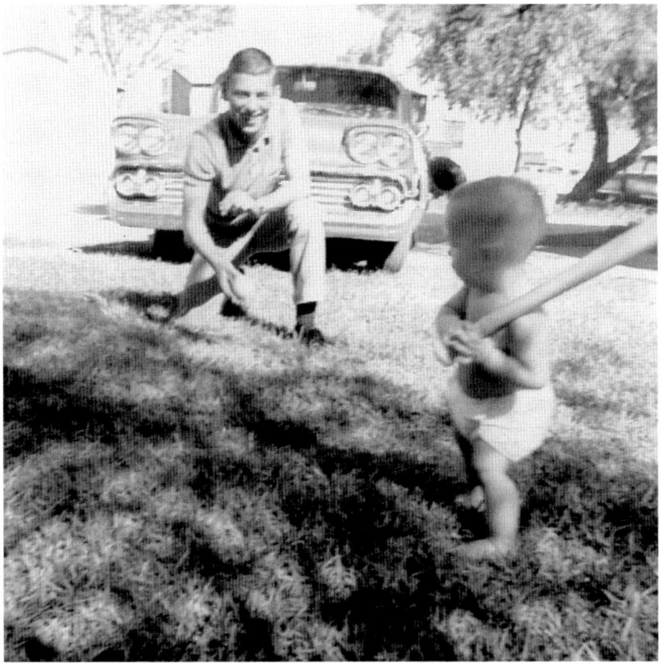

Edinburg ballplayer Jack Williams is seen introducing the coach's son Rubén Ayala Jr. to some of his first baseball action. Rubén Ayala Sr. served the community in numerous capacities, including setting time aside to coaching baseball. Rubén Jr. would go on to play baseball in his hometown of Edinburg in high school for the Bobcats and at Pan American College for the Broncs. Jack Williams went on to participate in the 1962 Hidalgo County Colt League World Series championship team. (Courtesy of Gloria Guerra Ayala.)

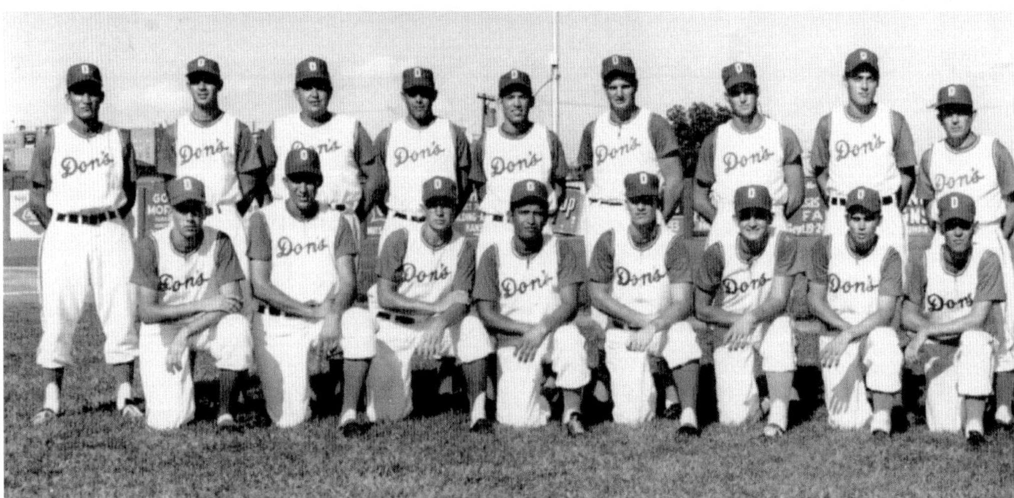

Semiprofessional baseball became extremely popular in the Rio Grande Valley. Baseball teams expanded throughout towns, as community after community wanted to showcase their talents. The McAllen Dons featured future Major Leaguer Ted Uhlaender and Major League prospect Camilo Estévis. Also playing for the Dons was football standout R.C. "Fito" Flores, who went on to play at the University of Colorado. This is a photograph of the McAllen Dons semiprofessional team around 1959–1960. Standing on the far left in the second row is Mike Maldonado, and standing next to him is Pancho Cavazos from Mission. Standing third and second from right are R.C. Flores and future Major Leaguer Ted Uhlaender. Kneeling second from left is Camilo Estévis, a future draftee of the Los Angeles Dodgers. This team was loaded with talent. (Courtesy of Vicente and Francisco Estévis.)

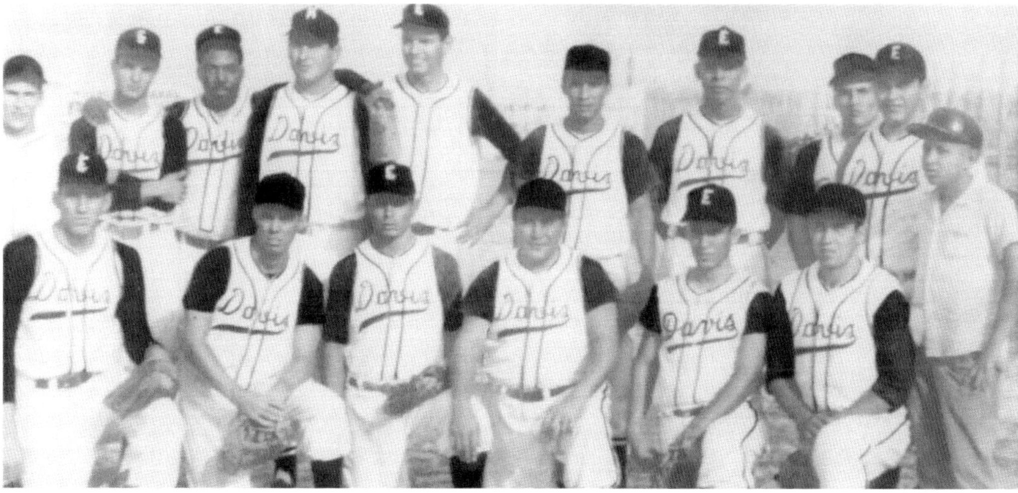

The Edinburg Joe Davis Ginners state playoff team is pictured in 1963. The origin of the Ginners goes back to 1946, when World War II veteran Ramón O. Cantu began to organize sandlot ball among his friends in Edinburg. That year, the Edinburg Merchants, a semiprofessional team, was born. From 1954 to 1966, the team became known as the Edinburg Joe Davis Ginners. Even though the sponsorship changed hands, Cantu remained a central figure. Among the shining stars who suited up for the Ginners were Major League scout and Japanese League professional Jack Bloomfield, coach Joe Rodríguez, Camilo and Francisco Estévis, and Lupe Salinas. The Los Angeles Dodgers signed Camilo Estévis to a contract. (Courtesy of Vicente and Francisco Estévis.)

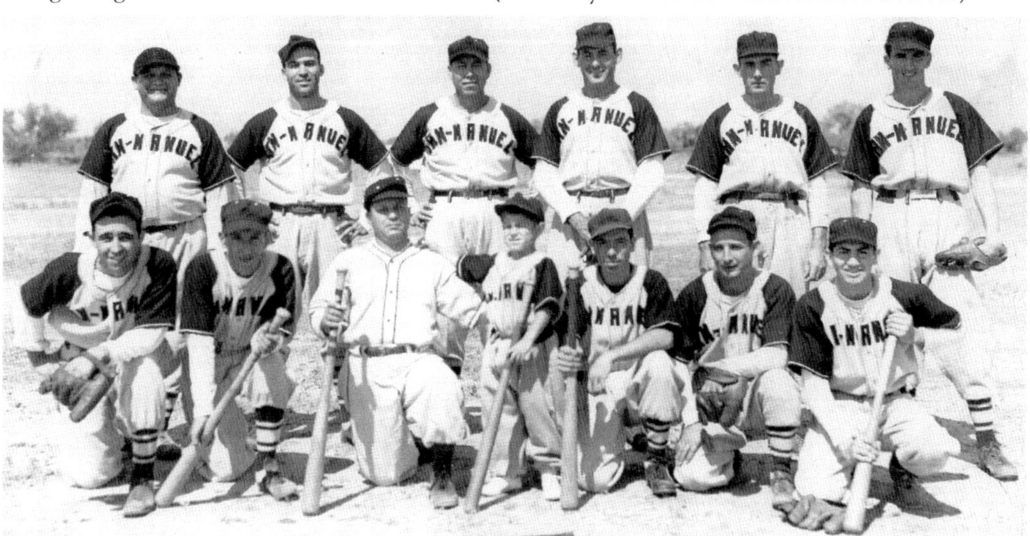

In the 1940s, baseball served as one of the few forms of leisure and entertainment in the rural community of San Manuel–Linn. Primarily known for its ranching and agriculture, laborers made time for the sport. It was common to see Sunday matinees as players gathered for an exciting outing. The manager for the squad was local entrepreneur Adolfo "Shorty" Guerra (first row, third from left), who, along with his two other brothers, owned Chorizo de San Manuel and Guerra's Country Club. (Courtesy of Gloria Guerra Ayala.)

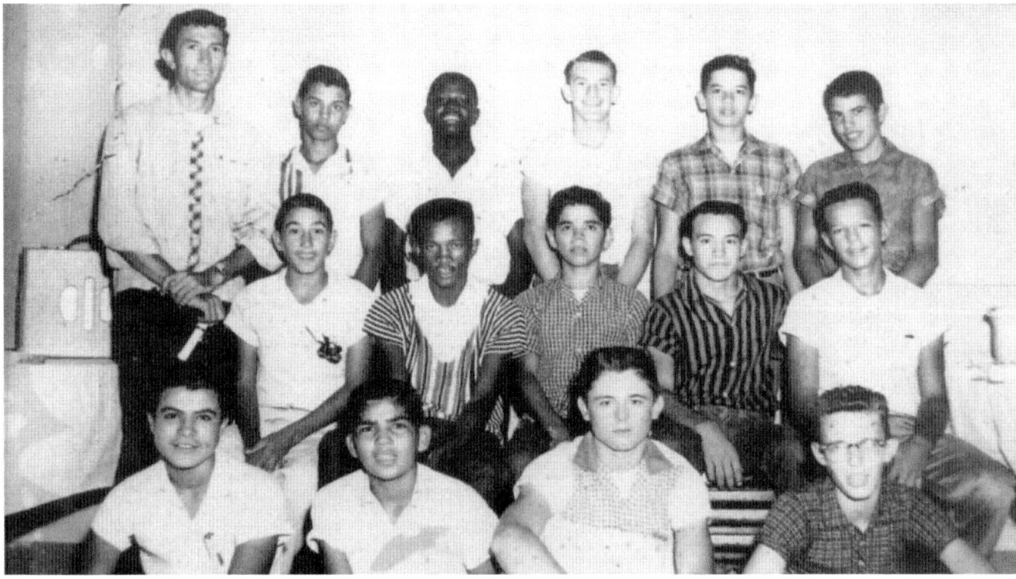

In South Texas in the 1950s, baseball served as an avenue for social and racial unification. During that time, there was a sizable African American presence in South Texas. In Edinburg, the African American community lived in the east part of town by Nineteenth Street and Van Week. Gary West and James (T-Bone) Heliton (not pictured) were among the African American students taught by Melissa Dotson Betts at the George Washington Carver School, which served the African American community in Edinburg from 1938 to 1961. While social and racial barriers existed, baseball tore down some of them through unity on the diamond. (Courtesy of Vicente and Francisco Estévis.)

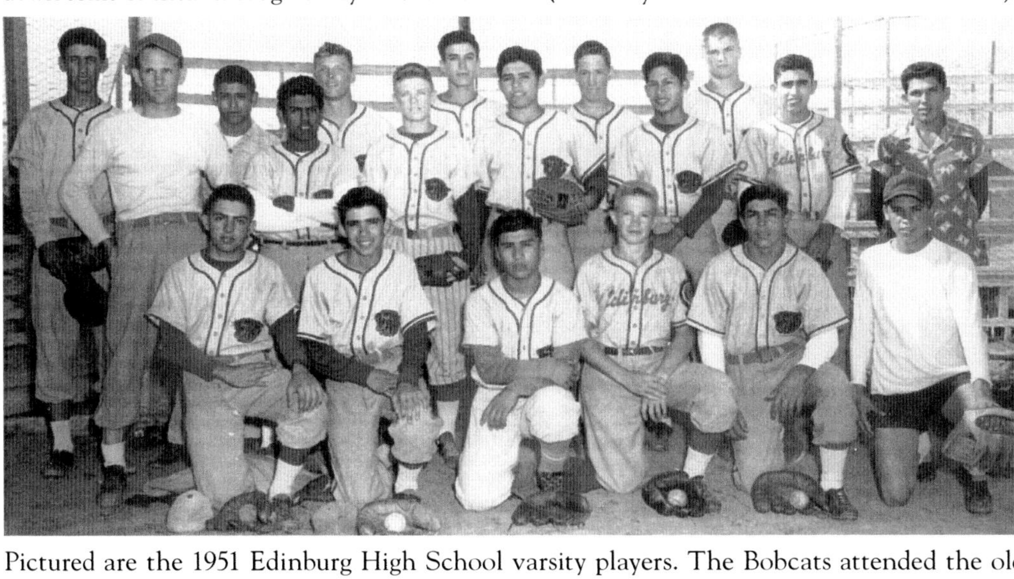

Pictured are the 1951 Edinburg High School varsity players. The Bobcats attended the old Edinburg High School, which went on to become the "old" Edinburg North Junior High School and now serves as the administration building for the Edinburg Consolidated Independent School District. Loaded with talent, this team went on to win the District 16 AA championship that year. (Courtesy of Vicente and Francisco Estévis.)

The Mission 30-30 Rifles baseball club was founded by former professional Leo Najo; Bernardo Peña and his teammates became one of the better-known semiprofessional teams in the region. José Carreón Garza, an avid hunter from Peñitas, came up with the name. Here, Mayor Logan Duncan (far right) prepares to throw the first pitch on opening day at 30-30 field in the summer of 1947. The stadium was built under the leadership of Matías Cavazos (third from right) and was supported by community leaders, who eventually owned shares in the park. Later, Leo Najo bought out the stockholders and became the sole owner. (Courtesy of José Mario Cavazos.)

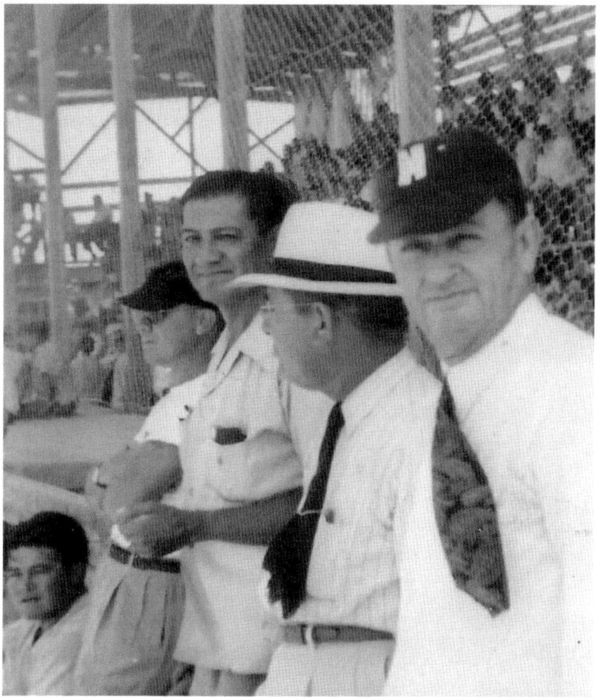

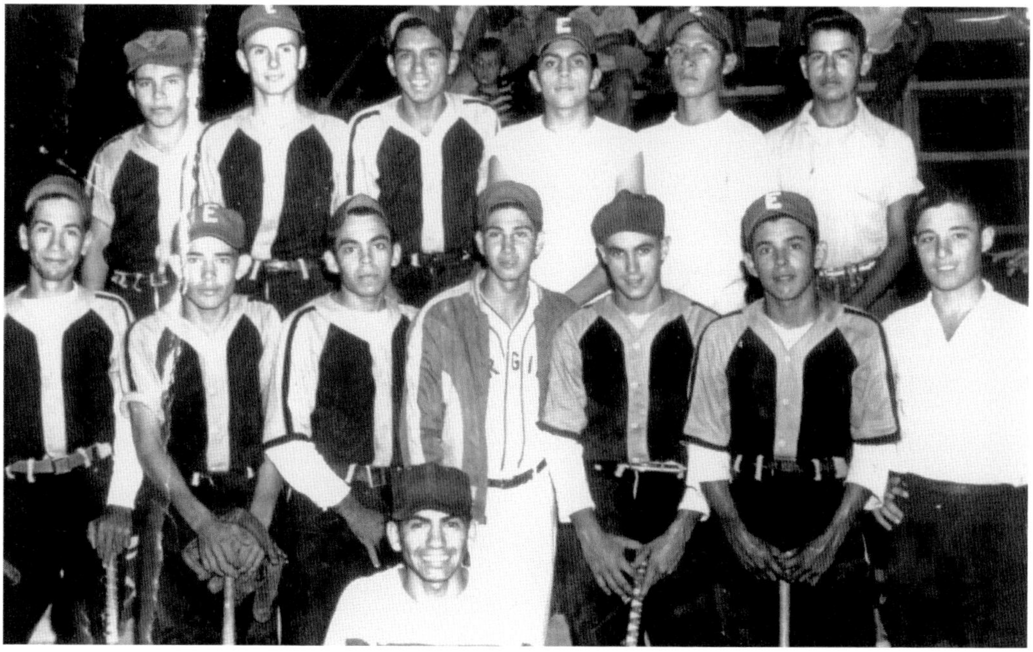

This 1951–1952 picture shows the Edinburg High School varsity baseball team. The Bobcats won District 16 AA that year. In the third row are, from left to right, Modesto Blanco, A. Garza, Camilo Estévis, unidentified, Francisco Estévis, and unidentified. Many of the ballplayers went on to play college and semiprofessional baseball. Camilo Estévis went on to play professionally and was signed by the Los Angeles Dodgers. (Courtesy of Vicente and Francisco Estévis.)

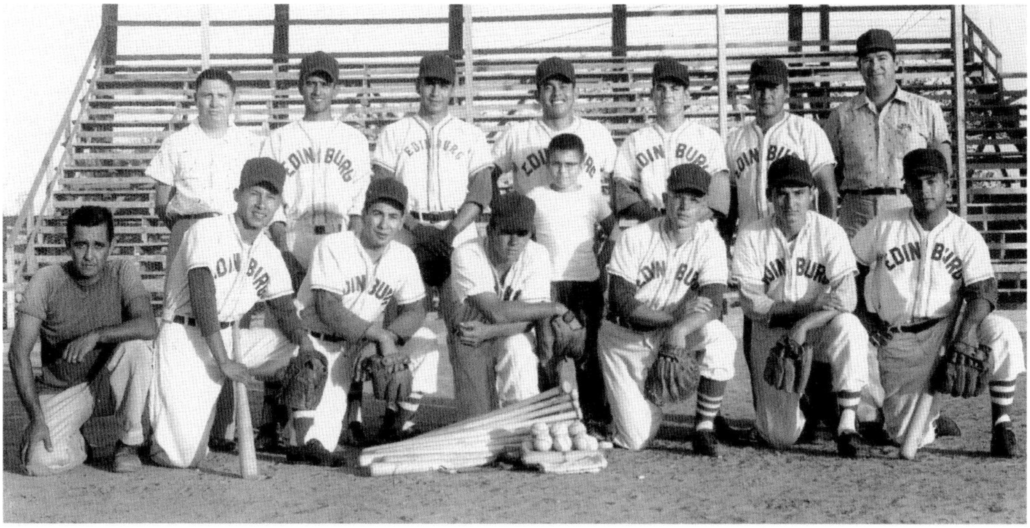

Among those pictured are Isaac Garza, Leo Garza, David Mosqueda, Lauro Guerra, Ramón Cantu, Pete de la Garza, Oscar Díaz, Francisco Estévis, Baltazar Salazar, Jimmy Green, Pablo Pérez, and Joe Alex Vela. Ramón Cantu served as a promoter/organizer of the Ginners. The Ginners played against teams from McAllen, Pharr, Mission, and the surrounding communities. They were an exceptional team that competed for state titles. Despite the team changing sponsors, Cantu remained a central figure with the club and took them to compete throughout the state and in Mexico. (Courtesy of Vicente and Francisco Estévis.)

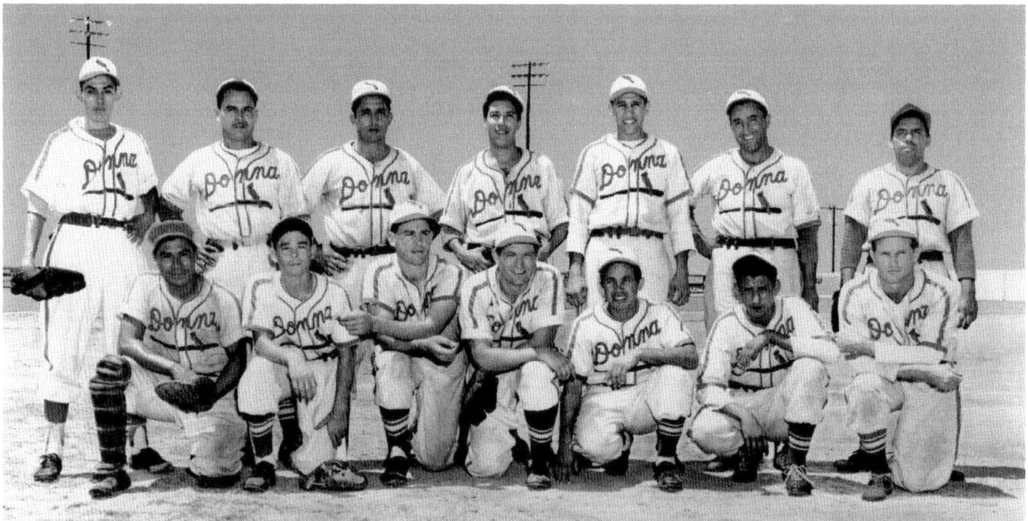

The 1957 Donna Cardinals were an outstanding team with a strong pitching staff, an excellent defense, and a powerful lineup of hitters. From left to right are (first row) "Chino" López; unidentified batboy; Ray Stewart, third base; Jeff Stewart, right field; Hector Casas, left field; ? Rodríguez, pitcher; and Mitch Bloomfield, second base; (second row) Lefty Sánchez, pitcher; Tomas Villa Gomez, pitcher; Amadeo Lozano; ? Reza, shortstop; Frank Maldonado, first base; Simon Saenz, centerfield; and Lefty Ríos, pitcher. (Courtesy of Francisco Maldonado.)

During a baseball tournament in San Antonio, a group of South Texas boys decided to do some sightseeing and visited the historical Alamo. The 200-plus mile journey brought the Valley boys into an urban setting that was different from home. However, they did not shy away from the competition and proved that the Rio Grande Valley could compete in these larger settings. For several of the boys, this was their first time traveling out of deep South Texas. Today, both boys' and girls' teams from the Valley compete in the Alamo City and beyond, carrying a rich legacy. Among those pictured here are Ramon Estévis, Francisco Estévis, and Rubén Lozado. (Courtesy of Vicente and Francisco Estévis.)

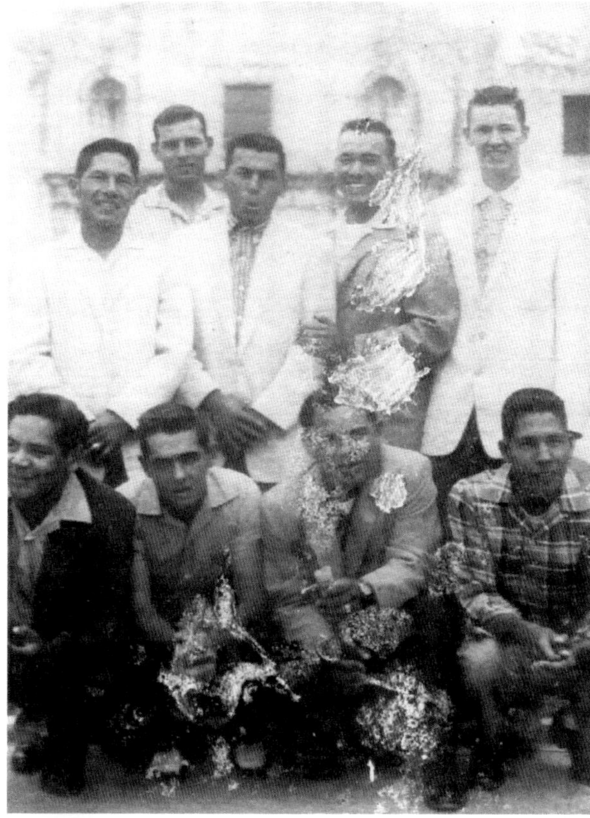

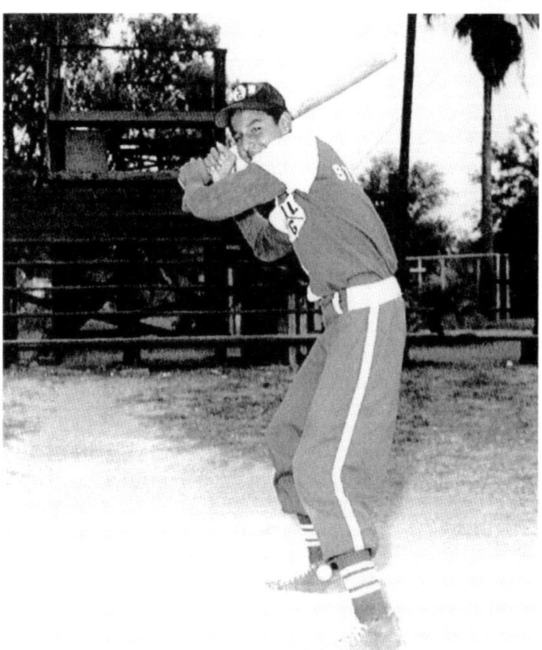

Fernando "Zapata" Rivera Jr. is pictured playing softball for Our Lady of Guadalupe Catholic School in Mission in 1955. He had the potential of pitching at the highest level; however, like many young men at the time, his priorities were to the family farm where his hands and arms were needed more. Rivera went on to serve in the US Army during the Berlin Crisis in 1961. Upon his return, he worked for a tractor implement company for 54 years. (Courtesy of Omar Rivera.)

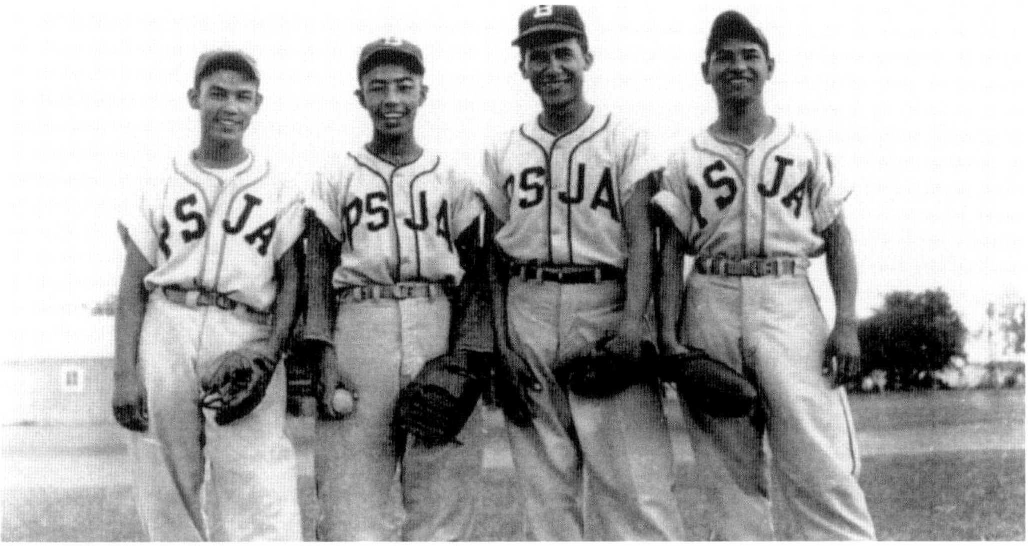

The 1952 Pharr–San Juan–Alamo (PSJA) High School Bears varsity baseball squad featured tremendous talent, including (from left to right) Mario Alañiz, Mario Gómez, Hipo Pruneda, and Lupe Abrego. Several players played college baseball for the Pan American College Broncs, and they all continued to play semiprofessional baseball. (Courtesy of Vicente and Francisco Estévis.)

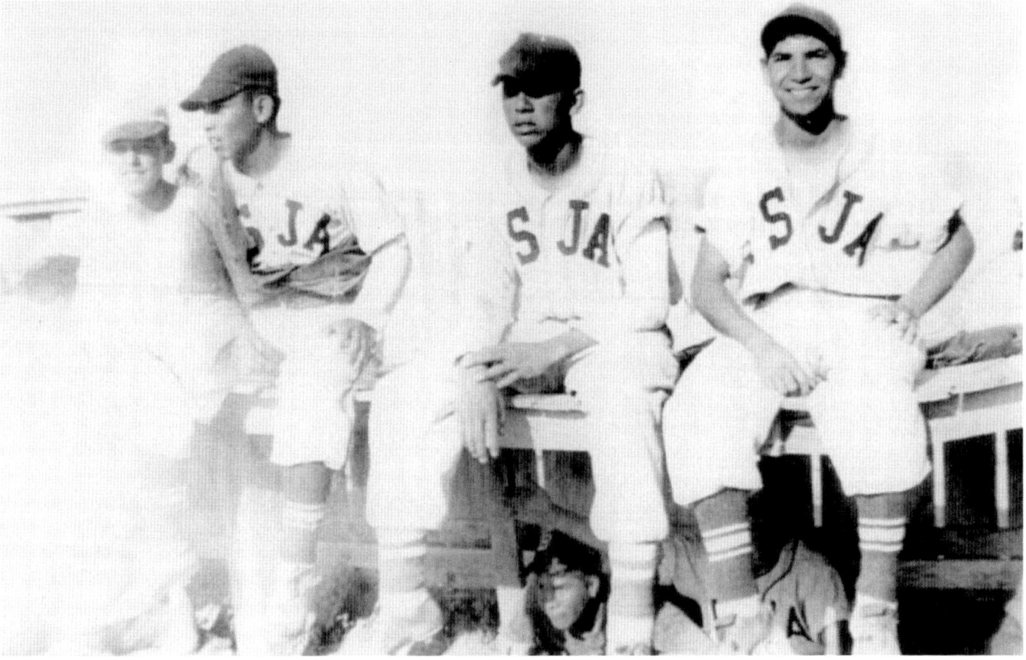

The 1951 PSJA High School Bears varsity squad featured Alonzo Sáenz, Fide Martínez, Mano Arcaute, and Lupe Abrego. The three neighboring towns along Highway 83 are connected by the highway and railroad, and also by a tradition of unity. Up to the early 1990s, the three communities shared one high school. Now over five high schools serve the PSJA School District. (Courtesy of Vicente and Francisco Estévis.)

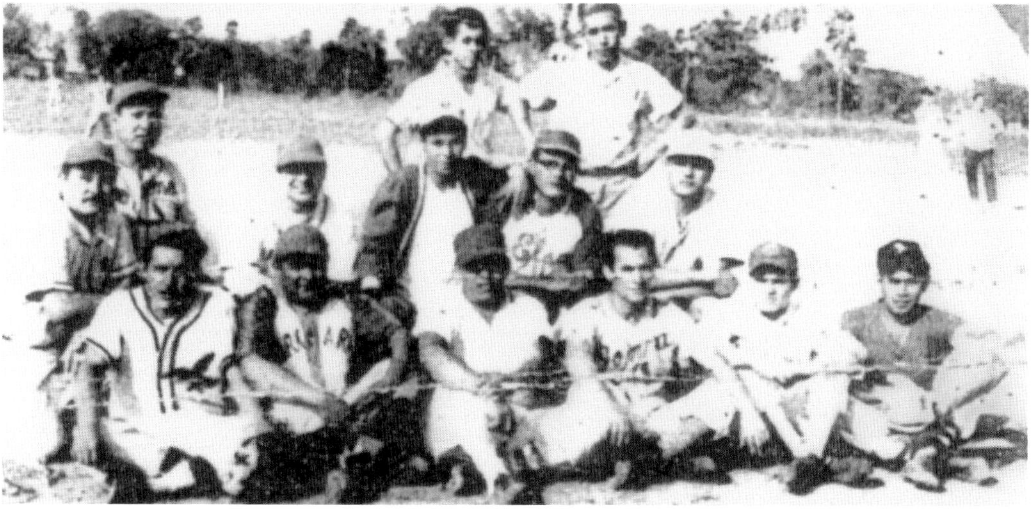

Pictured here are the 1958 Alamo Wildcats. From left to right are (first row) Artemio Robles, unidentified, Geronimo Nuñez, Solomon Villagomez, Guerrero? and unidentified; (second row) Ramon "El Aquacat" Hernandez, Rudy Uresti, Amador Guerrero, Tomas Villagomez, and Trino Farias; (third row) Severo Salinas and Crespin Rendon. (Courtesy of Vicente and Francisco Estévis.)

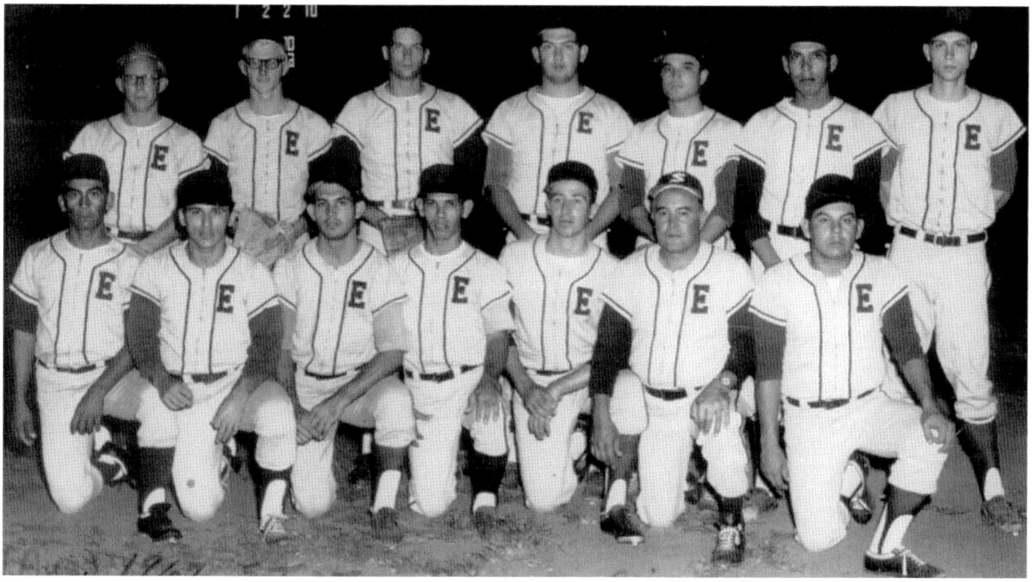

In August 1967, the National Baseball Congress Championship at Lubbock, Texas, tournament took place. This 1967 photograph shows the semiprofessional Salazar Grocery team of Edinburg, Texas. The team won the state championship in Lubbock that year. Under their former name, the Edinburg Davis Ginners, they had previously won the championship in 1963. Known as Mr. Baseball, Ramón Cantu, a local bookkeeper and owner of a Texaco Service Station, was active in putting a team together. (Courtesy of Vicente and Francisco Estévis.)

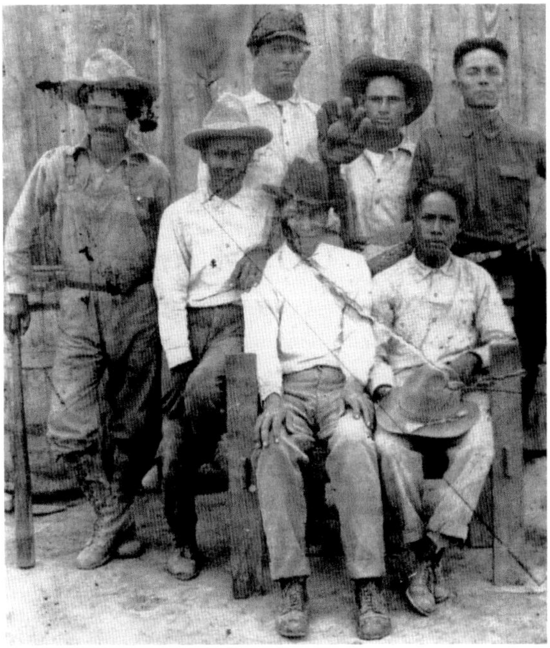

Pictured here are old-timers around 1918–1920. Brothers Francisco Estévis Sr. and Tomas Estévis played baseball along the Military Highway near the Rio Grande. Games such as this one were known as *el partido de la garra*, or pick-up sandlot ball. These were usually played after long days of work. (Courtesy of Vicente and Francisco Estévis.)

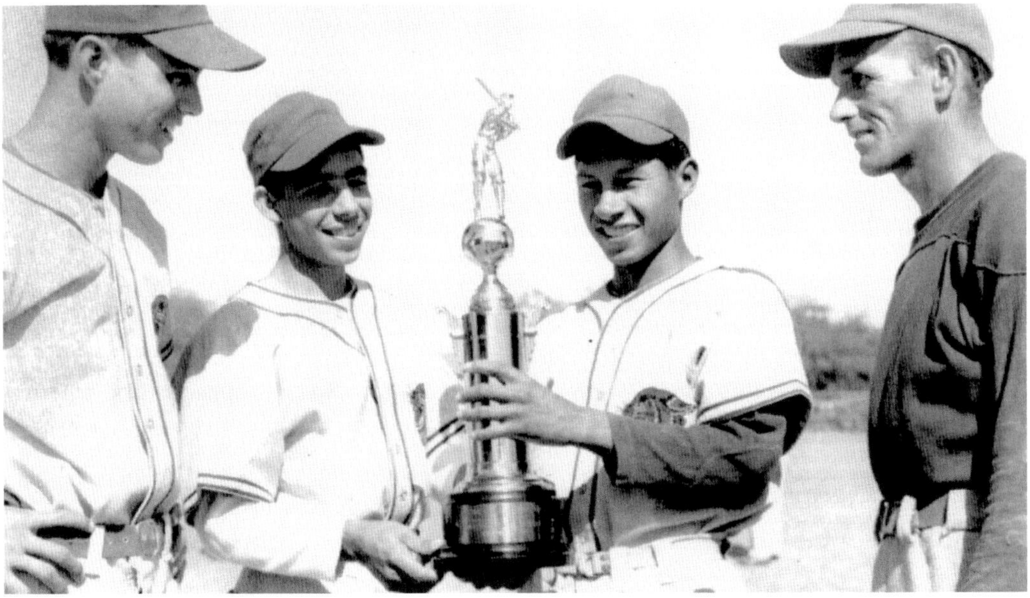

This is the 1952 Edinburg Bobcats varsity baseball team. After winning District 16 AA, the Bobcats faced the "Mighty" Mission Eagles, who dominated Single A ball. Both teams met for this trophy, and Francisco "Cisco" Estévis (holding trophy) claimed it for the victorious Bobcats. Estévis dueled it out against Reynaldo "Rey" Valadez (not pictured). After winning District 16 AA, Estévis, who was no longer eligible to pitch during his senior year of high school due to exceeding the age limit, went on to pitch for the Pan American Broncs while still in high school. Fellow rival Valadez, who faced a similar eligibility situation, ended up being Cisco's teammate with the Broncs. (Courtesy of Vicente and Francisco Estévis.)

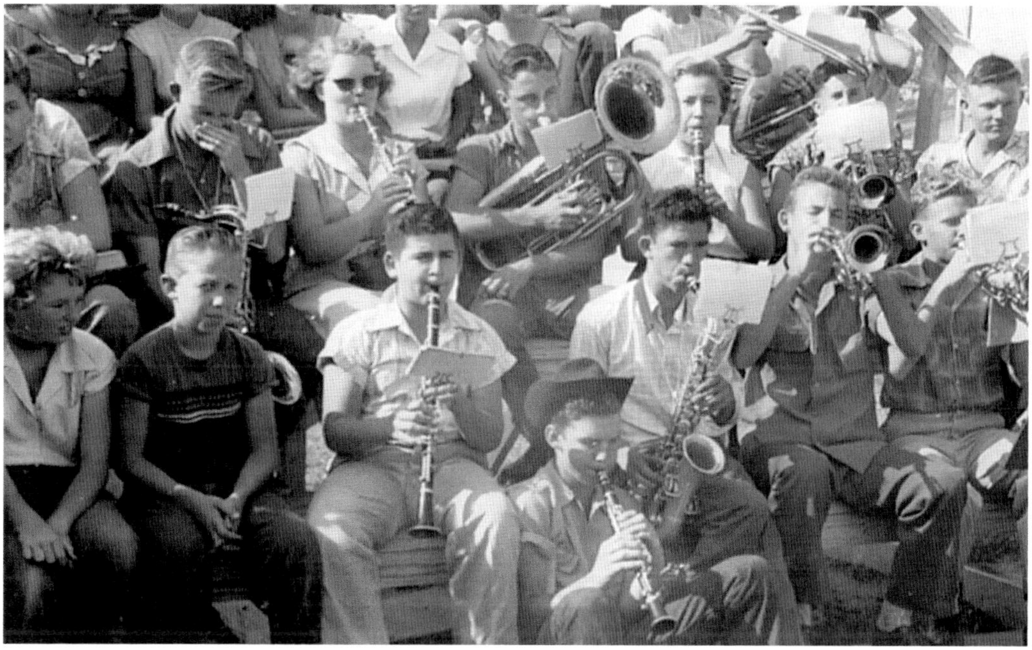

The band performed at the "old" Edinburg High School in the late 1940s to early 1950s. The field is now used during the spring as a practice field for local Little League teams. (Courtesy of Vicente and Francisco Estévis.)

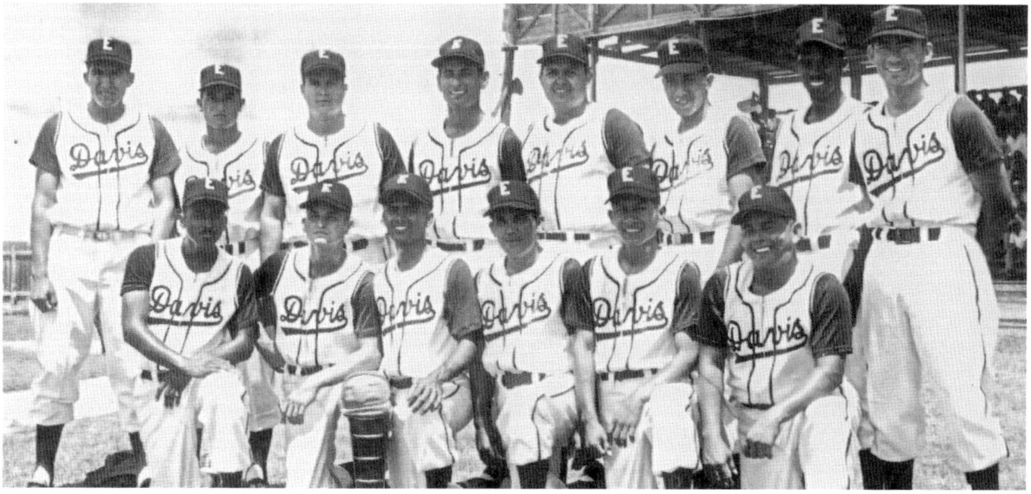

Here are the 1958–1959 Edinburg Joe Davis Ginners. Standing at far left is Camilo Estévis. Standing third from right is Vicente Estévis, and kneeling second from right is Francisco Estévis. The three brothers have remained very close to baseball. Camilo was signed by the Los Angeles Dodgers and played with their affiliates. After playing baseball in the military, Vicente played semiprofessional ball in South Texas. Francisco played at Pan American College and then attended New Mexico Highlands University, where he worked for his former coach Dr. John Donnelly. Coach Donnelly recruited a good number of ballplayers from South Texas to play at New Mexico Highlands. Francisco went on to coach baseball at various levels. (Courtesy of Vicente and Francisco Estévis.)

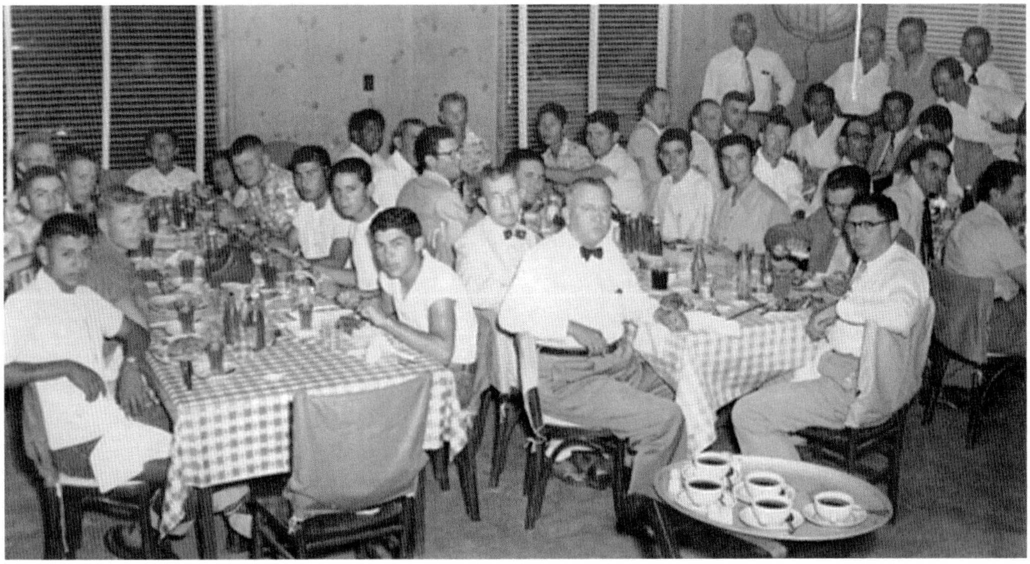

Dinner Time! Ballplayers, coaches, organizers, and community members come together and break bread after a long day of baseball. (Courtesy of Vicente and Francisco Estévis.)

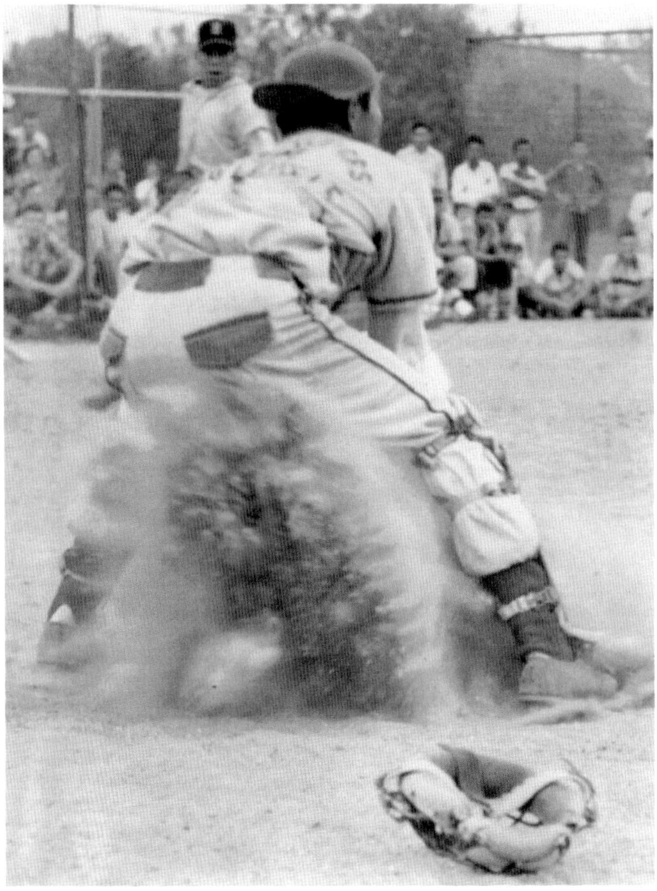

Hustle Plays! In a highly contested game between the Brownsville High School Golden Eagles and Edinburg High School Bobcats, neither side pulled any punches. As the Edinburg runner slides into home, it is a close call. Every at-bat proved to be vital, and the two rivals locked horns and tried to make the most of it. These boys played for the love and passion of the game. (Courtesy of Vicente and Francisco Estévis.)

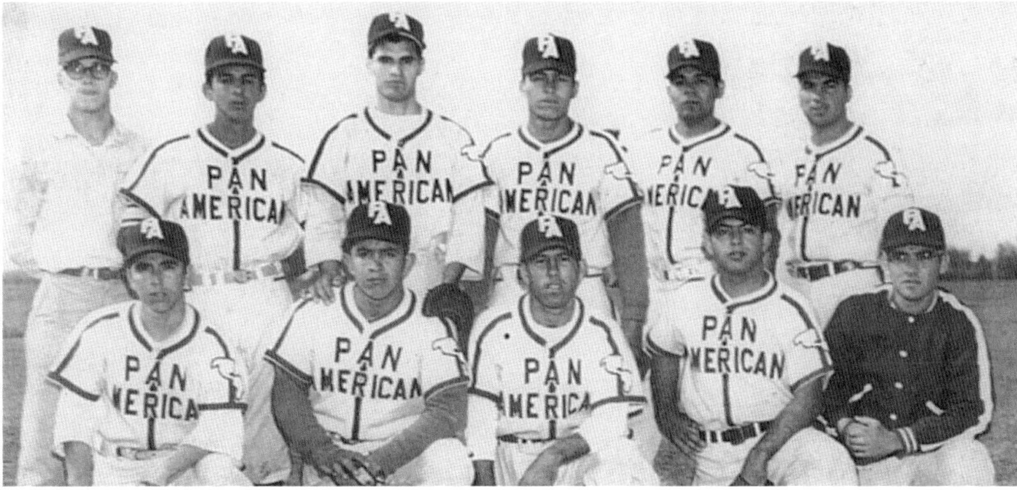

This c. 1955 photograph shows, from left to right, (first row) Alejos, Davis, Sauceda, Vela, and De León; (second row) Rand, González, Vento, Farias, Alemán, and Palacios. Refugio "Cookie" Alejos from Mission played with Pan American College from 1955 to 1958. Alejos played semiprofessional baseball and remained close to the game for the rest of his life. He also was an active member of the Leo Najo Hall of Fame Baseball Committee and served as a distinguished officer. The committee is responsible for holding an annual banquet commemorating baseball in South Texas and inducting new members to its hall of fame. (Courtesy of Vicente and Francisco Estévis.)

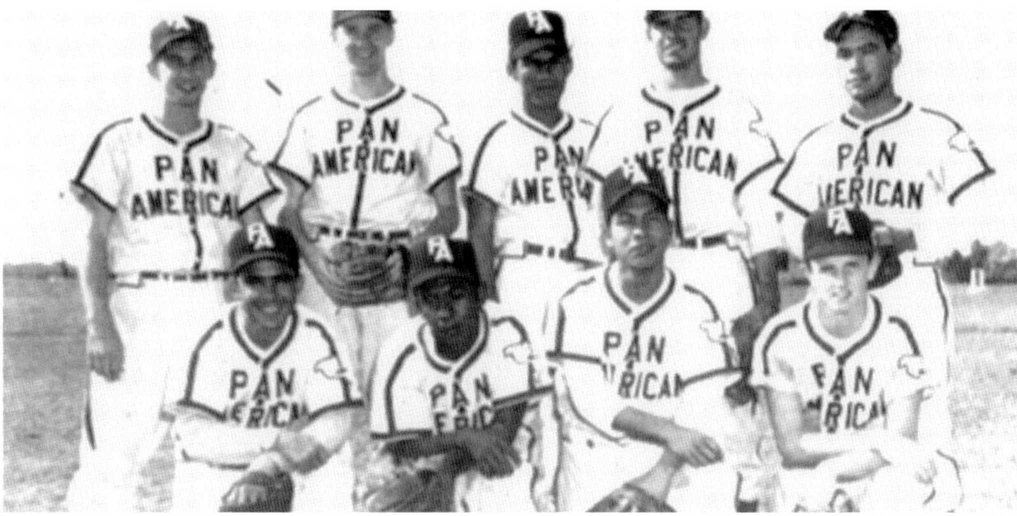

The 1958 Pan American College Broncs are, from left to right, (first row) Díaz, Mata, R. Estévis, and Gordon; (second row) Kaiser, Bolton, Estévis, Cavazos, and Alemán. The entire squad included pitchers Camilo Estévis, Cisco Estévis, Mike Maldonado, Pat Sáenz, Fito Salinas, and Jim Martínez; infielders Rey Chapa (first base), Romeo Díaz (second base), Don Bolton (shortstop), Frank Cavazos (third base), Ramón Estévis (third base), Joe Alemán (second base), Baldemar Farias (shortstop), Bob Gordon (second base), Ernesto Lugo (catcher), Adan Rodríguez (catcher), Jim Simpson (catcher); and outfielders Refugio "Cookie" Alejos, Joe Vela, Lefty González, Reuben Farias, Froben Losada, Héctor Palacios Raúl Sauceda, Joe Davis, and Arnold Vento. (Courtesy of Vicente and Francisco Estévis.)

Arturo Rivera is pictured in his Our Lady of Guadalupe Catholic School uniform in 1955. Arturo followed in the footsteps of his older brother Fernando playing for the Our Lady of Guadalupe Blackhawks softball team. Arturo served in the Marine Corps during Vietnam. He went on to study agronomy at Texas A&M in College Station and then worked for the FBI for 28 years. (Courtesy of Omar Rivera.)

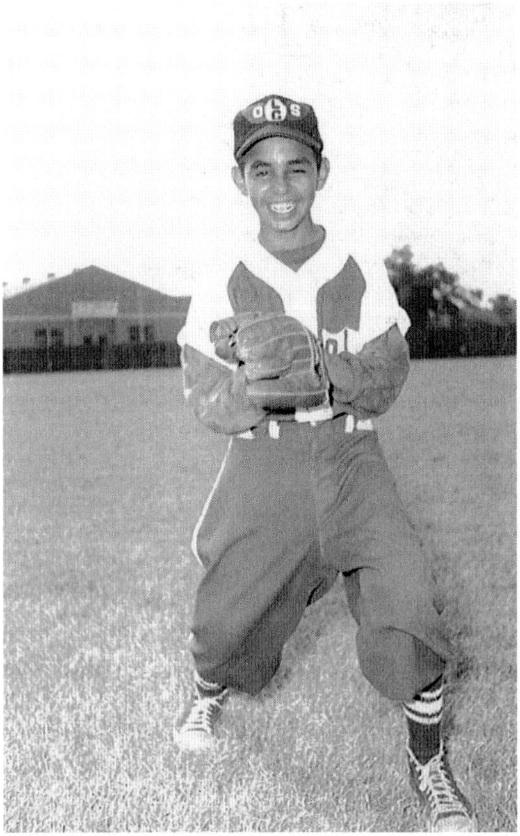

Members of the Mission High School baseball team for the 1920–1921 season are, from left to right, principal and coach Ernest Poteet, Joe Bryan, Hank Evans, "Pepe" Barrera, Olwyn Dooley, Theodore Conkwright, Lyndal Lehman, Doyt Lehman, Farrar "Cheesie" Dooley (later a business partner of Roy P. Conway), Leo Hilderbrandt, unidentified, and "Frenchy." (Courtesy of José Mario Cavazos.)

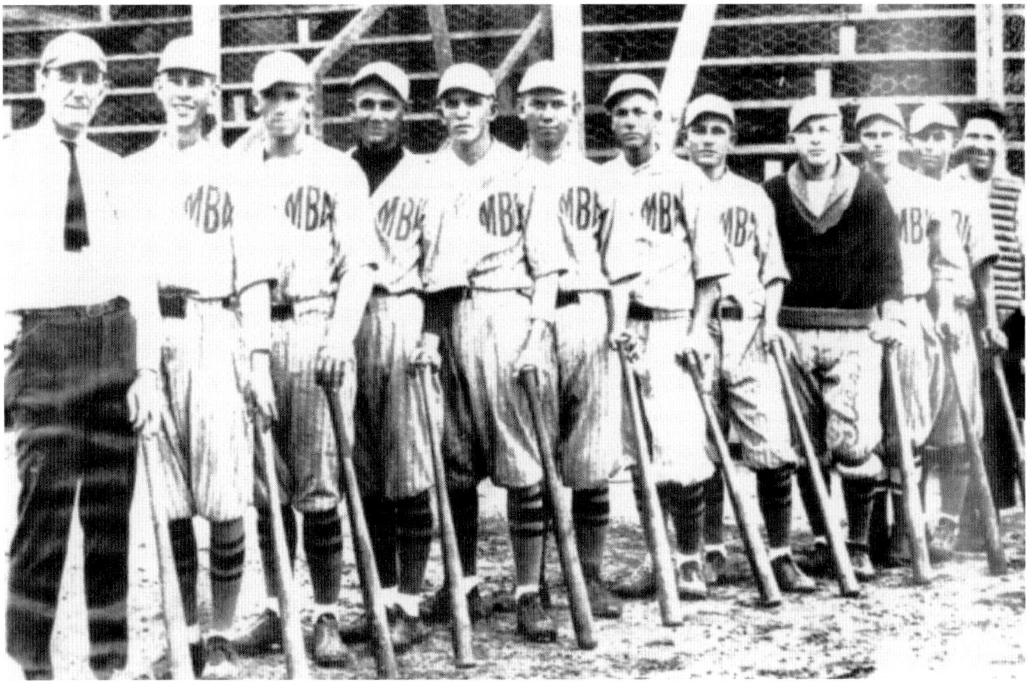

¡*Hay esta la bola!* Here is a walk-off home-run ball from a 1979 Edinburg Little League all-star game. It was hit by Librando Rolando Salinas, an Edinburg native whose family originated from La Palmita, Nuevo Leon, Mexico. Families in the Rio Grande Valley cherish and preserve baseball memorabilia from their youth. These artifacts are evidence of the passion and love Mexican Americans have for baseball in South Texas. (Courtesy of Guadalupe and Librando R. Salinas; photograph by Horacio Garza Jr.)

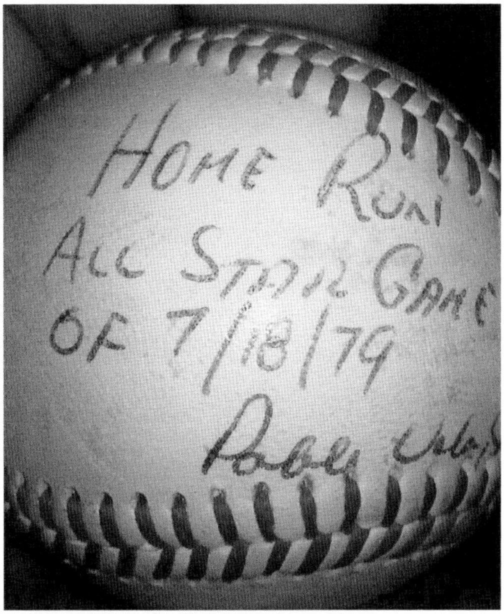

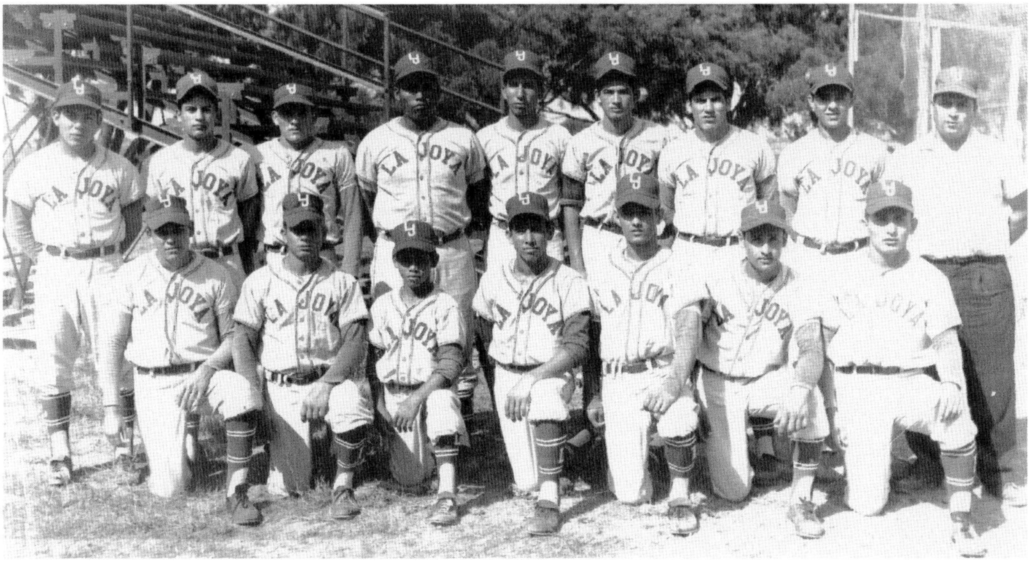

Pictured here are the 1964 regional champion La Joya High School Coyotes. Francisco Santiago (second row, far left) and Roberto Zamora (second row, third from left) played on the 1962 Hidalgo County Colt League World Series championship team. They started as freshmen and played from 1961 to 1964. The team played in the Texas regional state finals in 1961, 1963, and 1964. La Joya beat Del Rió San Felipe in 1961, lost to Shertz Cíbolo from San Antonio in 1963, and beat Crystal City in 1964. The regional state finals were as high as the teams could advance at that time. They were coached by Leo Garza (second row, far right) from Mission. Garza, Roberto Zamora, Francisco Santiago, José Guadalupe Reyna (second row, fourth from left), and Domingo Villarreal Jr. (front row, second from left) have been inducted into the Leo Najo Hall of Fame. Lindolfo Zamora (first row, far left) and Hector Zamora (first row, far right) also played on this team. (Courtesy of Evangelina Garza.)

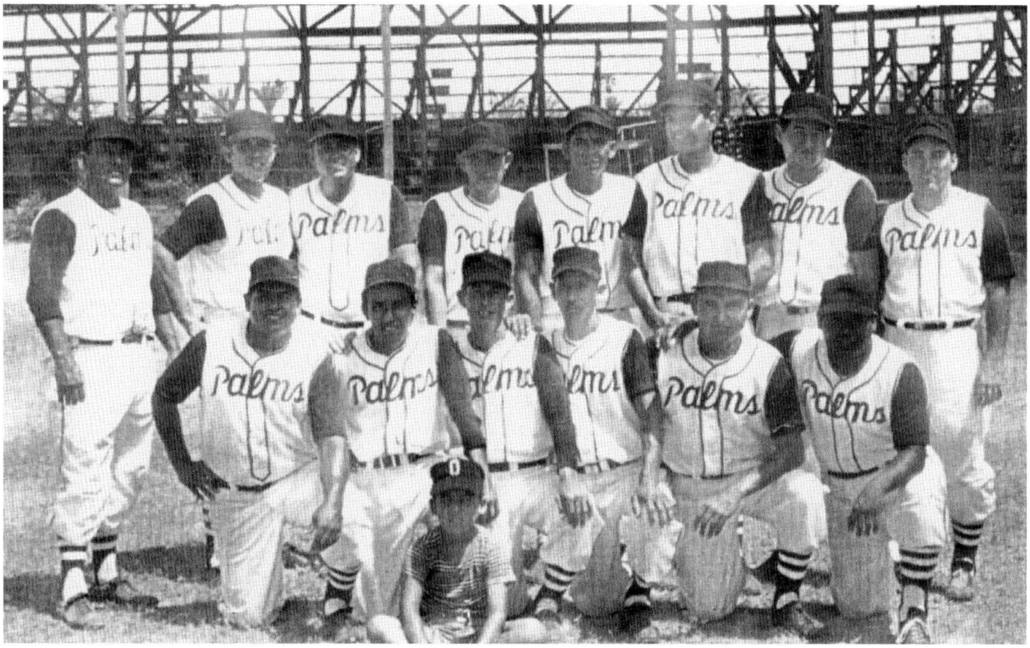

A 1950s McAllen Palms team is seen here. It was a semiprofessional team that played out of McAllen in the Old Class C Rio Grande League. The Palms played against semiprofessional teams from Edinburg, Mission, Pharr, and the surrounding communities. (Courtesy of José Mario Cavazos.)

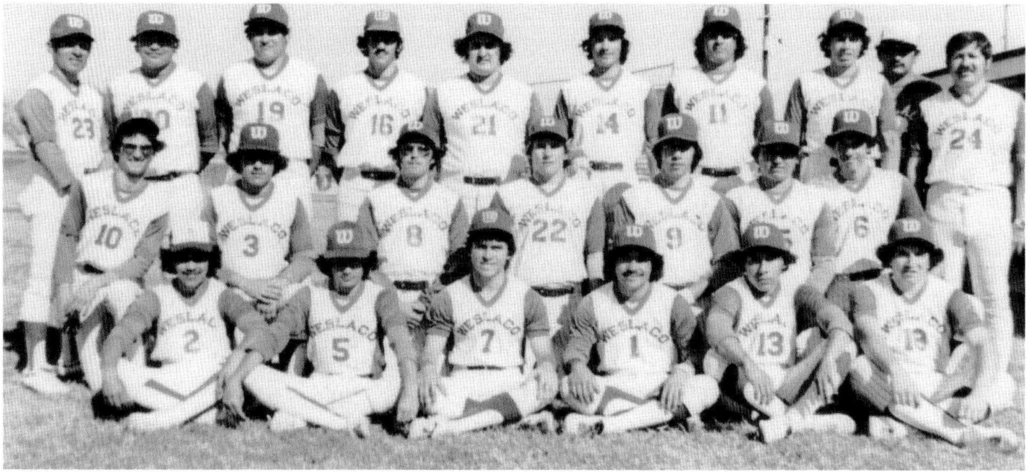

This Weslaco High School Panthers varsity team was coached by Francisco "Cisco" Estévis (standing, far left). After playing college and semiprofessional baseball, Estévis began to coach at the high school level. He served the Weslaco Independent School District as its varsity baseball coach for many years before moving on to teach special education and physical education for the South Texas Independent School District at its Edinburg Campus, formerly known as the Teaching Academy. Estévis, who dedicated his career to teaching, has yet to lose his passion for baseball and remains active with the Leo Najo group. (Courtesy of Vicente and Francisco Estévis.)

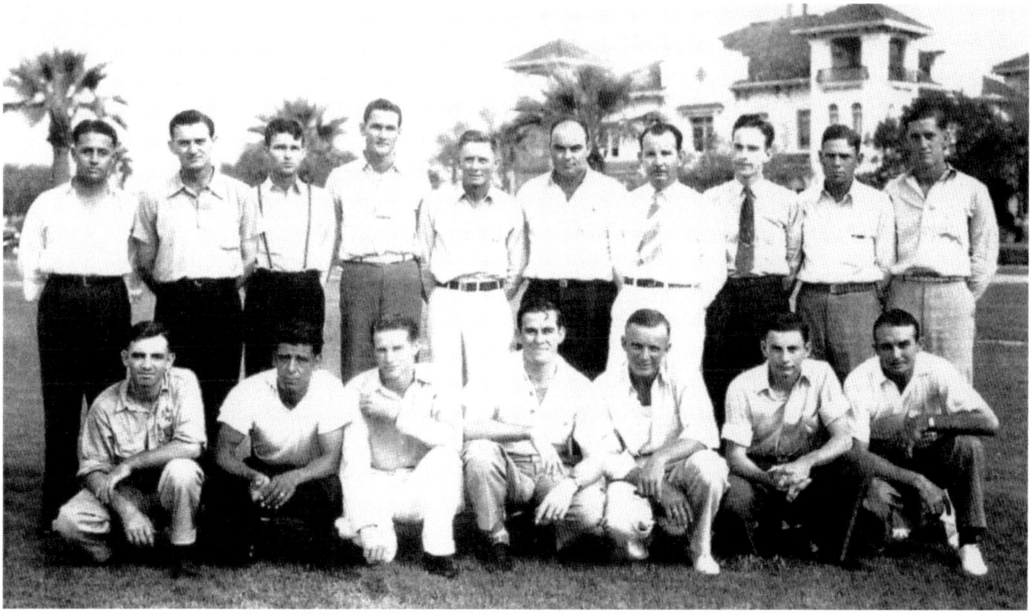

Pictured here from left to right are (first row) Stanley Cowan, catcher; Max Cavasos, catcher; Mitch Bloomfield, second base; Jerry Stephens, shortstop; Sid Wortham, outfielder; Alex Champion, outfielder; and Art Banworth, outfielder; (second row) Orvis Bernard, manager; Malcome Sellers, outfielder; Shin Young, third base; Melvin Hearne, first base; Layman Skinner, outfielder; Monti Hetrick, pitcher; Mike Mckinney, pitcher; Bill Southwell, pitcher; Putt Williams, outfielder; and Bill Snyder, outfielder. (Courtesy of Jack Bloomfield.)

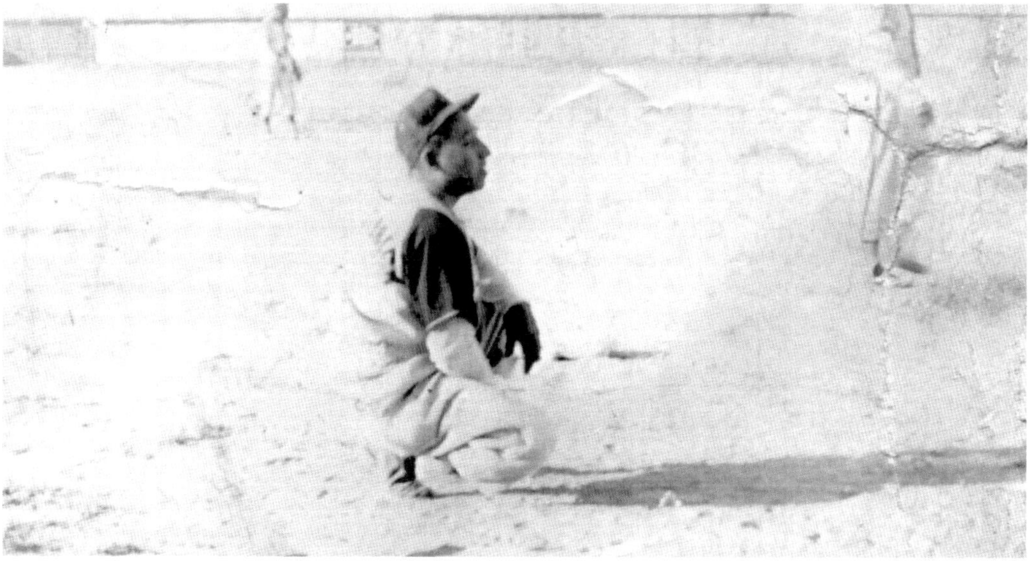

Fernando "Nango" Rivera Sr., manager of the Madero Valley Brickers, is seen around 1941. The Brickers played in the small farming community just south of Mission and along the Texas-Mexico border. Pancho and Ignacio Guerra played for the Brickers. (Courtesy of Omar Rivera and the Rivera family.)

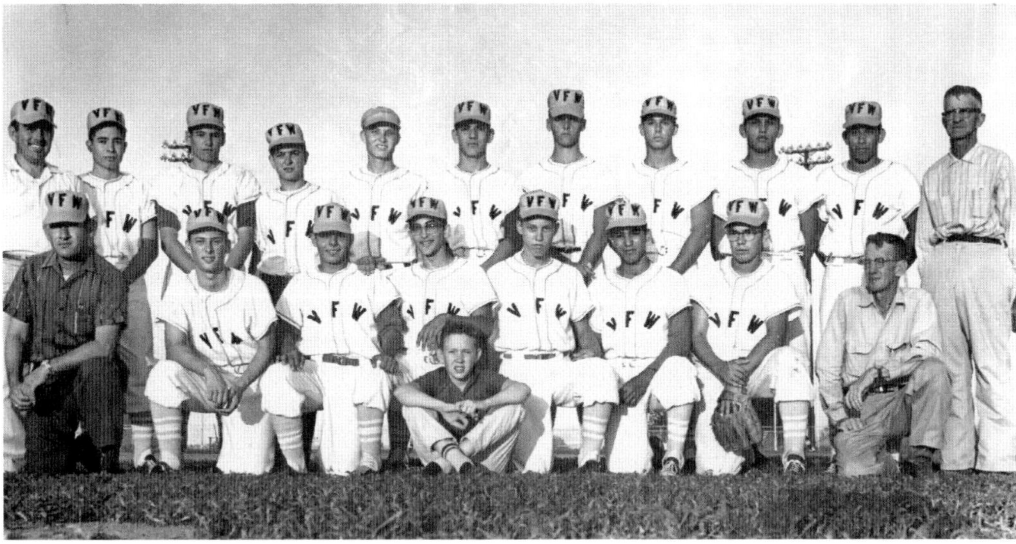

Sporting a first place 7-1 record in the Hidalgo County Colt League, the Edinburg entry was sponsored by the local Veterans of Foreign Wars. From left to right are (first row) coach Tommy Esparza, Jack Williams, Jaime Salazar, Noe Gorena, Richard Brady, Romeo Rodriquez, Pete de la Garza and George Lenig, commander of the VFW; (second row) coach Rubén Ayala, Arnold Ramos, Roy Lee Hinojosa, Richard Alamia, Carroll Brady, Ralph Garza, Jerry Tolliver, J.J. Avila, Robert Alañiz, Joe Vásquez, and M.H. Ballew, VFW trustee. In the foreground is James Williams, the batboy. During the three years Esparza coached the team, they posted a 26-6 record. Williams and Hinojosa were members of the Hidalgo County Colt League All Star world champions. Ronny Boney is not pictured. (Courtesy of Gloria Guerra Ayala.)

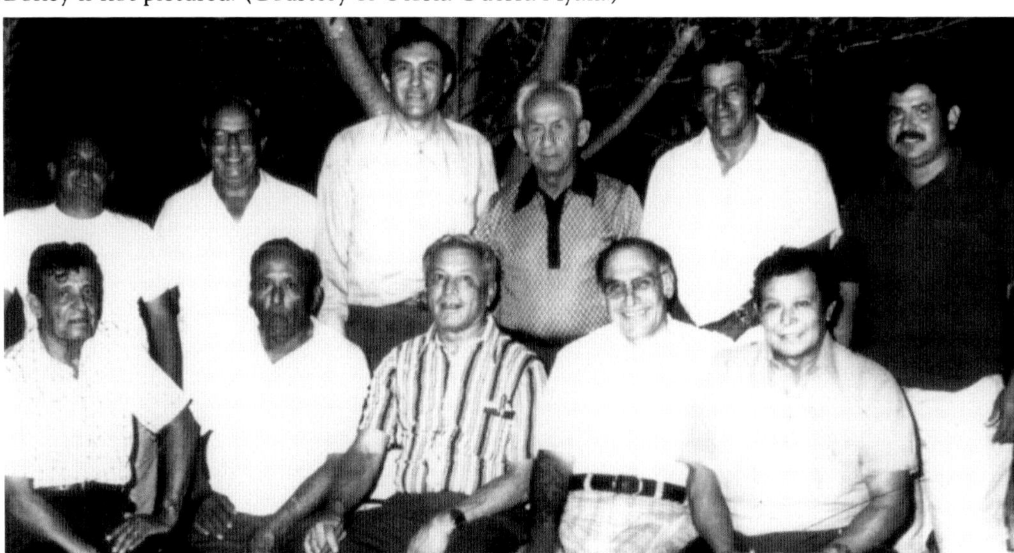

Pictured here from left to right are (first row) Nick Cavazos, unidentified, Dario García, Lefty Sánchez, and unidentified; (second row) Carlos de la Garza, Abel Casas, Camilo Estevís, Leo Najo, Jorge Gonzalez, and unidentified. (Courtesy of Vicente and Francisco Estevís.)

2

Lower Valley

The Lower Rio Grande Valley has a rich baseball history dating back to the post–Civil War years. Baseball continued to flourish throughout the 20th century. The Brownsville Brownies played in 1910–1911 as part of the Southwest Texas League. After being shut down for 17 years, the team was revived in 1928 and became the Brownsville Charros in 1938, when they played in the Texas Valley League. After 1938, the team was affiliated with different leagues, the last being United League Baseball, which closed at the end of the 2014 season. Minor league baseball was not limited to Brownsville. The neighboring city of Harlingen was home to professional baseball as early as 1931 when E.P. Ladd established the St. Louis, Brownsville & Mexico Railway.

Like the Brownsville team, the Harlingen team experienced changes in the team's name and was affiliated with different leagues. Other names by which this team was known included the Hubs, Capitals, Rio Grande Valley Giants, and Rio Grande Valley Whitewings. The Giants were a farm club of the San Francisco Giants. Future Hall of Famer and Cy Young winner Gaylord Perry played for the RGV Giants in 1960. Other RGV Giants who played in the Major Leagues were Bobby Bolin, Manny Mota, and José Tartabull.

In 1965, the Brownsville High School Golden Eagles, loaded with outstanding talent, came within a game of winning the state title. Edinburg native coach Joe Rodríguez coached a team led by a pair of left-handed pitchers, Charlie Vaughan and Tony Barbosa Jr. Vaughn played with the Atlanta Braves from 1966 to 1969, while Barbosa was drafted by the California Angels and also played in the Mexican League. One other player from that team, César de la Garza, signed to play with the Houston Astros rookie league. Other notable players on the 1965 Brownsville Eagles included Arnoldo Álvarez and Rene Torres, who both played for the Pan American College Broncs.

Continuing the rich baseball tradition in the Lower Rio Grande Valley were the 1977 Texas Southmost College Baseball team from Brownsville who played in the Junior College World Series in Grand Junction, Colorado. One of the many standout players on the team was Cesar Perez, a right-handed pitcher from Rio Grande City. Perez was inducted into the Leo Najo Hall of Fame in October 2015. The Lower Rio Grande may well be considered the birthplace of baseball in South Texas, as individual players and teams have set traditions here that future generations will continue to enrich.

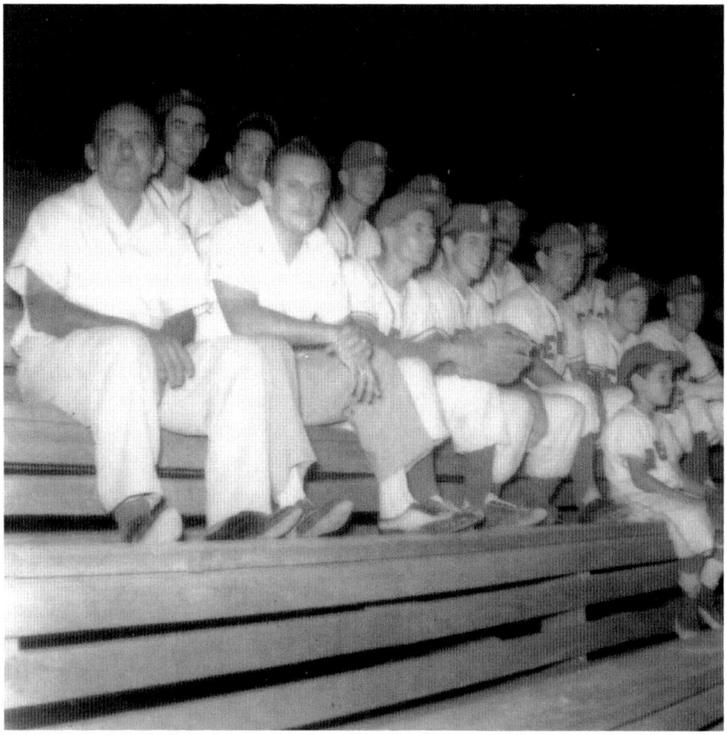

Hometown fans of the Brownsville Regals are seen at a game in 1957–1958. Home fans gathered in droves to support the Regals. Families gathered for Sunday matinees and cheered on Mexican American ballplayers. (Courtesy of Francisco Maldonado.)

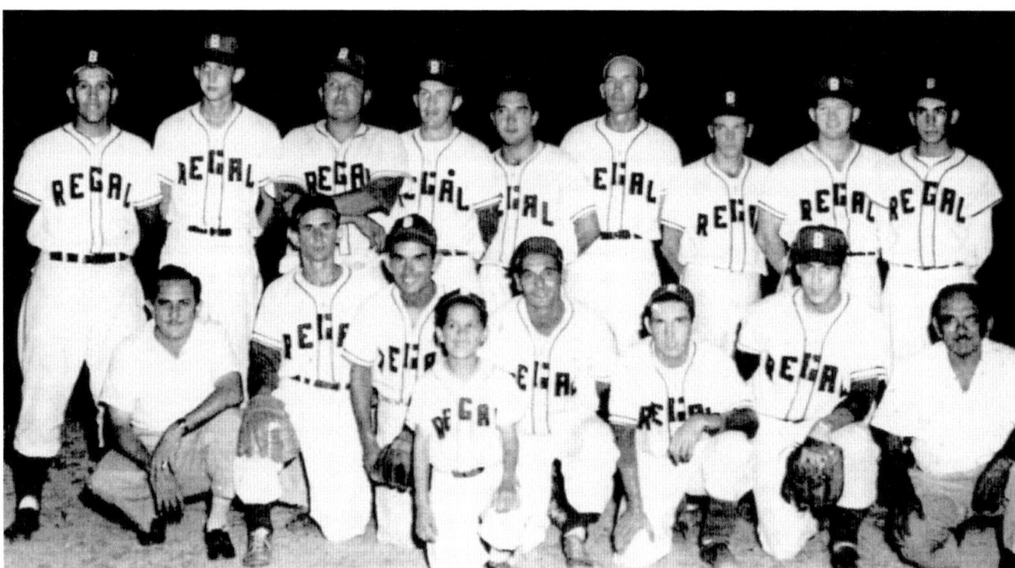

The Brownsville Regals participated in the very competitive Rio Grande Valley Semiprofessional League of 1956. The circuit included teams from throughout the valley, like those in San Benito, three squads from Harlingen, Weslaco, Pharr, and Edinburg. The Regals matured into a solid group that had a pitching staff comparable to any Class "C" professional team. The batboy in this photograph, Rene Torres, grew up to be a significant figure in valley baseball as well. (Courtesy of Rio Grande Valley Sports Hall of Fame.)

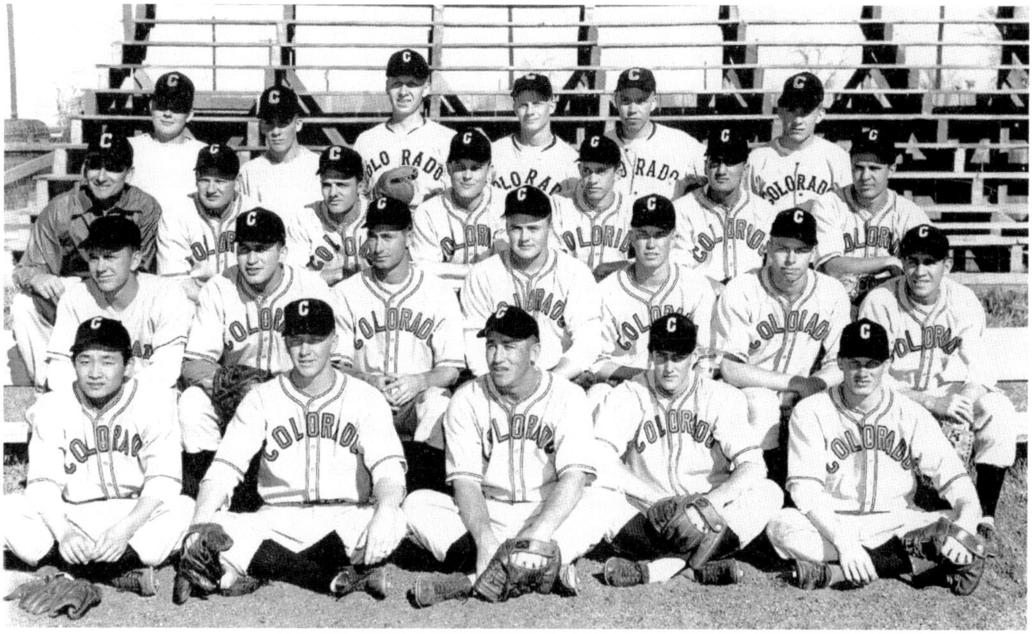

Seen here is the 1949 University of Colorado baseball team. Brownsville native Francisco Maldonado played first base and was the only Mexican American on the team. He is in the second row at far right. Also suiting up for the Buffaloes in 1949 are Ashton, Cox, Bierbaum, Pudlick, Pixlex, Grump, Thompson Fanning, Johnson, Ley, Manire, Narcisian, Krasovich, Hagin, Knoblock, Nix, Trick, Rogers, Bock, Graham, Evans, Beeny, and Codden. (Courtesy of Francisco Maldonado.)

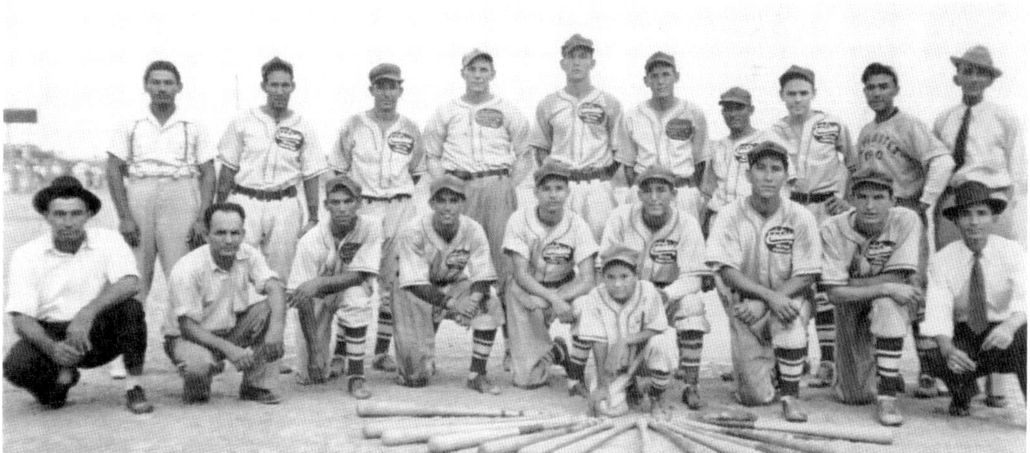

The Brownsville Edelstein All-Stars semi-pro team was formed in 1940. The squad was under the leadership of two veterans of the diamond—Tomas "Tito" Torres, who had plenty of credentials as a former player and manager, and his partner in the dugout Timo Cantu, another notable around Valley baseball circles. Fans who attended their Sunday doubleheaders were always treated to a solid game of hardball. (Courtesy of Rene Torres.)

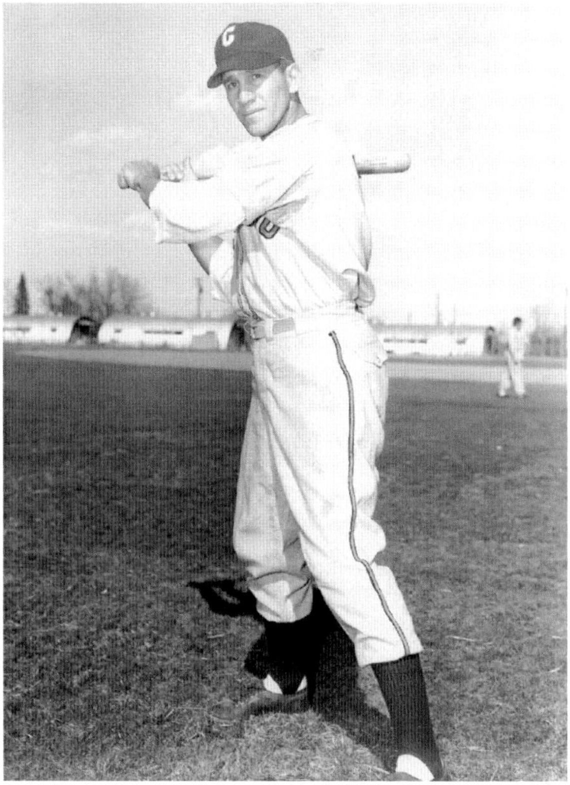

Here, Francisco Maldonado is at bat for the University of Colorado. Maldonado lettered in 1949 and 1950 for the Buffaloes. During those two seasons, the Buffaloes competed in the Big 7 Conference and played against Colorado State, Kansas, Kansas State, Nebraska, Utah, Missouri, Oklahoma, and Iowa State. (Courtesy of Francisco Maldonado.)

Francisco Maldonado is pictured at first base for the 1950 University of Colorado team. Maldonado became the regular first baseman for the Buffaloes and also became a threat at bat as he hit the ball with great force. (Courtesy of Francisco Maldonado.)

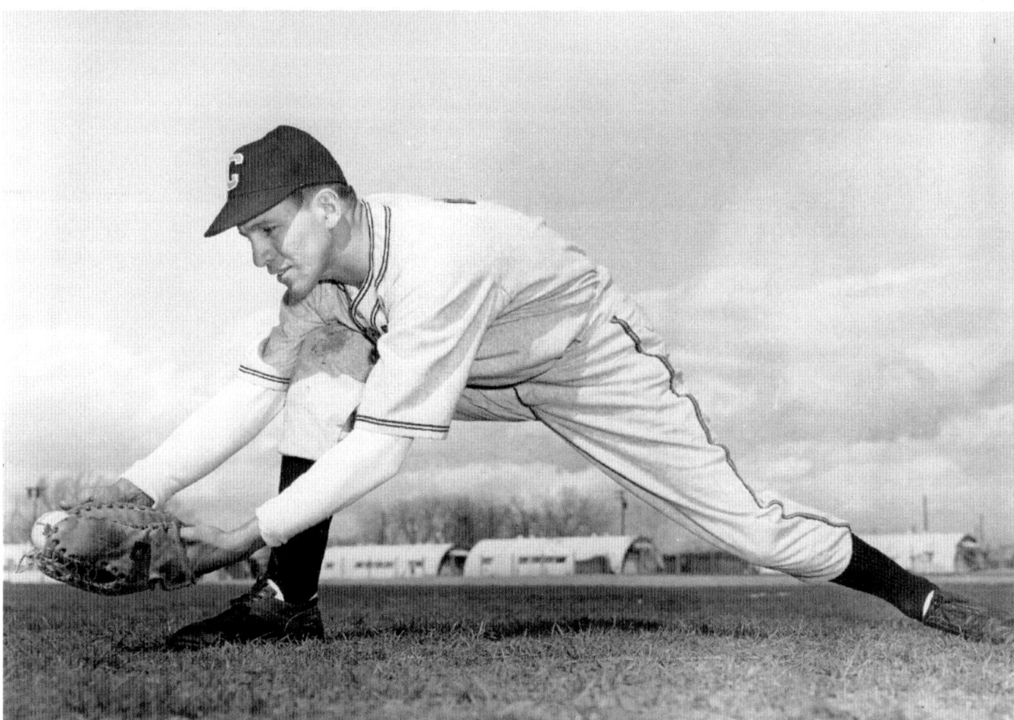

Francisco Maldonado stretches out for a ball during the 1949 season at the University of Colorado. Led by Coach Prentup, the Buffaloes competed in the Big 7 Conference. (Courtesy of Francisco Maldonado.)

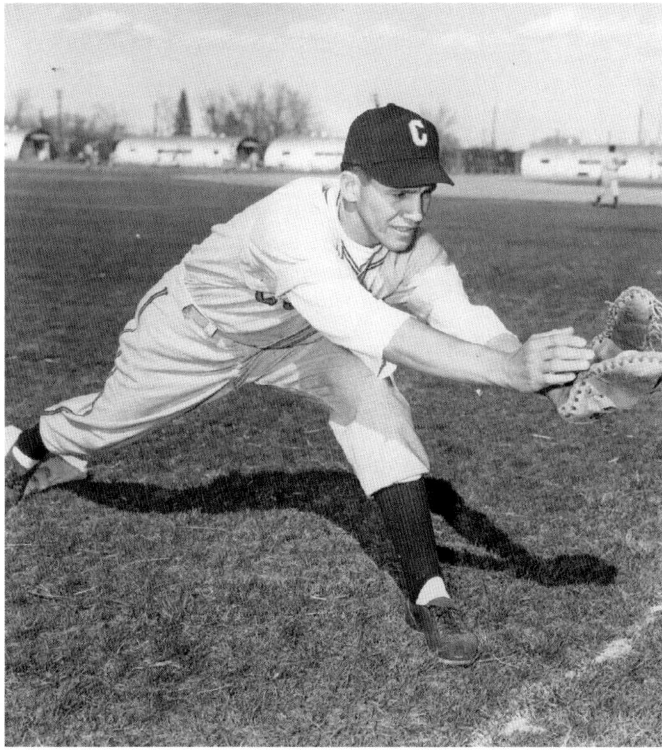

Shown in 1949, the University of Colorado Buffalo ballplayers gather for a strategic talk. From left to right are Ely Billy, Gene Rodgers, Jack Cowden, and Francisco Maldonado. (Courtesy of Francisco Maldonado.)

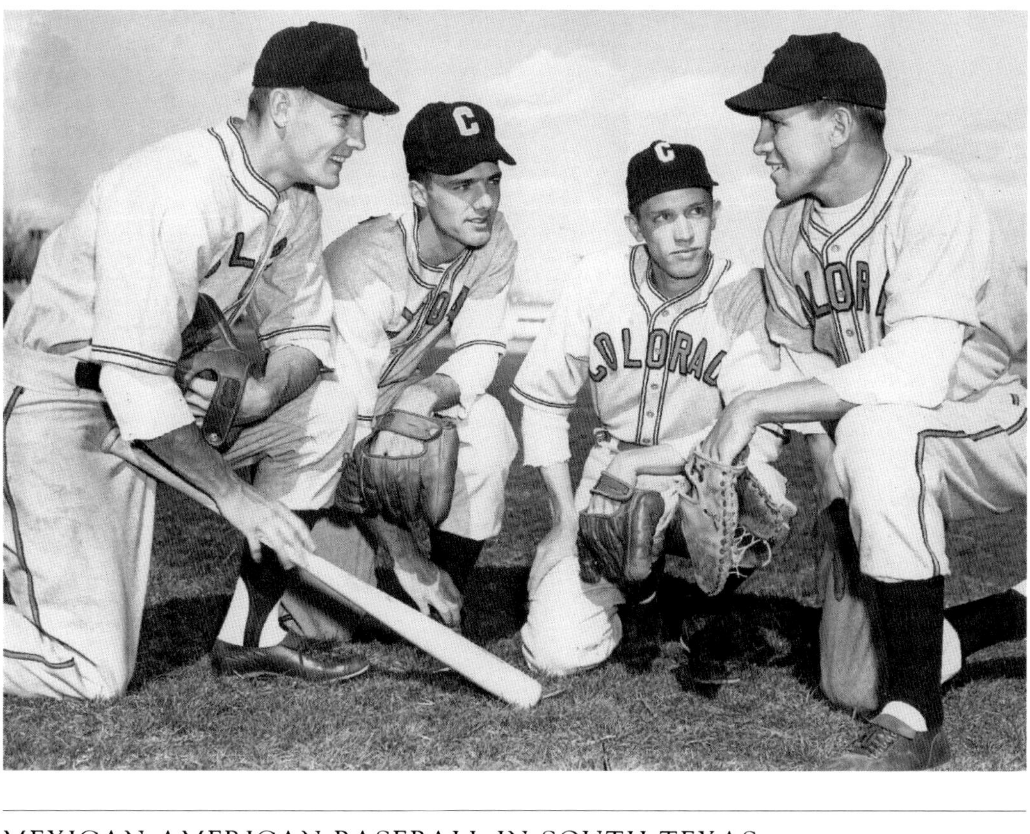

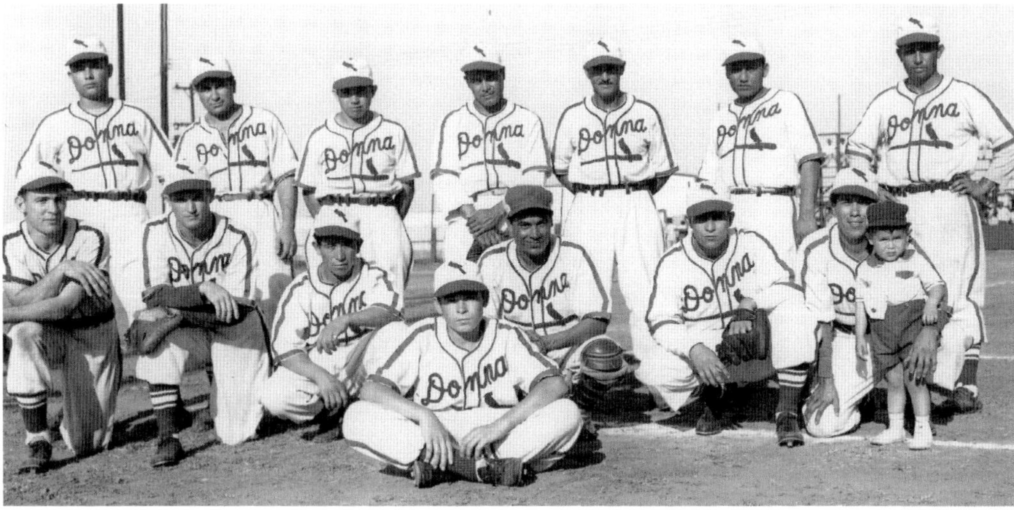

The 1947–1948 Donna Cardinals were under the direction of Pánfilo Ávila and later, Pete Lerma. The Cardinals were a semiprofessional team who played their home games at Ávila Field in East Donna, which became one of the first ballparks in the valley to get lights. Francisco Maldonado played for the Cardinals as the team brought players together from across the Rio Grande Valley. (Courtesy of Francisco Maldonado.)

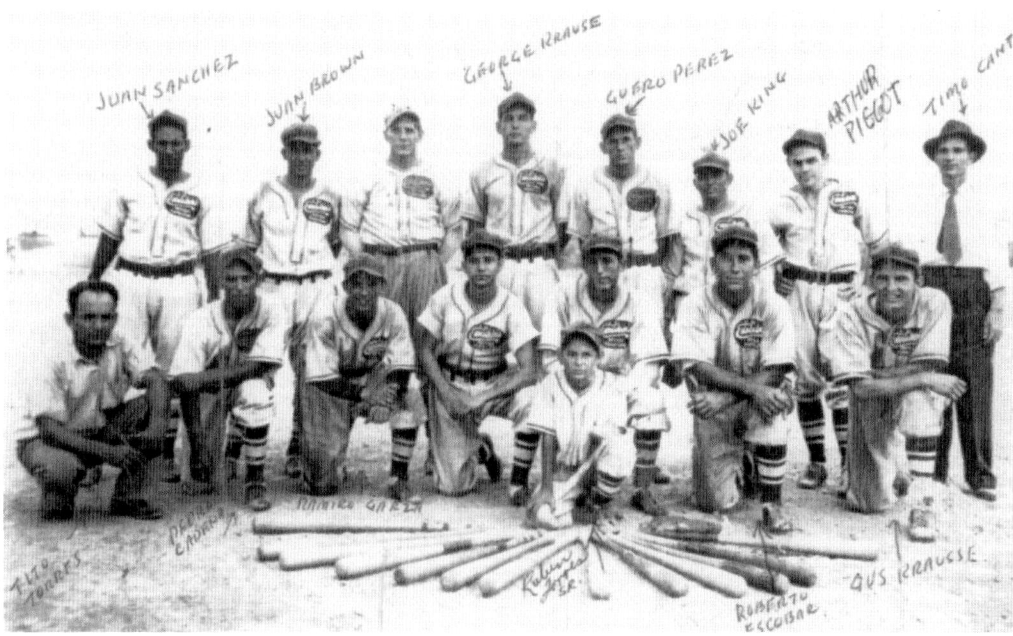

This semiprofessional team was sponsored by Edelstein Furniture. The team featured both Mexican Americans and Anglo Americans. In the early part of the 20th century, baseball was one of the few integrated activities. Shown here are, from left to right, (first row) Tito Torres, Pedro Cadena, Ramiro Garza, unidentified, Rubén Torres Sr., Roberto Escobar, and Gus Krausse; (second row) Juan Sánchez, Juan Brown, unidentified, George Krausse, "Guero" Pérez, Joe King, Arthur Piggot, and Timo Cantu. (Courtesy of Francisco Maldonado.)

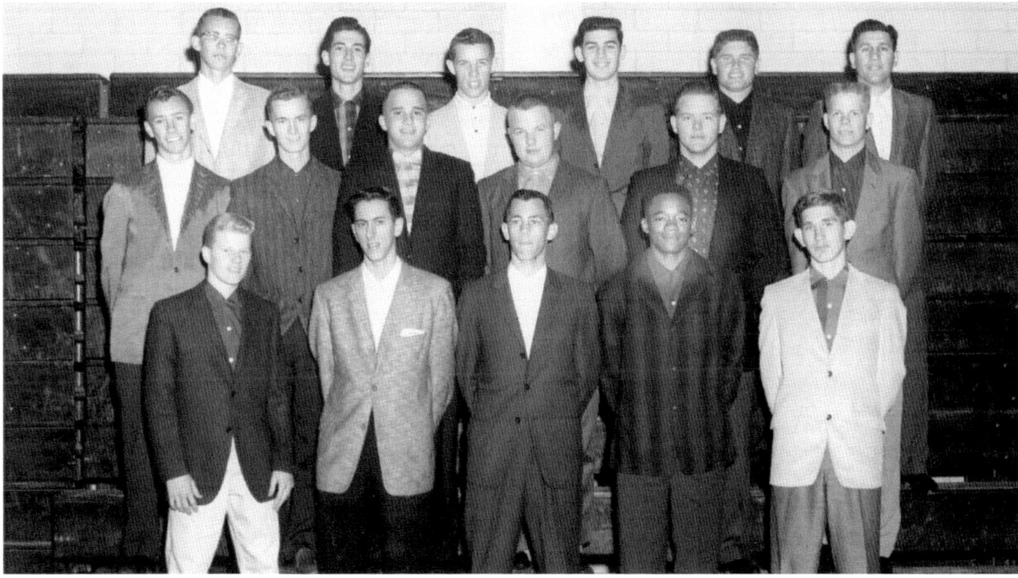

In 1950, Francisco Maldonado (third row, far right) became the coach of the McAllen High School Bulldogs varsity baseball team. Coach Maldonado led the team to its first district title in 10 years as the Bulldogs once again became relevant in Rio Grande Valley high school baseball. The Bulldogs played against other valley teams such as the Harlingen Cardinals, Brownsville Golden Eagles, PSJA Bears, and Edinburg Bobcats. (Courtesy of Francisco Maldonado.)

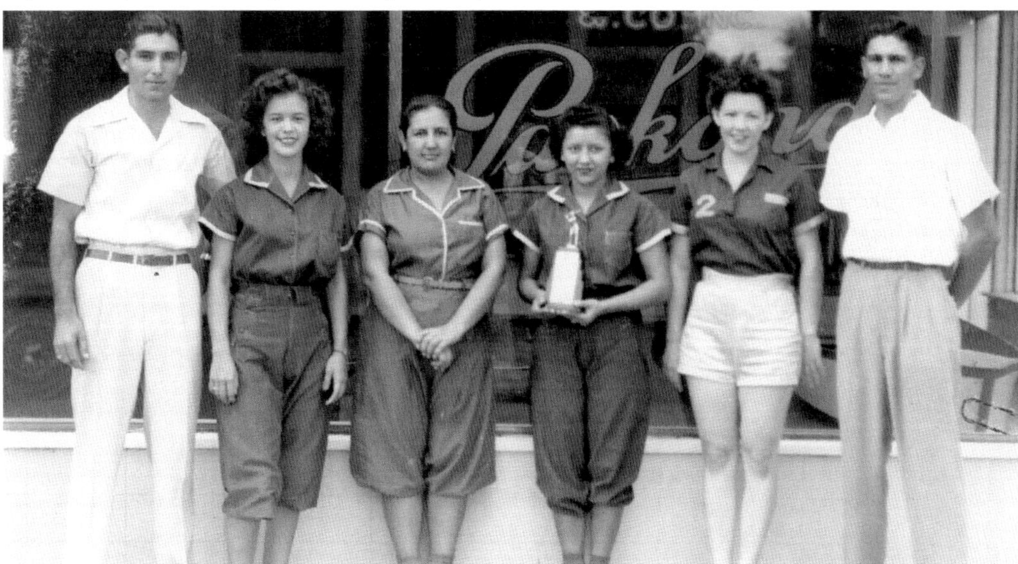

The Brownsville D.W. Simpson's Packard Clippers team was made up of female softball players from Brownsville who competed in the Valley Maid League. The Clippers played their home games at the Thirty-Sixth Street diamond in the late 1940s. Competing against the Clippers were the Lyford Red Birds, La Feria Graham Bombers, Mercedes Green Hornets, and Harlingen Palm Gardens. The communities of Edcouch and Alamo also fielded teams. (Courtesy of Francisco Maldonado.)

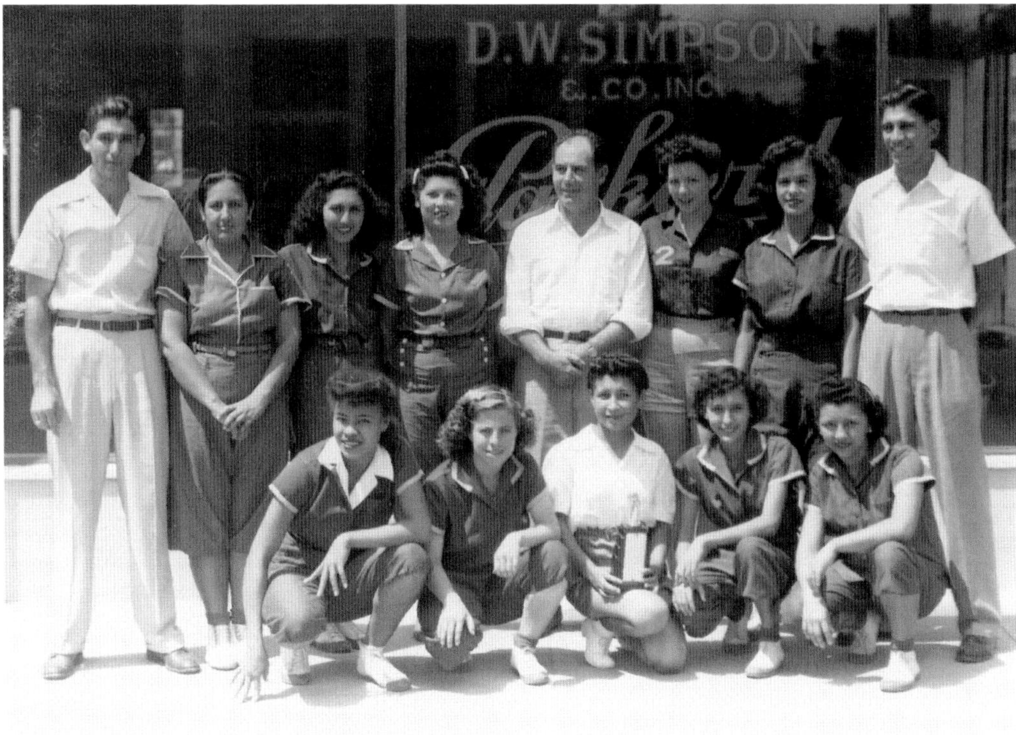

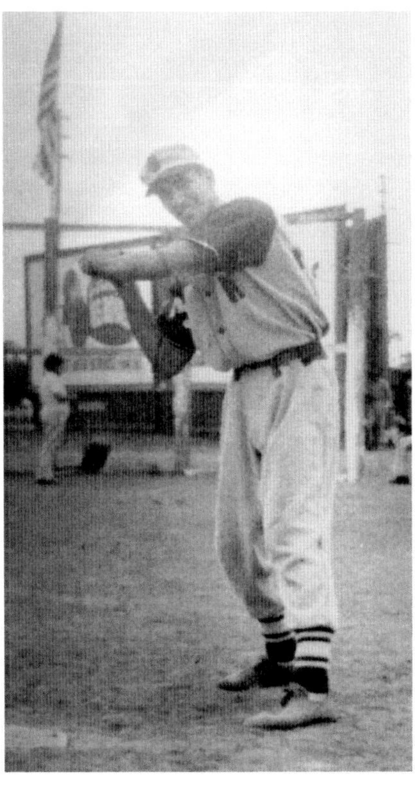

The Brownsville D.W. Simpson's Packard Clippers won the Texas Amateur Athletic Federation girls softball tournament in 1946. Playing for the Clippers that year were Julia Burst, Fela Flores, Frances Escobar, Ofelia Piña, Bertha Baker, Aurora López, Lupita Flores, H. Landis Consuelo García, Pime Montemayor, Ofelia Castillo, and Estephina Garza. Coaches were B. Stevens, Alfonso García, and M. Cantu, and the manager was Francisco Maldonado. (Courtesy of Francisco Maldonado.)

Francisco Maldonado is at the plate playing semiprofessional baseball in South Texas. After playing baseball in Brownsville, Maldonado served in World War II. Upon his return to the states in 1946, he had a tryout with the New York Giants and went on to play college baseball at the University of Colorado in 1949 and 1950. After college, he came back home to the Rio Grande Valley and dedicated his life to coaching. Maldonado continued to play ball semiprofessionally with teams like the Donna Cardinals and Brownsville Regals. (Courtesy of Francisco Maldonado.)

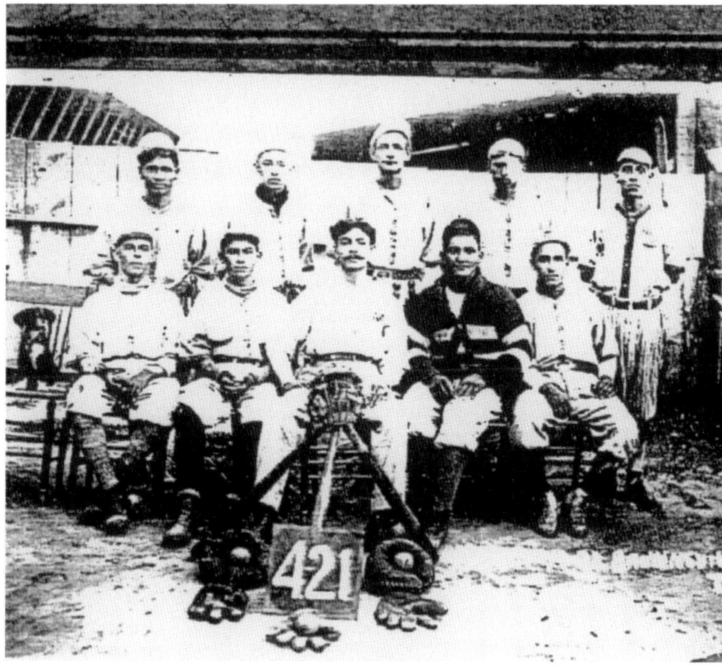

La 421 was a baseball club in a Mexican American *barrio* in Brownsville in the early 1900s. From left to right are (first row) Francisco Maldonado, Guadalupe "El Polvo" Olvera, manager Pedro Linares, Rogelio Padron, and Humberto Davila; (second row) Apolonio Martínez, Librado Macías, Amado "La Zorra" Robledo, Ibense Quintero, and unidentified. (Courtesy of Francisco Maldonado.)

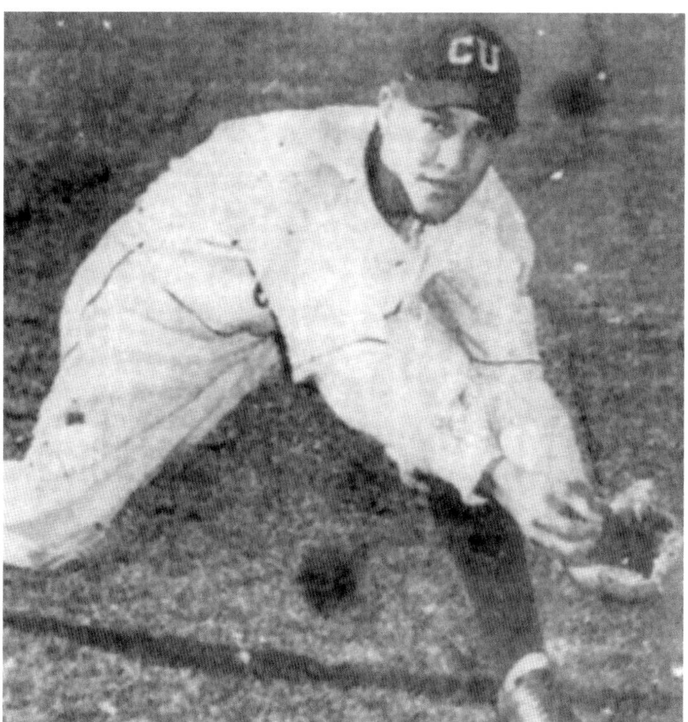

Francisco Maldonado played first base at the University of Colorado in 1949 and 1950. Maldonado grew up in Brownsville, where he played high school and semiprofessional baseball. During the 1950 season at Colorado, Maldonado was second on the team in RBIs. Maldonado was one of a few Mexican American athletes at the University of Colorado. Fellow Mexican American from Edinburg R.C. Fito Flores joined Maldonado at Colorado, as he played on the football team. (Courtesy of Francisco Maldonado.)

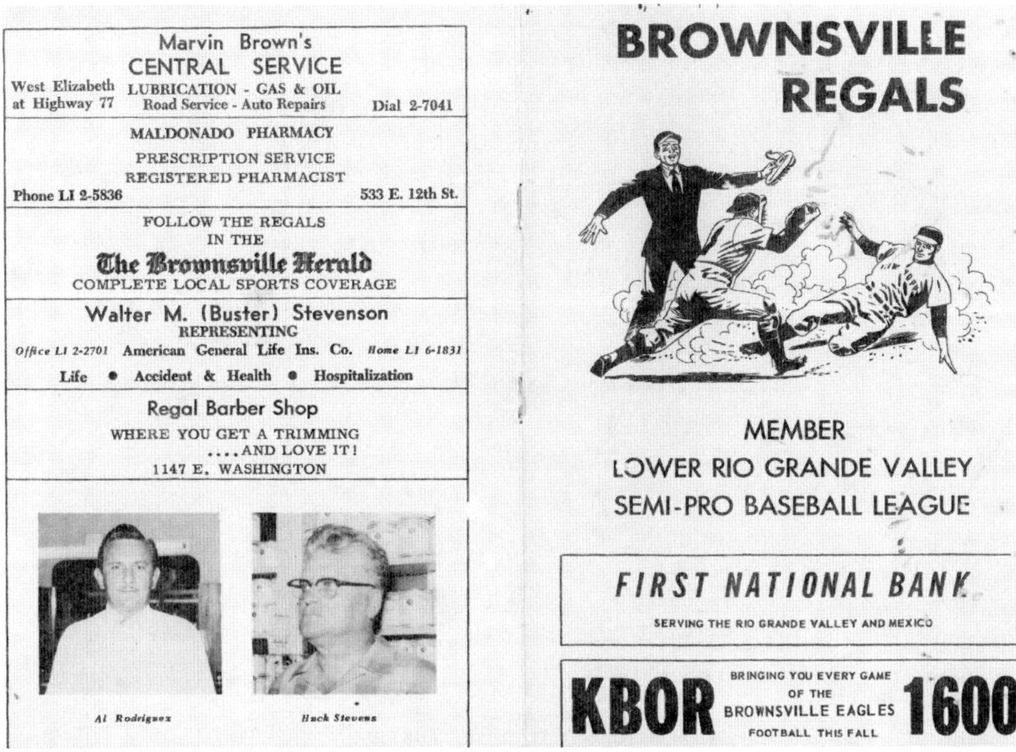

Marvin Brown's
CENTRAL SERVICE
West Elizabeth at Highway 77
LUBRICATION - GAS & OIL
Road Service - Auto Repairs
Dial 2-7041

MALDONADO PHARMACY
PRESCRIPTION SERVICE
REGISTERED PHARMACIST
Phone LI 2-5836
533 E. 12th St.

FOLLOW THE REGALS
IN THE
The Brownsville Herald
COMPLETE LOCAL SPORTS COVERAGE

Walter M. (Buster) Stevenson
REPRESENTING
Office LI 2-2701 American General Life Ins. Co. Home LI 6-1831
Life • Accident & Health • Hospitalization

Regal Barber Shop
WHERE YOU GET A TRIMMING
....AND LOVE IT!
1147 E. WASHINGTON

Al Rodriguez

Huck Stevens

BROWNSVILLE REGALS

MEMBER
LOWER RIO GRANDE VALLEY
SEMI-PRO BASEBALL LEAGUE

FIRST NATIONAL BANK
SERVING THE RIO GRANDE VALLEY AND MEXICO

KBOR
BRINGING YOU EVERY GAME OF THE BROWNSVILLE EAGLES FOOTBALL THIS FALL
1600

Pictured are a program and a scorecard from the 1956 Brownsville Regals. The Regals were members of the Lower Rio Grande Valley Semiprofessional Baseball League. Baseball was followed religiously from Little League to Pony League, to high school, and finally, to the semiprofessional level. Local businesses supported baseball through buying advertisements on the programs. The *Brownsville Herald* supported the sport and did a tremendous job in covering baseball at all levels. (Both, courtesy of Francisco Maldonado.)

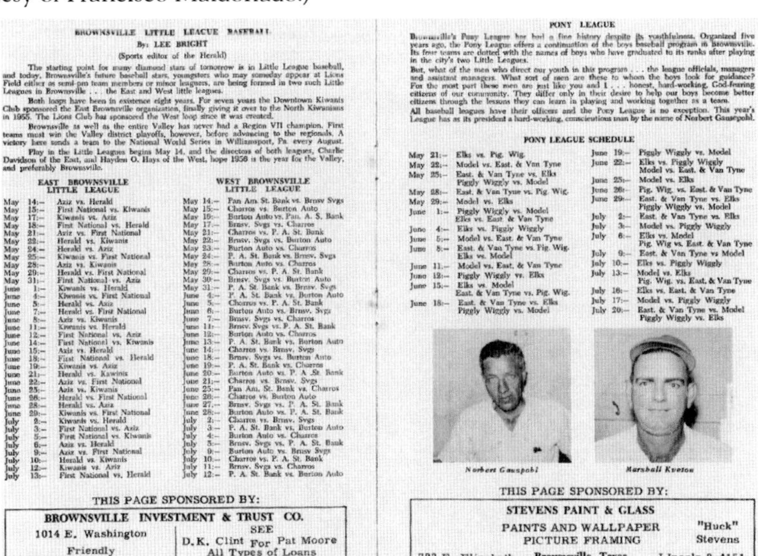

BROWNSVILLE LITTLE LEAGUE BASEBALL
By: LEE BRIGHT
(Sports editor of the Herald)

The starting point for many diamond stars of tomorrow is in Little League baseball, and today, Brownsville's future baseball stars, youngsters who may someday appear at Lions Field either as semi-pro team members or minor leaguers, are being formed in two such Little Leagues in Brownsville . . . the East and West little leagues.

Both loops have been in existence eight years. For seven years the Downtown Kiwanis Club sponsored the East Brownsville organization, finally giving it over to the North Kiwanians in 1955. The Lions Club has sponsored the West loop since it was created.

Brownsville as well as the entire Valley has never had a Region VII champion. First teams must win the Valley district playoffs, however, before advancing to the regionals. A victory here sends a team to the National World Series in Williamsport, Pa. every August.

Play in the Little Leagues begins May 14, and the directors of both leagues, Charlie Davidson of the East, and Hayden O. Hays of the West, hope 1956 is the year for the Valley, and preferably Brownsville.

EAST BROWNSVILLE LITTLE LEAGUE

May 14:–	Aziz vs. Herald
May 15:–	First National vs. Kiwanis
May 17:–	Kiwanis vs. Aziz
May 18:–	First National vs. Herald
May 21:–	Aziz vs. First National
May 22:–	Herald vs. Kiwanis
May 24:–	Herald vs. Aziz
May 25:–	Kiwanis vs. First National
May 28:–	Aziz vs. Kiwanis
May 29:–	Herald vs. First National
May 31:–	First National vs. Aziz
June 1:–	Kiwanis vs. Herald
June 4:–	Kiwanis vs. First National
June 5:–	Herald vs. Aziz
June 7:–	Herald vs. First National
June 8:–	Aziz vs. Kiwanis
June 11:–	Kiwanis vs. Herald
June 12:–	First National vs. Aziz
June 14:–	First National vs. Kiwanis
June 15:–	Aziz vs. Herald
June 18:–	First National vs. Herald
June 19:–	Kiwanis vs. Aziz
June 21:–	Herald vs. Kawinis
June 22:–	Aziz vs. First National
June 25:–	Aziz vs. Kiwanis
June 26:–	Herald vs. First National
June 28:–	Herald vs. Aziz
June 29:–	Kiwanis vs. First National
July 2:–	Kiwanis vs. Herald
July 3:–	First National vs. Aziz
July 5:–	First National vs. Kiwanis
July 6:–	Aziz vs. Herald
July 9:–	Aziz vs. First National
July 10:–	Herald vs. Kiwanis
July 12:–	Kiwanis vs. Ariz
July 13:–	First National vs. Herald

WEST BROWNSVILLE LITTLE LEAGUE

May 14:–	Pan Am. St. Bank vs. Brnsv Svgs
May 15:–	Charros vs. Burton Auto
May 16:–	Burton Auto vs. Pan. A. S. Bank
May 17:–	Brnsv. Svgs vs. Charros
May 21:–	Charros vs. P. A. St. Bank
May 22:–	Brnsv. Svgs vs. Burton Auto
May 23:–	Burton Auto vs. Charros
May 24:–	P. A. St. Bank vs. Brnsv. Svgs
May 28:–	Burton Auto vs. Charros
May 29:–	Charros vs. P. A. St. Bank
May 30:–	Brnsv. Svgs vs. Burton Auto
May 31:–	P. A. St. Bank vs. Brnsv. Svgs
June 4:–	P. A. St. Bank vs. Burton Auto
June 5:–	Charros vs. P. A. St. Bank
June 6:–	Burton Auto vs. Brnsv. Svgs
June 7:–	Brnsv. Svgs vs. Charros
June 11:–	Brnsv. Svgs vs. P. A. St. Bank
June 12:–	Burton Auto vs. Charros
June 13:–	P. A. St. Bank vs. Burton Auto
June 14:–	Charros vs. Brnsv. Svgs
June 18:–	Brnsv. Svgs vs. Burton Auto
June 19:–	P. A. St. Bank vs. Charros
June 20:–	Burton Auto vs. P. A. St. Bank
June 21:–	Charros vs. Brnsv. Svgs
June 25:–	Pan Am. St. Bank vs. Charros
June 26:–	Charros vs. Burton Auto
June 27:–	Brnsv. Svgs vs. P. A. St. Bank
June 28:–	Burton Auto vs. P. A. St. Bank
July 2:–	Charros vs. Brnsv. Svgs
July 3:–	P. A. St. Bank vs. Burton Auto
July 4:–	Burton Auto vs. Charros
July 5:–	Brnsv. Svgs vs. P. A. St. Bank
July 9:–	Burton Auto vs. Brnsv Svgs
July 10:–	Charros vs. P. A. St. Bank
July 11:–	Brnsv. Svgs vs. Charros
July 12:–	P. A. St. Bank vs. Burton Auto

THIS PAGE SPONSORED BY:

BROWNSVILLE INVESTMENT & TRUST CO.
1014 E. Washington
Friendly
Confidential Service
SEE
D.K. Clint For Pat Moore
All Types of Loans
and Insurance

PONY LEAGUE

Brownsville's Pony League has had a fine history despite its youthfulness. Organized five years ago, the Pony League offers a continuation of the boys baseball program in Brownsville. Its four teams are dotted with the names of boys who have graduated to its ranks after playing in the city's two Little Leagues.

But, what of the men who direct our youth in this program . . . the league officials, managers and assistant managers. What sort of men are these to whom the boys look for guidance? For the most part these men are just like you and I . . . honest, hard-working, God-fearing citizens of our community. They differ only in their desire to help our boys become better citizens through the lessons they can learn in playing and working together as a team.

All baseball leagues have their officers and the Pony League is no exception. This year's League has as its president a hard-working, conscientious man by the name of Norbert Gausepohl.

PONY LEAGUE SCHEDULE

May 21:–	Elks vs. Pig. Wig.
May 22:–	Model vs. East. & Van Tyne
May 25:–	East. & Van Tyne vs. Elks Piggly Wiggly vs. Model
May 28:–	East. & Van Tyne vs. Pig. Wig.
May 29:–	Model vs. Elks
June 1:–	Piggly Wiggly vs. Model Elks vs. East. & Van Tyne
June 4:–	Elks vs. Piggly Wiggly
June 5:–	Model vs. East. & Van Tyne
June 8:–	East. & Van Tyne vs. Pig. Wig. Elks vs. Model
June 11:–	Model vs. East. & Van Tyne
June 12:–	Piggly Wiggly vs. Elks
June 15:–	Elks vs. Model East. & Van Tyne vs. Pig. Wig.
June 18:–	East. & Van Tyne vs. Elks Piggly Wiggly vs. Model
June 19:–	Piggly Wiggly vs. Model
June 22:–	Elks vs. Piggly Wiggly Model vs. East. & Van Tyne
June 25:–	Model vs. Elks
June 26:–	Pig. Wig. vs. East. & Van Tyne
June 29:–	East. & Van Tyne vs. Elks Piggly Wiggly vs. Model
July 2:–	East. & Van Tyne vs. Elks
July 3:–	Model vs. Piggly Wiggly
July 6:–	Elks vs. Model Pig. Wig vs. East. & Van Tyne
July 9:–	East. & Van Tyne vs Model
July 10:–	Elks vs. Piggly Wiggly
July 13:–	Model vs. Elks Pig. Wig. vs. East. & Van Tyne
July 16:–	Elks vs. East. & Van Tyne
July 17:–	Model vs. Piggly Wiggly
July 20:–	East. & Van Tyne vs. Model Piggly Wiggly vs. Elks

Norbert Gauspohl

Marshall Kveton

THIS PAGE SPONSORED BY:

STEVENS PAINT & GLASS
PAINTS AND WALLPAPER
PICTURE FRAMING
"Huck" Stevens
723 E. Elizabeth Brownsville, Texas LIncoln 2-4151

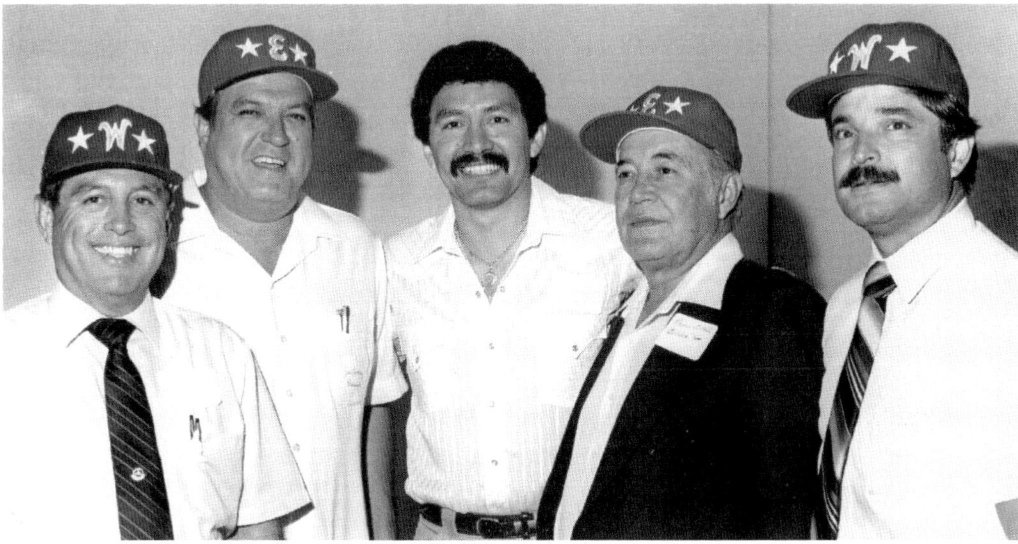

The East-West Showcase All-Star Baseball Game was held on June 18, 1983, at Jody Ramsey Stadium on the Pan American University campus in Edinburg. The game was played in honor of longtime baseball promoter and supporter Ramón "Mr. Baseball" Cantu. From left to right are Rubén Ayala Sr., who went on to serve Edinburg as municipal judge; Joe Rodríguez, who coached the 1965 Brownsville High School state finalist team; sponsor Lupe Salinas, a pitcher for the Pan American Broncs; Ramón Cantu; and coach Luís "Prince of Thieves" Alamia Jr., who played college ball at Pan American and New Mexico Highlands before coaching the Edinburg Bobcats varsity team. Not pictured is former Major Leaguer from Brownsville Charlie Vaughan, who was coaching the Eastern All-Stars. (Courtesy of Gloria Guerra Ayala.)

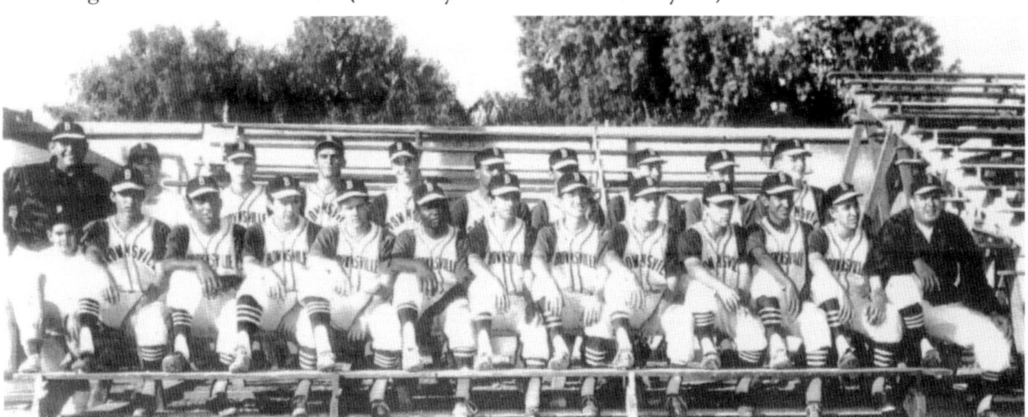

The 1965 Brownsville High School baseball team made the state finals. The Golden Eagles are, from left to right, (first row) batboy Roddy Rodríguez, Cesar de la Garza, Rubén Delgado, Sergio Manzano, Jack Harding, Louis Huff, Prax García, Albert Solitaire, Rene Torres, Arnoldo Álvarez, Henry Martínez, Tony Barbosa, and head coach Joe A. Rodríguez; (second row) assistant coach Ramón Rodríguez, team trainer Manuel Torres, Tommy Hughston, Ramiro Barreda, Charlie Vaughan, Art Galván, Raúl Barreda, Tony Tamayo, Chris Carpenter, and Ronnie Humphreys. (Courtesy of Rene Torres via Charlie Vaughan.)

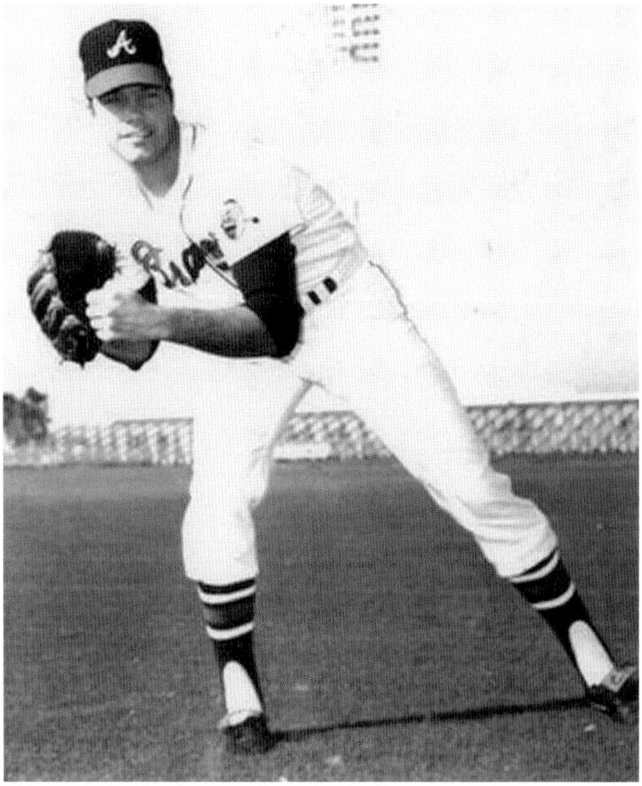

From the 1965 Brownsville Golden Eagles state finalist team, several players continued to play ball at the next level. Among them was left-handed pitcher Charlie Vaughan, who was drafted by the Milwaukee Braves in 1965. After spending time in the minor leagues, Vaughan debuted the following year in 1966 after the organization moved to Atlanta. In Atlanta, he rubbed elbows with elite stars such as Hank Aaron, Eddie Mathews, and Felipe Alou. Catching for Vaughan was Joe Torre. (Courtesy of Charlie Vaughan.)

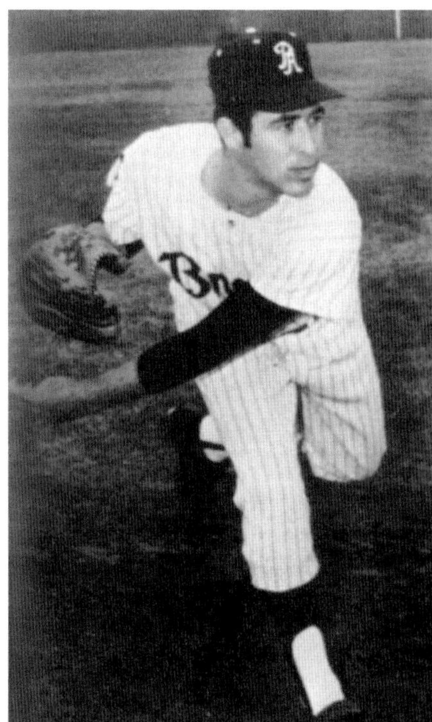

Between 1967 and 1970, Tony Barbosa Jr. pitched for Pan American College (today's University of Texas–Rio Grande Valley), becoming the first pitcher in the program's history to beat the University of Texas at Austin. Barbosa's career at Pan American College was a great one, and his finishing record included 290 innings pitched, 351 strikeouts, career 1.24 ERA, and .89 ERA single season (1968). In 1969, he was an NCAA All-American, pitching a no-hitter versus the University of Houston and, a year later, a one-hitter versus Houston Baptist. He was drafted by the California Angels. (Courtesy of Rio Grande Valley Collection, University of Texas–Pan American.)

If anyone can be called "Mr. Baseball," it is Rene Torres, who played centerfield for Pan American College from 1965 to 1969. Torres is a scholar of all South Texas sports and has single-handedly recovered the history of baseball on the Texas borderlands. Torres has served his community as a member of the Texas Southmost College board of trustees leading the Hispanic serving institution to a new road. Most people can only dream of affecting the world the way Rene Torres has. (Courtesy of Rene Torres.)

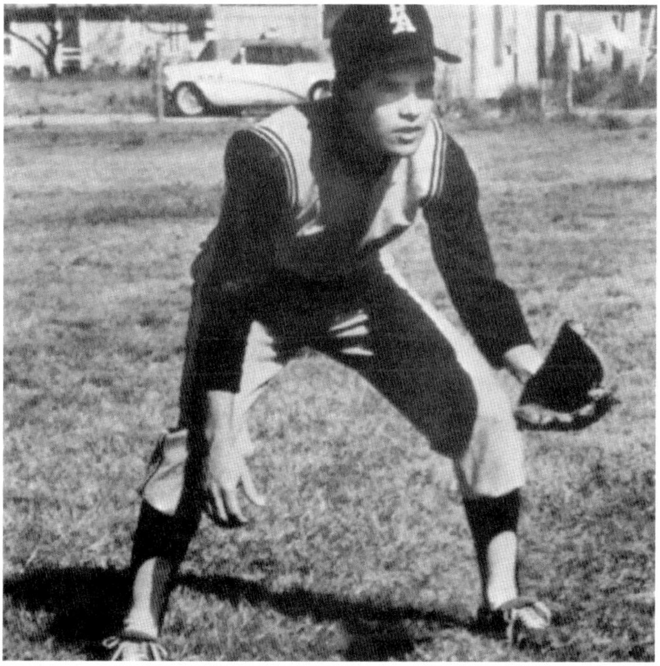

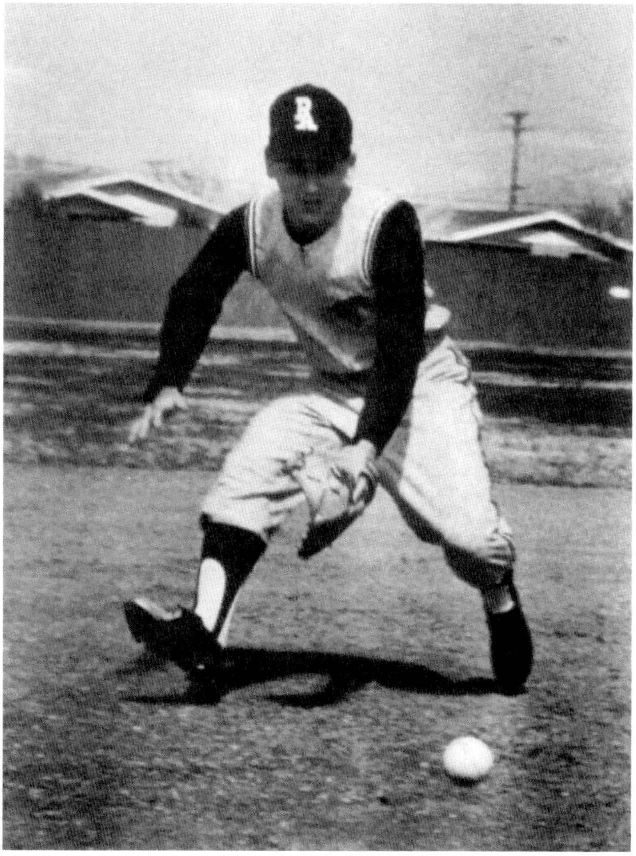

Arnoldo Álvarez played baseball for Pan American College between 1967 and 1970. The Brownsville, Texas, native played infield for the Broncs. Álvarez is the only man to be part of the University Interscholastic League state tournament both as player and a coach. In 1965, he played third base for Brownsville High School and was a coach with Mercedes High School in 1974. (Courtesy of Rio Grande Valley Collection, University of Texas–Pan American.)

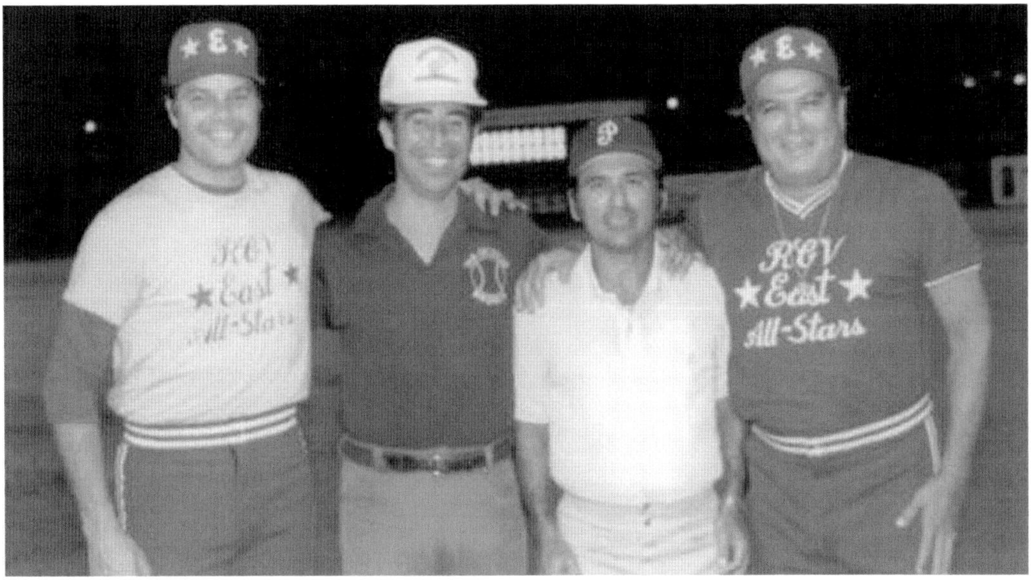

From left to right are Charlie Vaughan, Tony Barbosa, Arnoldo Álvarez, and coach Joe Rodríguez. The East-West Showcase All-Star Baseball Game, held on June 18, 1983, at Jody Ramsey Stadium at Pan American University, served as an unofficial reunion for several members of the 1965 Brownsville Golden Eagles, who reached the state finals. Charlie and Coach Joe coached the East squad. Fellow teammates Barbosa and Álvarez had notable coaching careers as Barbosa went on to coach at Brownsville Pace High School, and Álvarez respectively coached at Mercedes High School and Brownsville Porter High School. (Courtesy of Charlie Vaughan.)

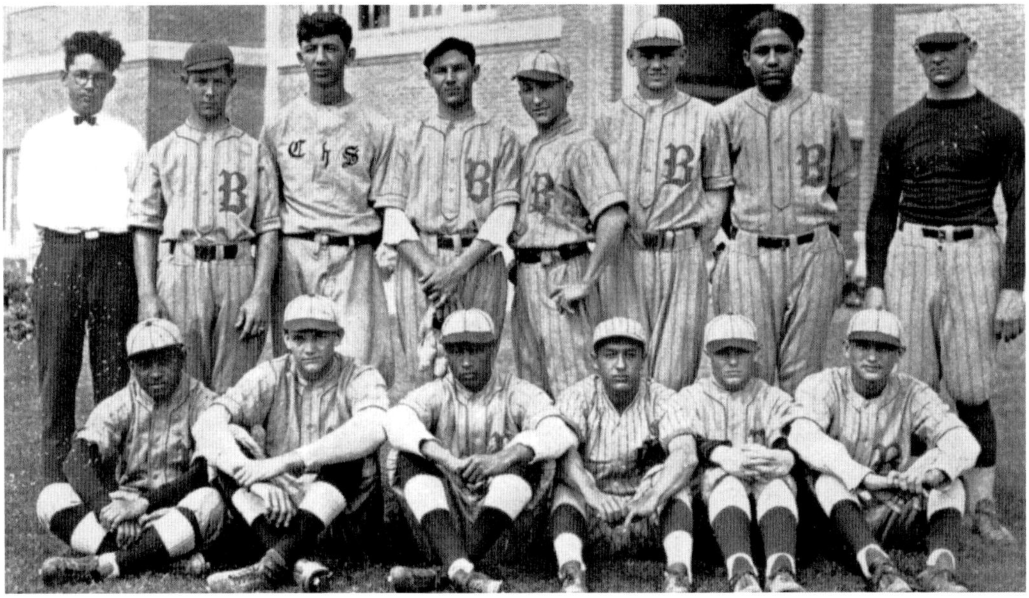

Since the early days of high school baseball, Brownsville High School had struggled on the diamond. But the 1925 team, pictured here, was a first-class squad. With brand new uniforms and a good coach, the aggregation gave Brownsville a team to be proud of. (Courtesy of Rene Torres.)

3

Baseball on the Border and Beyond

In the South Texas border region, baseball became an inclusive social activity in a society that was fragmented by a political border and by de facto segregation. The popularity of baseball was a transnational phenomenon. Teams from México including the 1957 Little League World Series champions from Monterrey, Nuevo León, México, traveled north across the Rio Grande to challenge their South Texas neighbors, and Mexican teams hosted games as well, as American teams traveled to México for a competitive contest.

Semiprofessional teams, such as the Mission 30-30 Rifles, set a precedent for integration and a limited interaction among Mexican Americans and Anglo Americans. The legendary Tom Landry, also a Mission native, suited up for the 30-30s. Through the early 1960s, Mission, like most valley towns, remained segregated as the Anglo community lived north of the railroad tracks and the Mexican American community lived south of the tracks. During the 1960s, teams were organized, managed, and coached by Ramón Cantu and traveled into Mexico to play in the cities of Monterrey, Saltillo, Montemorelos, La Fama, Cadereyta, and Miguel Aleman. They were comprised of Pan American College players and other Rio Grande Valley standouts who excelled at the game, including some who had played on teams organized by Leo Najo.

Sports served as an avenue for interaction between both groups, which eased racial tensions. During the 1946 season, the 30-30s played primarily on the road, as they lacked a home field. The team eventually settled at the Mission 30-30 Rifles Ballpark, located in Southwest Mission in what traditionally was the Mexican American part of town. The Anglo American community soon found itself cheering for the 30-30s in South Mission. The times were changing, and these transformations were evident on the baseball diamonds.

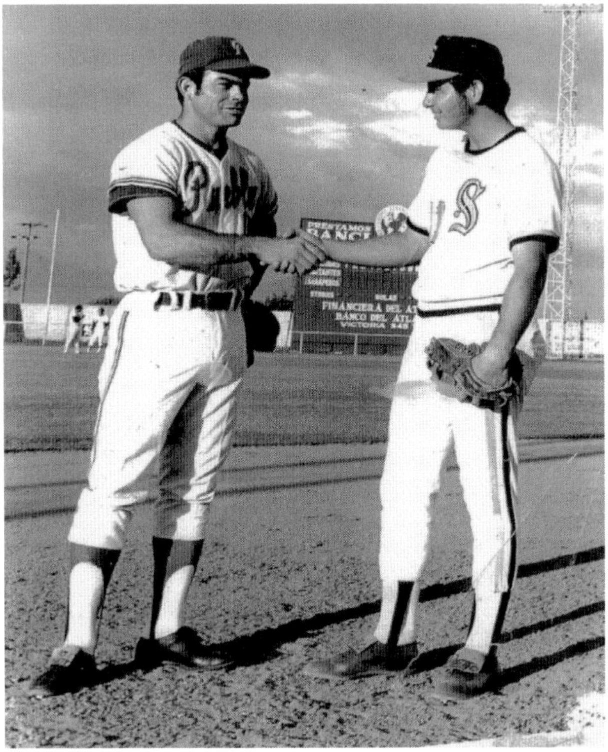

These are the García brothers from Faysville, Texas, a small rural community near Edinburg. On the left is Alonzo "Knot" García, and on the right is Humberto "Beto" García. The photograph is from when the brothers played in the Mexican Triple A League. Alonzo was the leader in stolen bases. Humberto was respected for his power hitting. Alonzo García was posthumously inducted to the Rio Grande Valley Sports Hall of Fame on June 27, 2015. (Courtesy of Vicente and Francisco Estévis.)

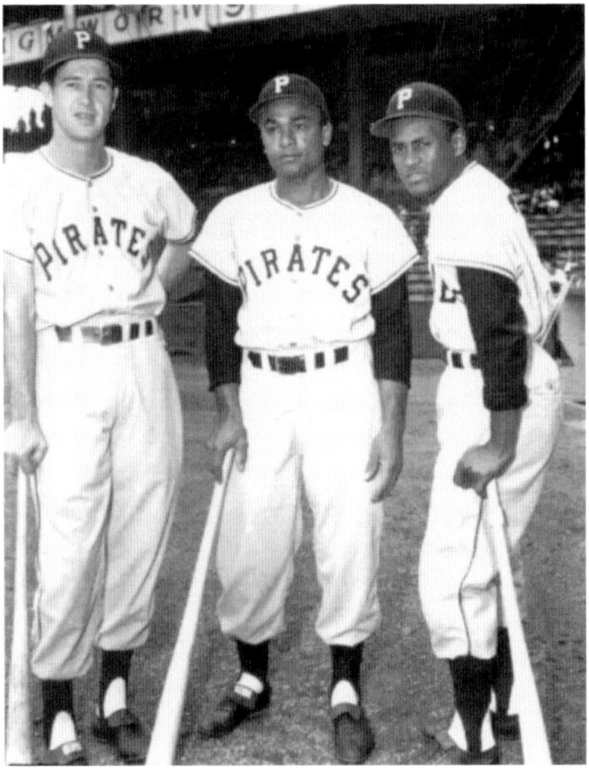

From left to right are Felipe Montemayor, Ramón Mejías, and the legendary Roberto Clemente. A native of Monterrey, Nuevo León, Mexico, Montemayor debuted for the Pittsburgh Pirates on April 14, 1953. After the 1955 season, the left-handed outfielder/first-baseman returned to Mexico where he continued to play professionally. In 1983, he was inducted to the Mexican Baseball Hall of Fame. He was often respectfully referred to as "the Mexican Ted Williams." Ironically, Ted Williams's mother is believed to have been a Mexican American from El Paso; hence, both were of Mexican descent. Montemayor was honored at the Leo Najo Hall of Fame induction ceremony on October 3, 2015, in Mission. (Courtesy of Bert Lozano.)

This c. 1934 photograph shows the 4th Cavalry stationed at Fort Ringgold in the border town of Rio Grande City. Soldiers stationed there from all over the United States played baseball in their free time. During World War II, soldiers stationed at the Moore Field Air Base in Mission and Harlingen Army Airfield continued the tradition. (Courtesy of Vicente and Francisco Estévis.)

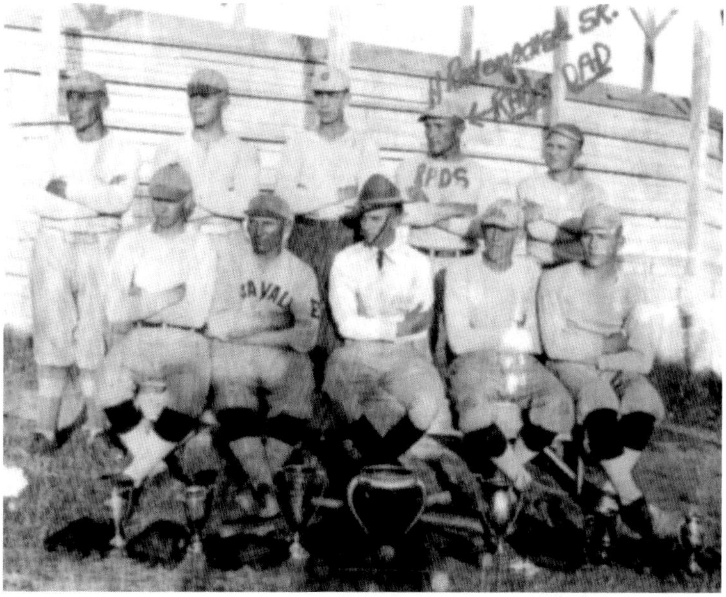

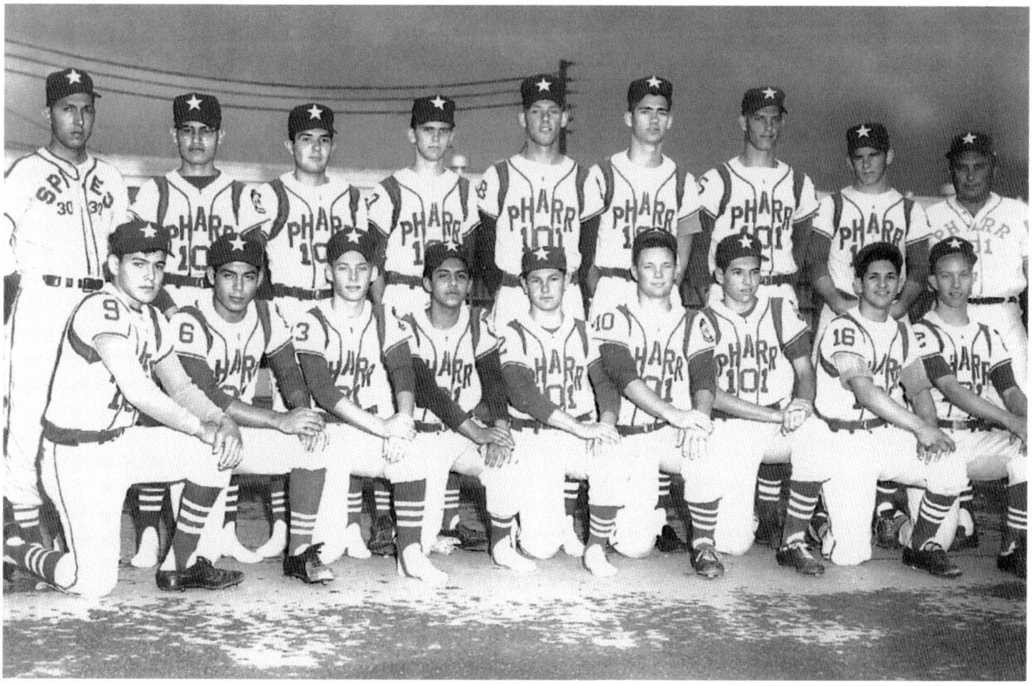

The 1962 Hidalgo County Colt League All Star team was composed of eight Mexican American and eight white players, and one Mexican American manager and one white coach. Players were selected from teams representing five Hidalgo County cities: Edinburg, McAllen, Mercedes, Mission, and Pharr. Francisco Santiago and Roberto Zamora from Penitas played with the Mission team. All team members and coaches were inducted into the Leo "Najo" Alanis Hall of Fame in 2012, on the 50th anniversary of winning the Colt League World Series in Shawnee, Oklahoma. The team had outstanding pitching. (Courtesy of Rey Valadez and Roberto Zamora.)

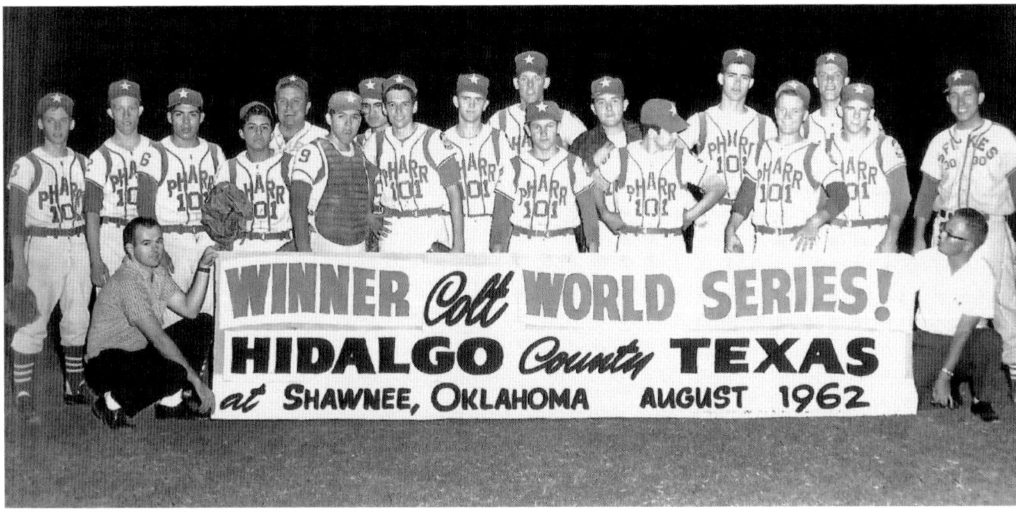

The 1962 Colt League World Series champions celebrate their victory over Riverside, California, in Shawnee, Oklahoma, on August 25, 1962. Upon returning to the Rio Grande Valley, the public celebrated the youngsters. The following May, the team was honored at the Mission Chamber of Commerce banquet where they were introduced to Texas governor John Connally. State representative and former Mission 30-30 Rifles ballplayer Kika de la Garza delivered on his promise made the previous summer and cemented a political career that would shortly take him to the US House of Representatives. (Courtesy of Roberto Zamora.)

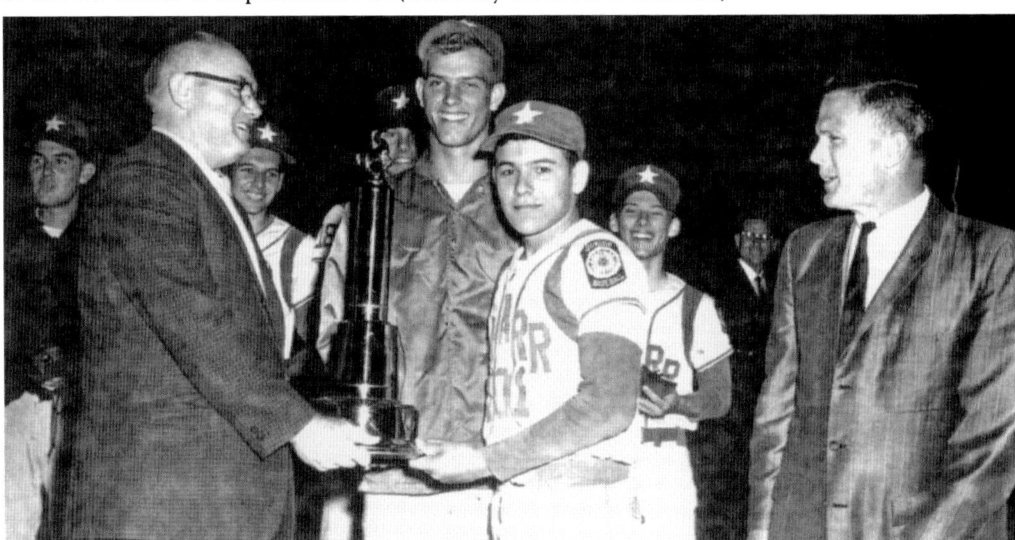

Co-captains Roberto Zamora (right) and Sherwood Lucas accept the championship trophy for the Colt League World Series on August 25, 1962. Zamora and Lucas gave tremendous symbolic representation to the 1962 Hidalgo County team. Despite the social barriers, inequality, and extreme poverty that existed at the time in their communities in South Texas, the team played in absolute harmony and came together as a true underdog, committed to achieving a Cinderella story. (Courtesy of José Alfredo Valadez.)

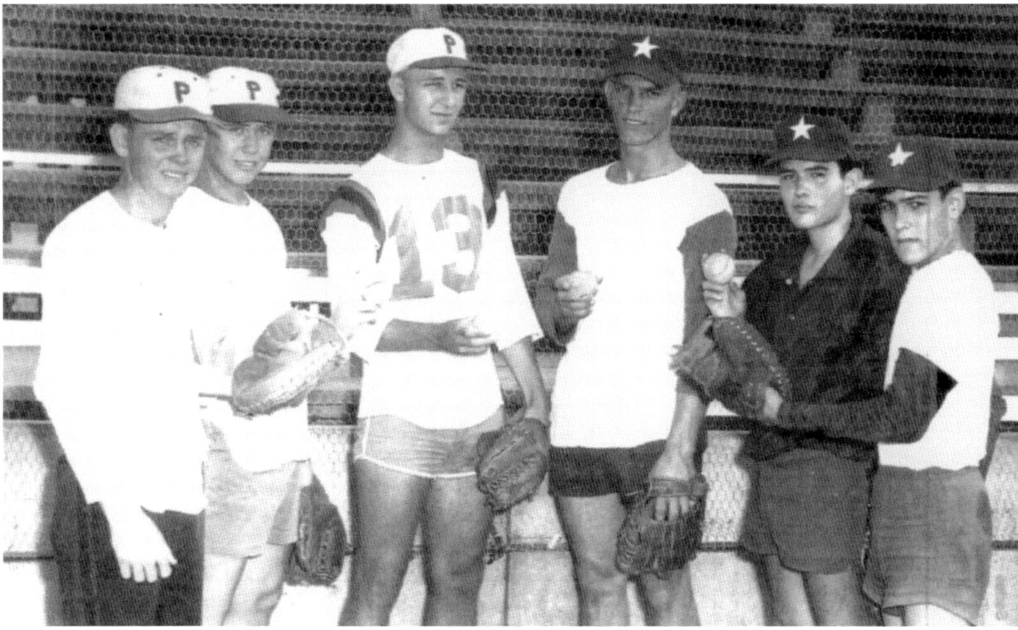

Here, pitchers and catchers for Hidalgo County (right) meet their counterparts from Pensacola, Florida. The teams met in Shawnee, Oklahoma, and the winner would represent the Southern Division in the 1962 Colt League World Series. Kindly referred to as the "Border Bandits" by the home crowd, the Texans went on to win and later faced the Northern Division champion Hamtramck, Michigan, a Detroit team that had previously won the Pony League World Series; Eastern Division champion Norfolk County, Virginia; and the Western Division champion Riverside, California, which then starred future Major Leaguer Bobby Bonds. (Courtesy of José Alfredo Valadez.)

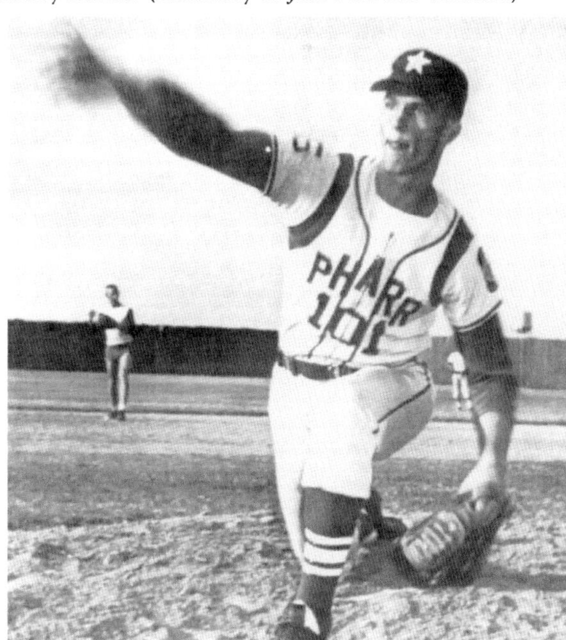

Hidalgo County pitcher Ted Larson from Edinburg warms up at the Colt League World Series in August 1962. Players from the entire county represented not just South Texas, but the entire state. Players from Mission, Peñitas, McAllen, Edinburg, Pharr, and Mercedes participated. Living in one of the most impoverished counties in the whole country, the Hidalgo County team could not afford new uniforms. Team manager Glen Robbie, who assisted head coach Rey Valadez, borrowed the best uniforms available from a team he managed at the American Legion Post No. 101 in Pharr, Texas. (Courtesy of José Alfredo Valadez.)

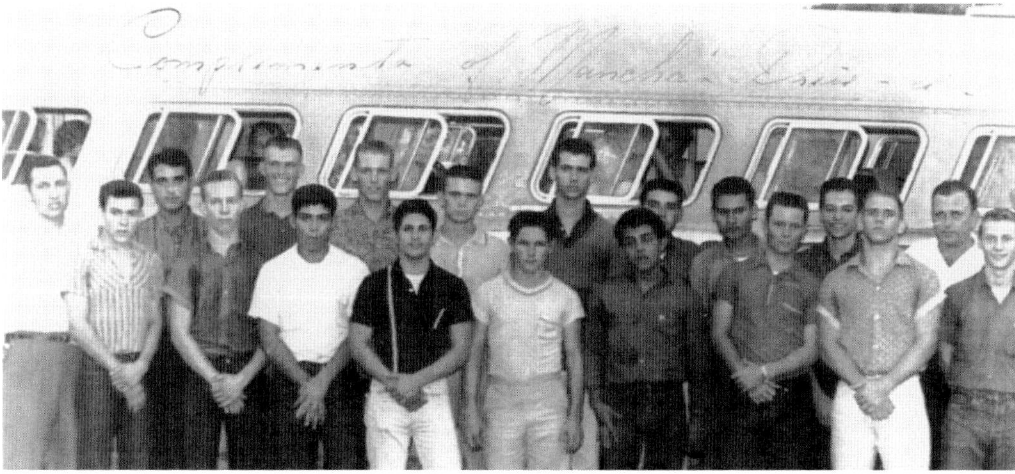

The 1962 Hidalgo County All-Stars pose in front of their bus before they embark on a trip that will change their lives forever. The players left the valley as aspiring youngsters who were underdogs; however, they returned as world champions and learned that they could accomplish anything in life. Johnny Economedes volunteered as the bus driver and equipment manager. After seeing the bus that was to transport the team, he went and found more suitable transportation, a school bus from Edinburg Consolidated Independent School District. (Courtesy of José Alfredo Valadez.)

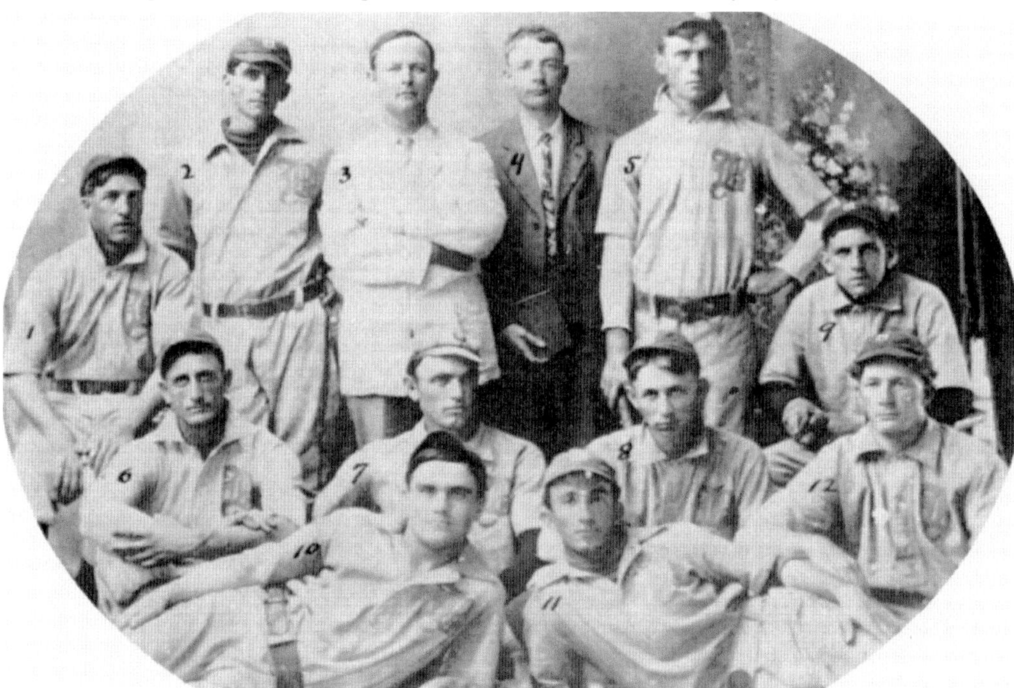

By 1904, the same year the St. Louis, Brownsville & Mexico Railway rattled into town—the city baseball nine made its debut. The Brownsville City Team developed a healthy following as they went through the season without a blemish. Unofficially, the border town boys were declared South Texas champions of 1904. (Courtesy of José Mario Cavazos.)

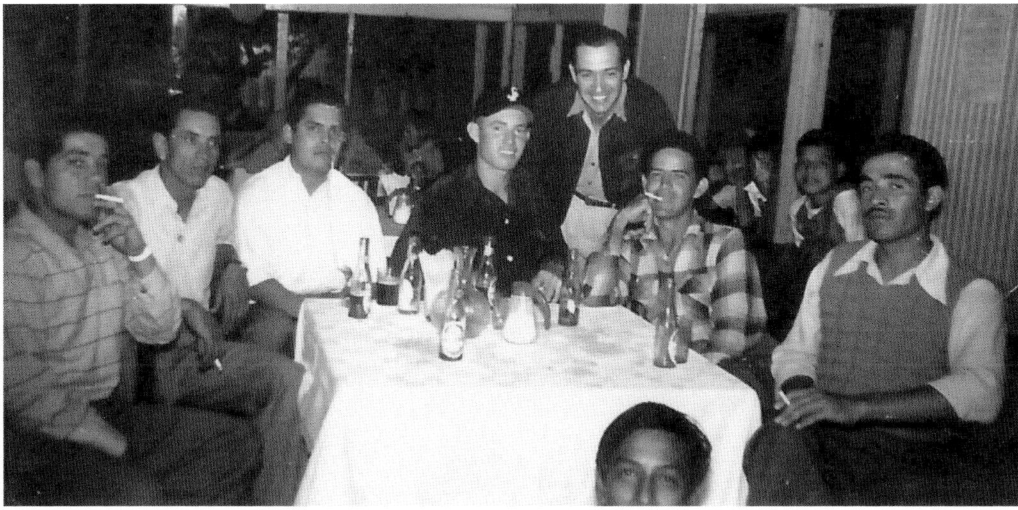

Manuel Cavazos is pictured with team members enjoying a cold refreshment after a game. Cavazos started to play baseball semi-professionally and professionally at the age of 18. He played for the Robstown team, McAllen Palms, Edinburg Ginners, Mission 30-30s, and Laredo Apaches. He also played winter ball in Veracruz, Mexico, and in La Liga Petrolera. (Courtesy of José Mario Cavazos.)

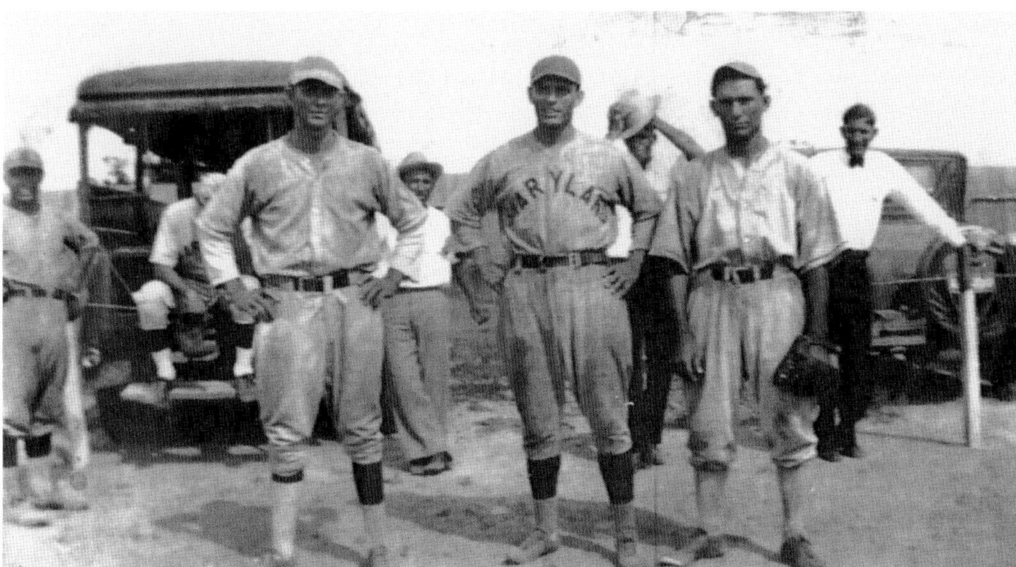

This picture, taken on November 30, 1923, shows baseball in the Mission area of Sharyland. The warmer climates in South Texas attracted Midwesterners. Tired of the cold, they relocated to not just warmer climates, but also to very fertile lands. John H. Shary, a transplant in the 1910s, was responsible for developing the farming community of Sharyland. Shary flourished in the citrus industry of South Texas. Today, Midwesterners continue to travel to South Texas during the winter months and join softball leagues such as the Senior Texan Softball League. (Courtesy of Pikey Rodríguez.)

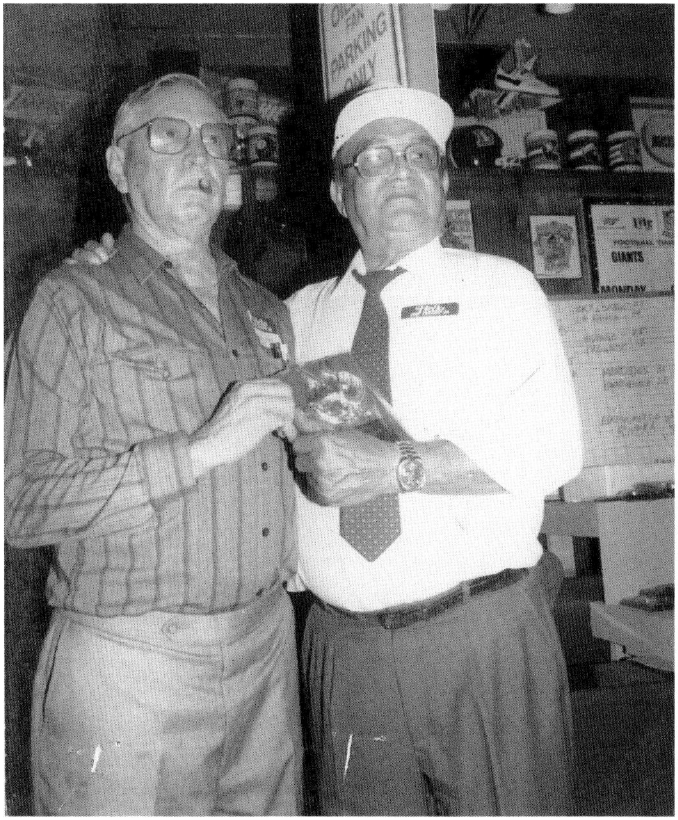

Camilo Rodríguez Sr. (left) worked as a baseball scout for the Houston Astros. Rodríguez spent a career searching for potential baseball talent throughout Texas and Northern Mexico. Prior to his work with the Houston Astros organization, Rodríguez played semiprofessional baseball in Mexico and Texas from 1934 to 1950. His son Camilo "Bucky" Rodríguez Jr. (not pictured) went on to play baseball for the Pan American College Broncs and coached high school baseball and football. Both have been enshrined in the Rio Grande Valley Sports Hall of Fame. (Courtesy of Pikey Rodríguez.)

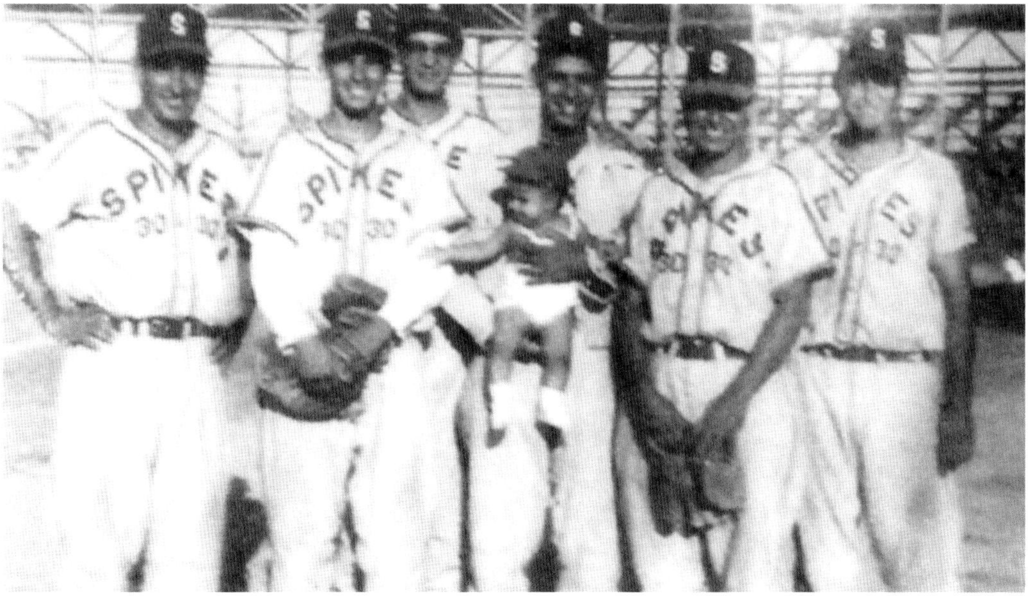

The Cavazos brothers are, from left to right, Manuel "Meme," Francisco "Pancho," José Angel "Joey," Mateo, and Tino. They played for the Mission Spikes 30-30 Rifles. (Courtesy of José Mario Cavazos.)

José Mario Cavazos was the first to go beyond elementary school in his family and was the first to graduate from the University of Texas at Austin. He was a pitcher, catcher, and first baseman for the Mission American Legion team and the Mission High School Eagles. These teams were undefeated in the Valley. Cavazos played two years (1949–1950) for the Edinburg Junior College Broncs. The Broncs won both of the junior college baseball tournaments, which included junior college teams from Brownsville, Laredo, San Antonio, Wharton, and Houston. (Courtesy of José Mario Cavazos.)

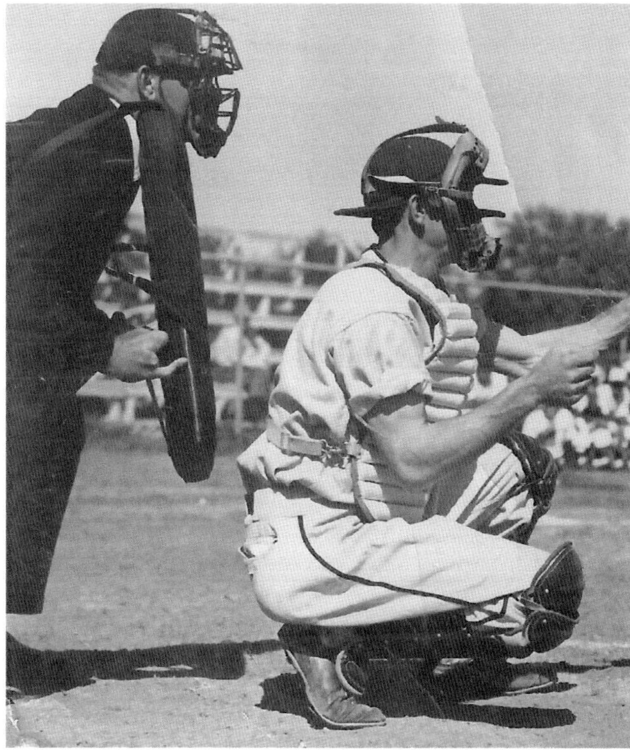

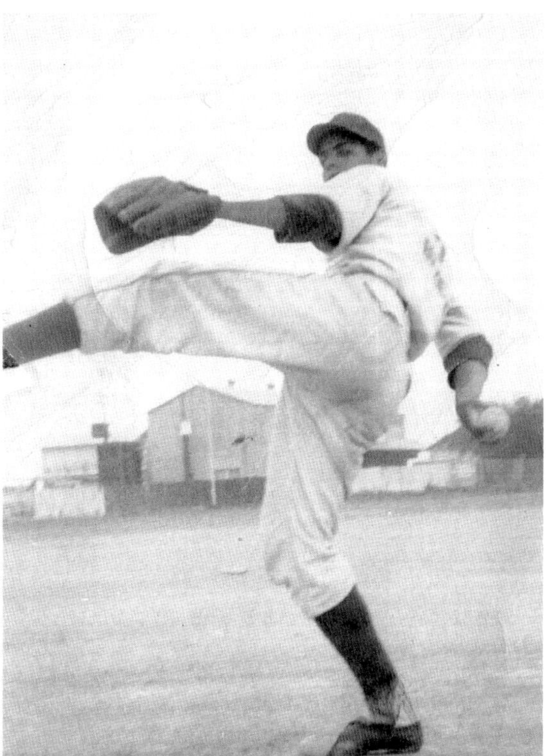

José Mario Cavazos tried out for the Texas Longhorns, but soon realized that academics and athletics do not mix easily. He played semi-pro and winter league baseball in Mexico. His best memories are playing for manager Leo Najo with the Mission 30-30s. He played second base on a heavily talented team. Cavazos also played for the Edinburg Ginners, where he was selected twice as All-District Player and twice played at the semi-pro state tournament, where the Ginners won the state championship. (Courtesy of José Mario Cavazos.)

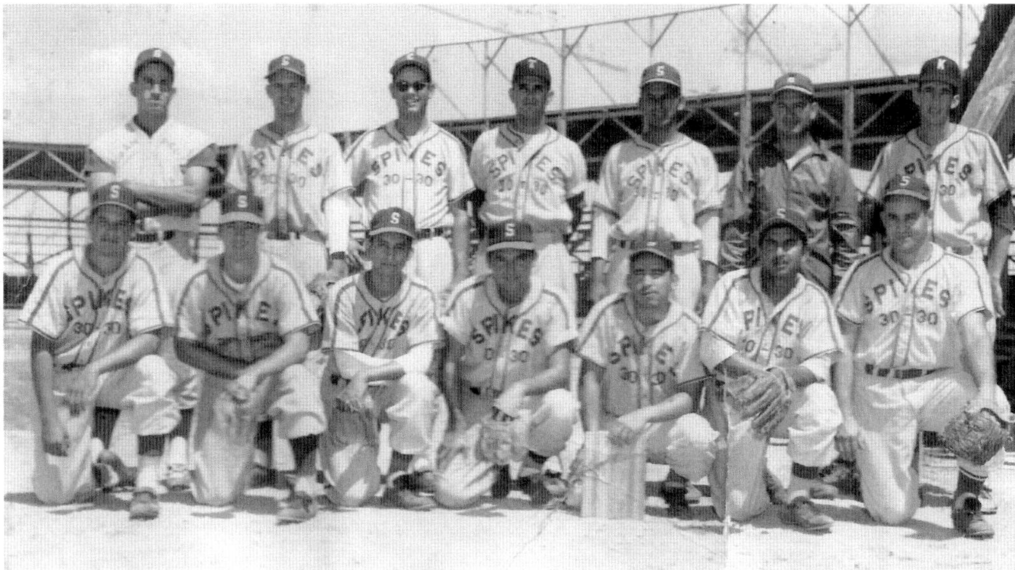

Players of the Mission Spikes 30-30 Rifles are seen here. They are, from left to right, (first row) Mateo Cavazos, Lonnie Anderson, Pete Pérez, Pablo Pérez, Ignacio García, José Flores, and Mundo Sánchez; (second row) Luís Sánchez, Francisco Cavazos, José Mario Cavazos, Faustino Cavazos, José Angel Cavazos, Manuel Cavazos, and Jimmy Edwards. (Courtesy of José Mario Cavazos.)

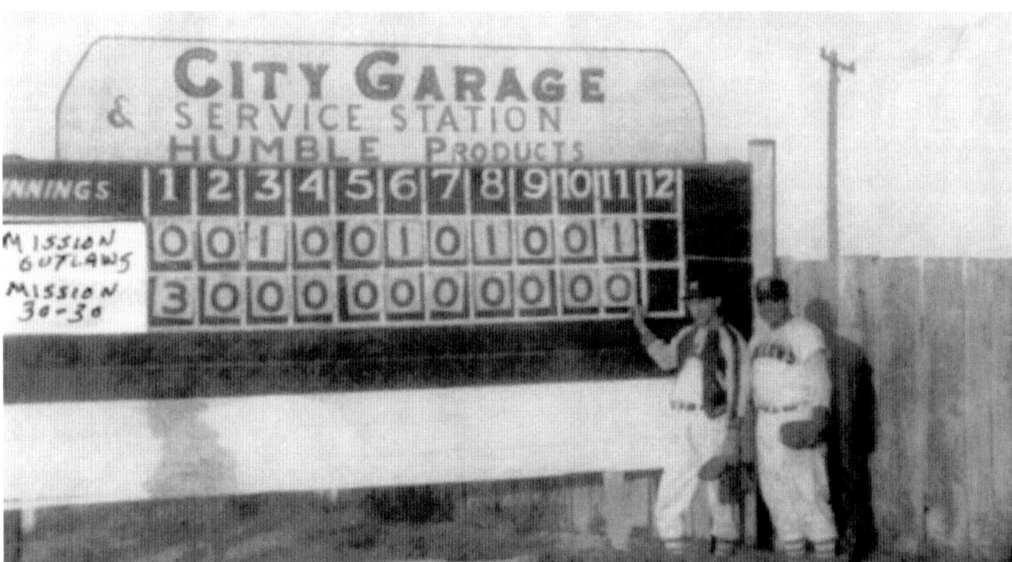

The Mission Derby between the Mission Outlaws and the Mission 30-30 Rifles was played on Labor Day, September 7, 1953. The fans were treated to 11 innings of baseball during which a very dominant Reynaldo "Rey" Valadez pitched a phenomenal outing. Major League prospect Mundo Sánchez, who was signed by the Detroit Tigers, played for the 30-30s. As major stars played on each side, Borrado Flores also played that day. Pictured are Outlaw and Bronc teammates Cisco Estévis (left) and Reynaldo Valadez. (Courtesy of Vicente and Francisco Estévis.)

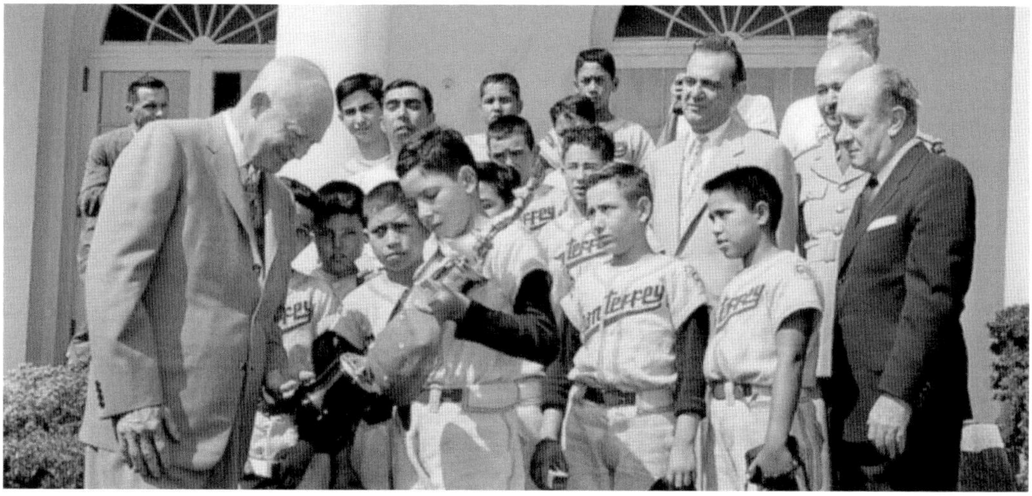

The 1957 Little League World Series champions were from Monterrey, Nuevo León, Mexico. Before the ambidextrous Ángel Macias pitched a perfect game clinching the Little League title and before being hosted by President Eisenhower at the White House, the Monterrey team crossed the border into the Rio Grande Valley where they were hosted by Judge Darío García Sr. In South Texas, the Monterrey team faced some fierce competitors from valley teams en route to the World Series title in Williamsport, Pennsylvania. (Courtesy of Juan D. Coronado.)

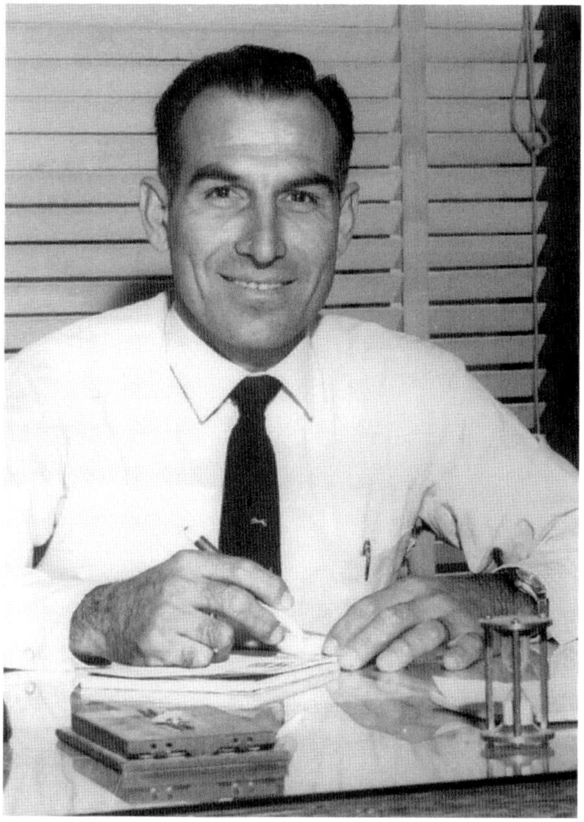

At a time when the border between the United States and Mexico was much more open, baseball teams crossed easily in both directions and partook in friendly yet competitive outings. Judge Darío García Sr., a former ballplayer who played for several semiprofessional teams including the Mecca Café from Reynosa, Tamaulipas, Mexico, the Mission 30-30 Rifles, the McAllen Palms, and the Donna Cardinals, had a passion not only for baseball, but also to see young children succeed. Judge García hosted the 1957 Monterrey team, providing them with room and board on their way to Pennsylvania. (Courtesy of Pikey Rodríguez.)

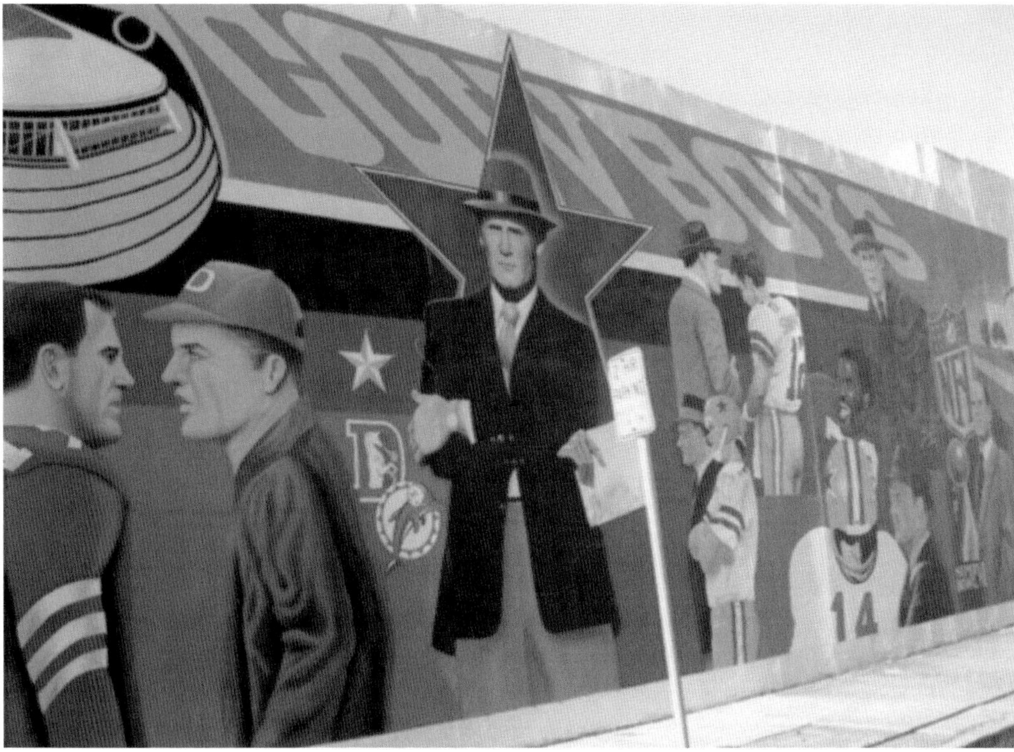

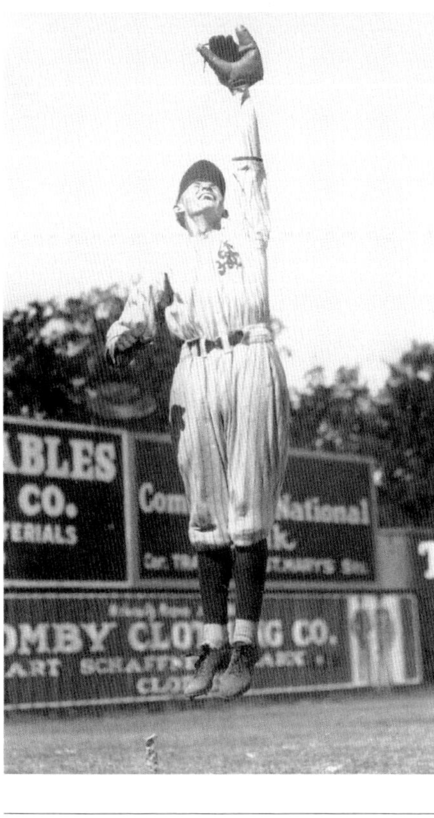

Tom Landry was a native of Mission. Before becoming the legendary coach of America's Team, the Dallas Cowboys, a team he led to two Super Bowl championships, Landry was a star athlete for the Mission High School Eagles. He is credited with hitting the first home run at the 30-30 ballpark in Mission in 1947. It is believed he was given a ring in commemoration of the feat. (Courtesy of Juan D. Coronado.)

Leonardo "Leo Najo" Alanis was born in La Lajilla, Nuevo Leon, Mexico, but grew up in Mission. He was an accomplished player in local leagues, playing with the Mission 30-30 Rifles and also in Mexico until 1926. He eventually signed with the San Antonio Missions and had a spring training tryout with the Chicago White Sox. Unfortunately, he broke his leg in July 1926 and never again had a chance to make the big leagues. He remained active as a player and played in Oklahoma, Mexico, and Texas. He also managed teams until the late 1950s. (Courtesy of Bert Lozano.)

Here is the October 14, 1956, program for the Major League All-Stars vs. Rio Grande Valley All-Stars game. On numerous occasions, Major Leaguers came down to the Rio Grande Valley to face local talent. During the 1950s, the valley was flooded with baseball talent, and semiprofessional teams were active in numerous South Texas towns. The warmer temperatures in South Texas made it attractive for both professional and college teams to come down for an outing. The game's proceeds went to charity. (Courtesy of Evangelina Garza.)

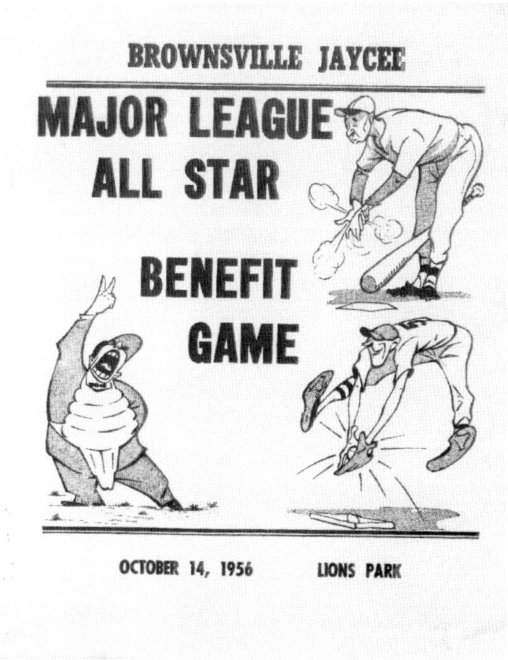

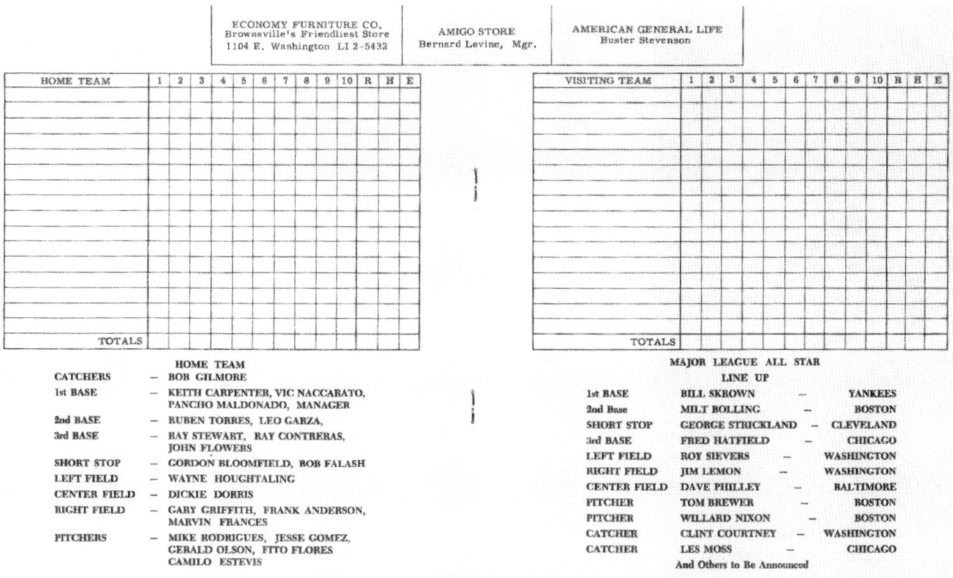

ECONOMY FURNITURE CO.
Brownsville's Friendliest Store
1104 E. Washington LI 2-5432

AMIGO STORE
Bernard Levine, Mgr.

AMERICAN GENERAL LIFE
Buster Stevenson

HOME TEAM	1	2	3	4	5	6	7	8	9	10	R	H	E
TOTALS													

VISITING TEAM	1	2	3	4	5	6	7	8	9	10	R	H	E
TOTALS													

HOME TEAM

CATCHERS	–	BOB GILMORE
1st BASE	–	KEITH CARPENTER, VIC NACCARATO, PANCHO MALDONADO, MANAGER
2nd BASE	–	RUBEN TORRES, LEO GARZA,
3rd BASE	–	RAY STEWART, RAY CONTRERAS, JOHN FLOWERS
SHORT STOP	–	GORDON BLOOMFIELD, BOB FALASH
LEFT FIELD	–	WAYNE HOUGHTALING
CENTER FIELD	–	DICKIE DORRIS
RIGHT FIELD	–	GARY GRIFFITH, FRANK ANDERSON, MARVIN FRANCES
PITCHERS	–	MIKE RODRIGUES, JESSE GOMEZ, GERALD OLSON, FITO FLORES CAMILO ESTEVIS

MAJOR LEAGUE ALL STAR
LINE UP

1st BASE	BILL SKROWN	–	YANKEES
2nd Base	MILT BOLLING	–	BOSTON
SHORT STOP	GEORGE STRICKLAND	–	CLEVELAND
3rd BASE	FRED HATFIELD	–	CHICAGO
LEFT FIELD	ROY SIEVERS	–	WASHINGTON
RIGHT FIELD	JIM LEMON	–	WASHINGTON
CENTER FIELD	DAVE PHILLEY	–	BALTIMORE
PITCHER	TOM BREWER	–	BOSTON
PITCHER	WILLARD NIXON	–	BOSTON
CATCHER	CLINT COURTNEY	–	WASHINGTON
CATCHER	LES MOSS	–	CHICAGO

And Others to Be Announced

Here is the October 14, 1956, program for the all-star benefit game. Baseball in the Rio Grande Valley during the 1950s was central to most towns. Communities gathered not only to see how local ballplayers did against themselves, but also how they fared against professionals. Major League squads had scouted several ballplayers by this point, as the talent in the valley was truly remarkable. While few made it professionally, all had the passion and heart to try to make it all the way. (Courtesy of Evangelina Garza.)

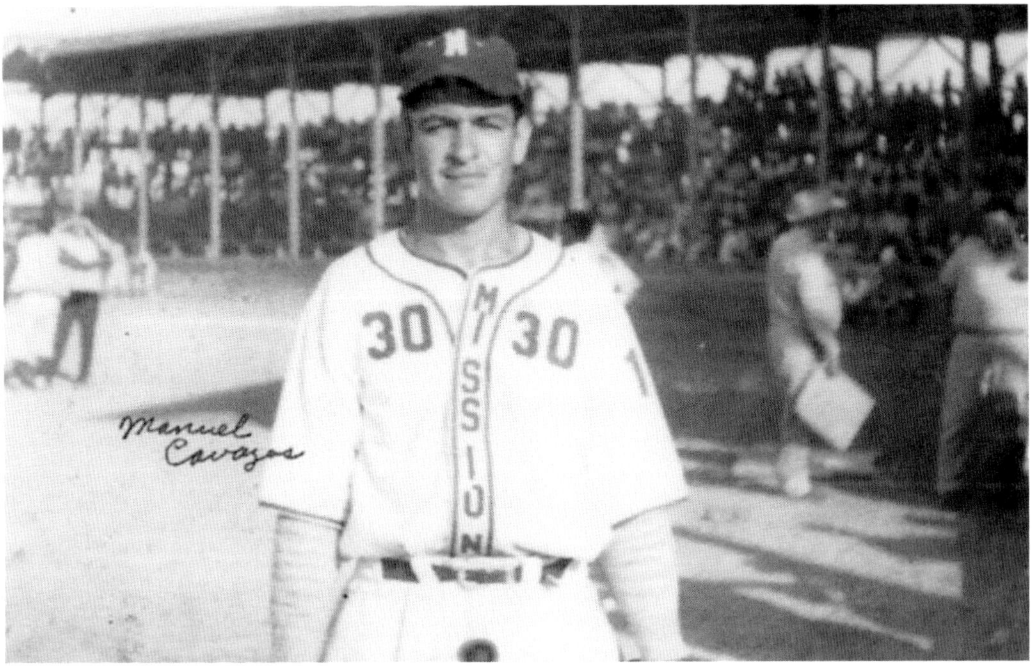

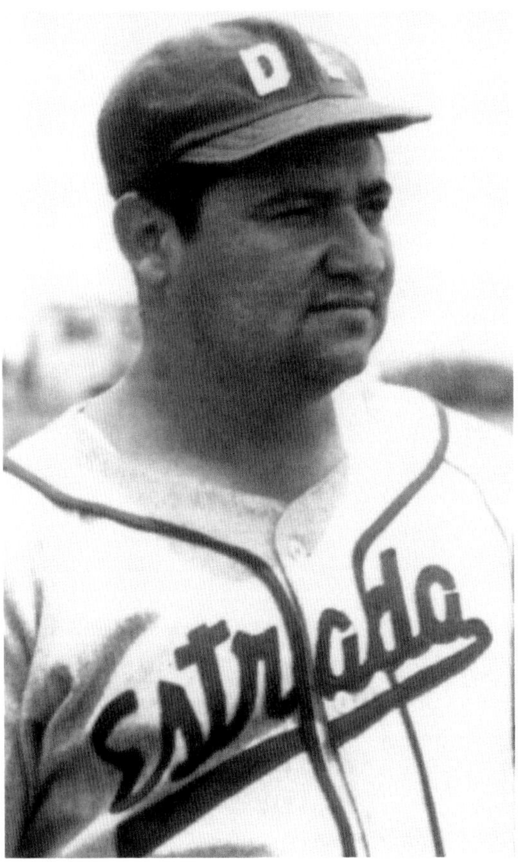

Manuel "Meme" Cavazos played for the Mission Spikes 30-30 Rifles. Having just played in his hometown of Mission, Cavazos also played in Mexico. He is pictured at the famous 30-30 ballpark in Southwest Mission. Both Anglo Americans and Mexican Americans played for the 30-30s and followed and supported the team with great dedication. (Courtesy of José Mario Cavazos.)

This is the legendary Arturo Estrada Sánchez who, aside from playing in the Mexican League, dedicated 40 years as an umpire. Sánchez was instrumental in developing the sport in his home state of Nuevo León as he served as founder of the "Carta Blanca" Baseball Club. In 1935, he formed a squad of Mexican and international players who hosted a baseball tournament in Monterrey, Nuevo León, Mexico. The best Mexican and Río Grande Valley teams participated in the tournament as did the Kansas City Royals and the Mineola Black Spiders, an African American team. (Courtesy of Evangelina Garza.)

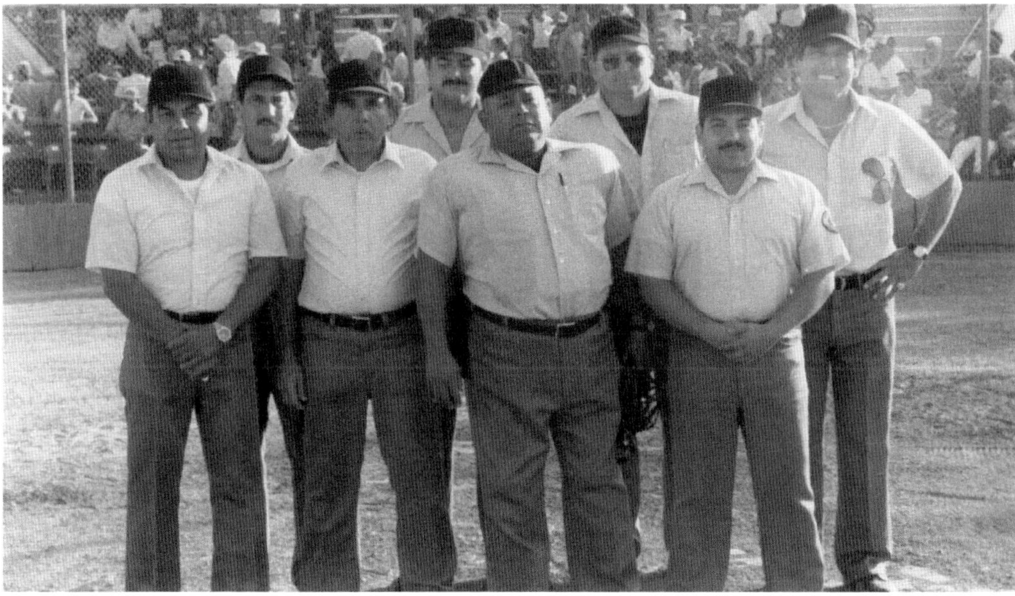

Umpires are instrumental to organized baseball. Most started as ballplayers, and many played high school, college, and semiprofessional baseball. This is a picture of the umpiring crew that called the first Rio Grande Valley High Schools Senior East-West all-star game in 1983, sponsored by Lupe Salinas, the former standout pitcher for the Pan American Broncs team and the Professional Mexican Baseball League. (Courtesy of Bert Lozano.)

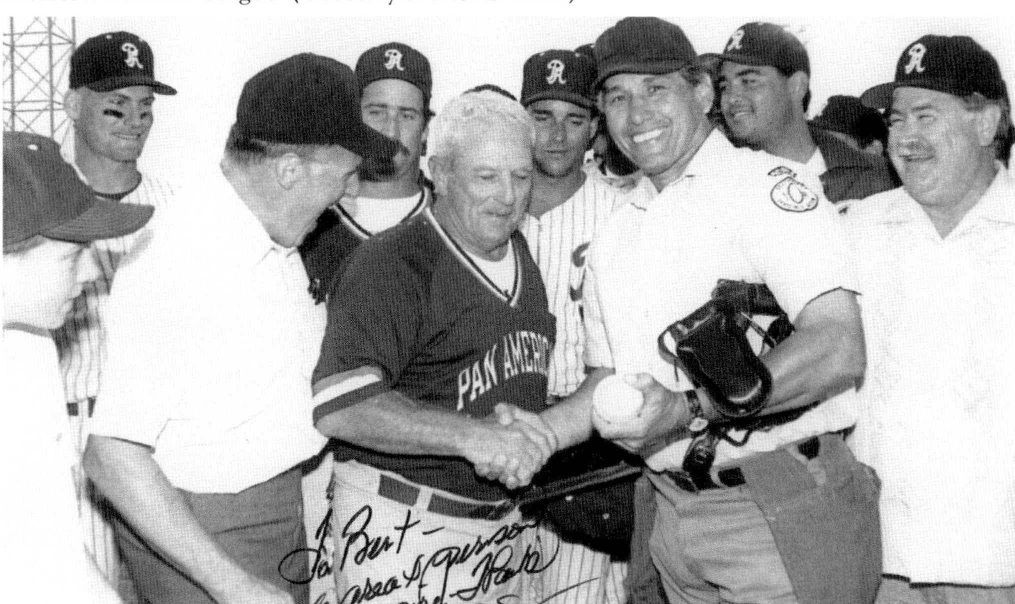

Coach Alfred H. "Al" Ogletree (center) and Bert Lozano (right) are seen here. Coach Ogletree headed Pan American University, later known as the University of Texas–Rio Grande Valley. In 1971, Coach Ogletree led the Broncs to their first College World Series and finished fourth in the tournament, the best finish in school history. (Courtesy of Bert Lozano.)

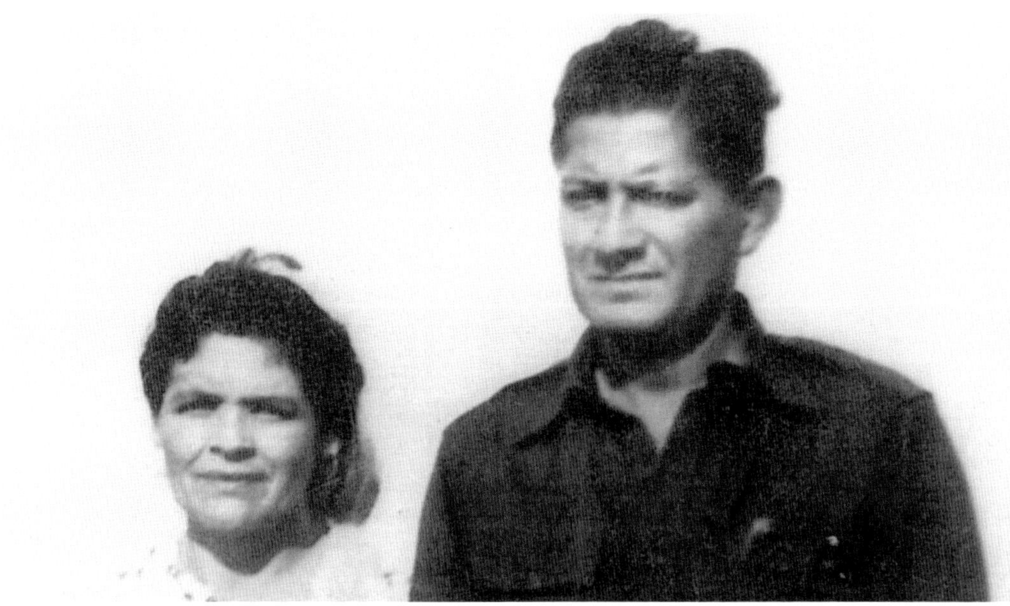

Calixtra Cadena and Matias H. Cavazos started their family in Mercedes, Texas. They moved to Mission in 1929. They ended up with 12 sons and four daughters. Matias was the driving force getting community leaders to build the last 30-30 baseball park west of Mission on old US Highway 83. The park was used by the 30-30 team, the high school team, and the Mission American Legion team. It was constructed under the supervision of Matias H. Cavazos in 1945. (Courtesy of José Mario Cavazos.)

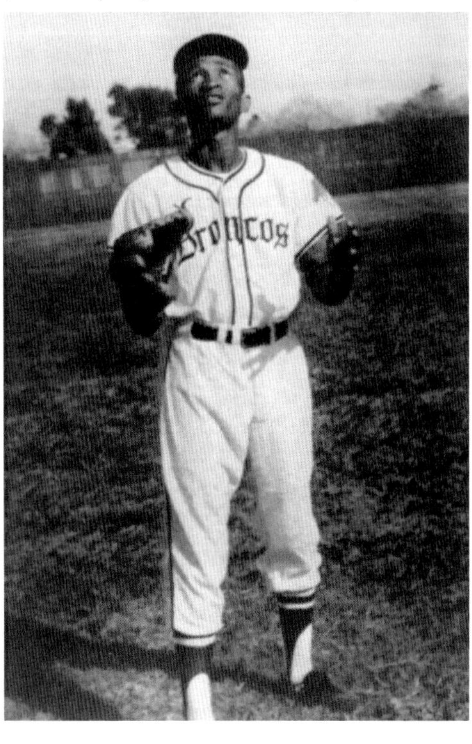

Gary West, along with fellow African American ballplayer James "T-Bone" Heliton (not pictured) from Edinburg, would travel into Mexico with Mexican American ballplayers led by Ramón Cantu. West, a remarkable talent at centerfield, felt at home as Mexican crowds in Nuevo Leon, Coahuila, and Tamaulipas cheered him on. West recalls receiving hats full of pesos from fans in Mexico after hitting home runs. The praise was so delightful that West wished at times that he had stayed in Mexico. (Courtesy of José Mario Cavazos.)

4

THE LONE STAR STATE

In the first Texas-based book in this series, the authors discussed how baseball and softball were (and are) a critical part of the daily experience in *communidades* throughout the Lone Star State. This chapter, with its photographs from the various regions, provides further support of this contention. From places such as Zapata, San Ygnacio, Dallas, San Diego, El Paso/Juárez, and elsewhere, the photographic testimony is clear that, at the workplace (factories, farmlands, and oil fields) and during precious leisure time, Mexican Americans utilized baseball to demonstrate athletic, strategic, and organizational acumen, as well as strengthening ethnic bonds. Moreover, the chapter highlights a few teams from Mexico that often engaged Texas teams on the diamond. The history of Texas baseball is linked to its longtime rivalry with teams from south of the border.

A 1950 thesis from Hardin-Simmons University, in its own condescending way, supports much of the argument presented in this and other works dealing with Mexicans and baseball. In a short work on the status of "Latin Americans" in the city of Melvin (about 60 miles southeast of San Angelo), Floyd Leslie Marshall notes the impact of the game on children both male and female. In his patronizing tone, Marshall acknowledged the value of the sport because such students "became proficient in this sport as a result of having played at home before entering school. Further, the game helped players break down barriers by playing with, and against, white schoolmates. Finally, the game built up in these students a chance to develop good sportsmanship . . . [and] provide a place for them on the Anglo American teams after they reach high school or the [upper] grades."

Although his terminology does not suit today's sensibilities, Marshall's work proffers insight as to the value of baseball in the lives of Mexican Americans in this small community. Surely, if a researcher who did not necessarily embrace Mexican Americans as equals could see the usefulness of the sport to the next generation, baseball and its surrounding events had to be of even greater import to Spanish-speakers. The images that follow buttress this claim as they display the pride and athleticism that were and are a vital part of the Mexican American communities throughout Texas.

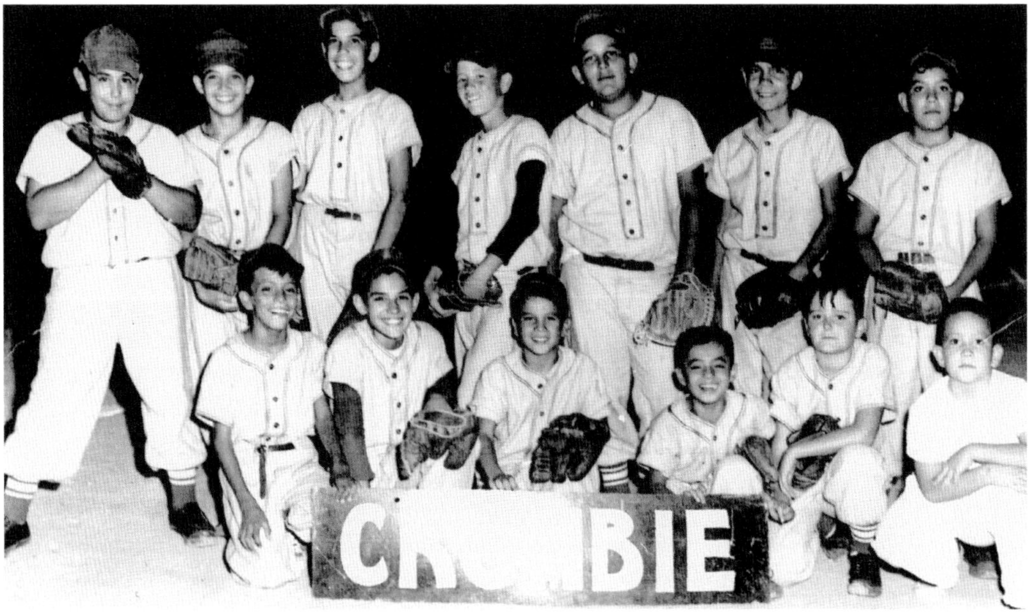

Pictured in the early 1950s, the Crombie team was part of the El Paso West Side Little League. Armando "Muggins" Ruiz practically grew up in the Little League program. He played second base for this team, and with his strong athletic abilities, went on to play numerous levels in the league. Pictured are, from left to right, (first row) Gilbert Meléndez, Júnior Herron, Armando "Muggins" Ruiz, Alonso Gonzáles, Louis Hogge, and David Sosa; (second row) Aténió García, Rudy Ortiz, Amador González, Red ?, Joe Porras, Eddie Mapula, and Stan Sosa. (Courtesy of Armando "Muggins" Ruiz.)

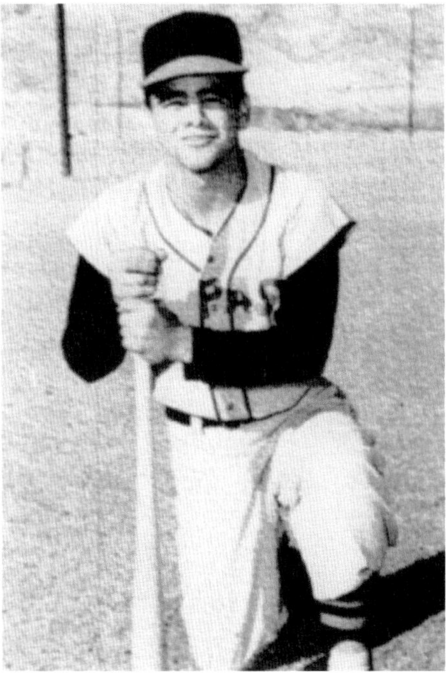

Armando "Muggins" Ruiz grew up in El Paso and graduated from El Paso High School, where he lettered in baseball for four years. He received his bachelor's and master's degrees from Texas Western, now the University of Texas at El Paso. Ruiz taught special education in Texas and California. He later became an administrator before moving to the Coast Community College District in Orange County, California, where he served on the board of trustees for 25 years. He passed away in 2015 and is survived by his wife, Cathy Ruiz; his three children, Jaime, Mandy, and Armando Jr.; and multiple grandchildren. (Courtesy of Armando "Muggins" Ruiz.)

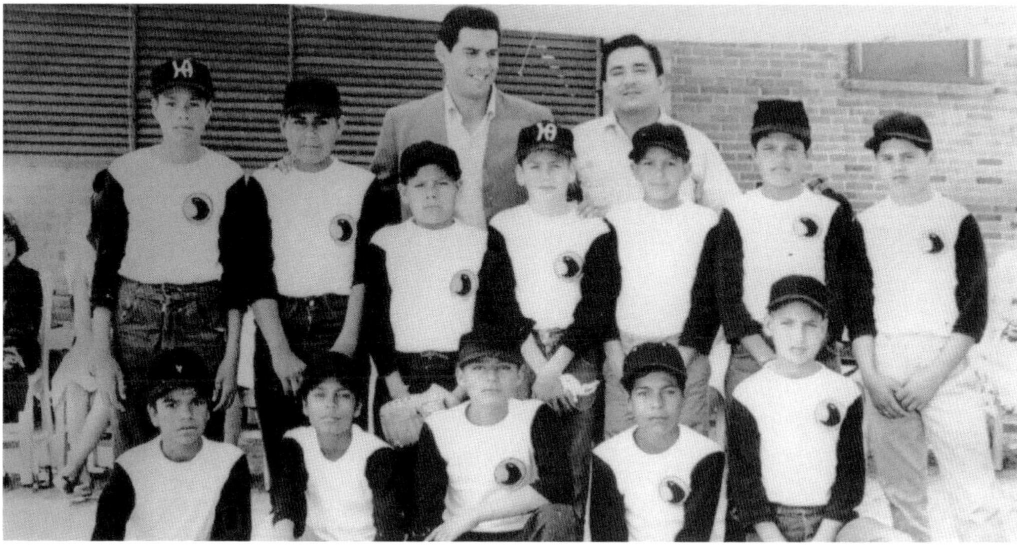

Ray Loya is seen here in the third row, far left in 1967 in Laredo, Texas. The manager asked Loya to help his players. He was living in Laredo and coaching for the Tecolotes de Nueva Laredo in Mexico. He met his wife in Laredo and played and coached in Mexico. He played in Vera Cruz and later in Reynosa, where his pitching debut was against Los Diablos Rojas. Loya played for the Los Mayos de Navojoa, Los Cachorros de Jalisco, and Los Sultanes de Monterey until he retired in 1969. (Courtesy of Ray Loya.)

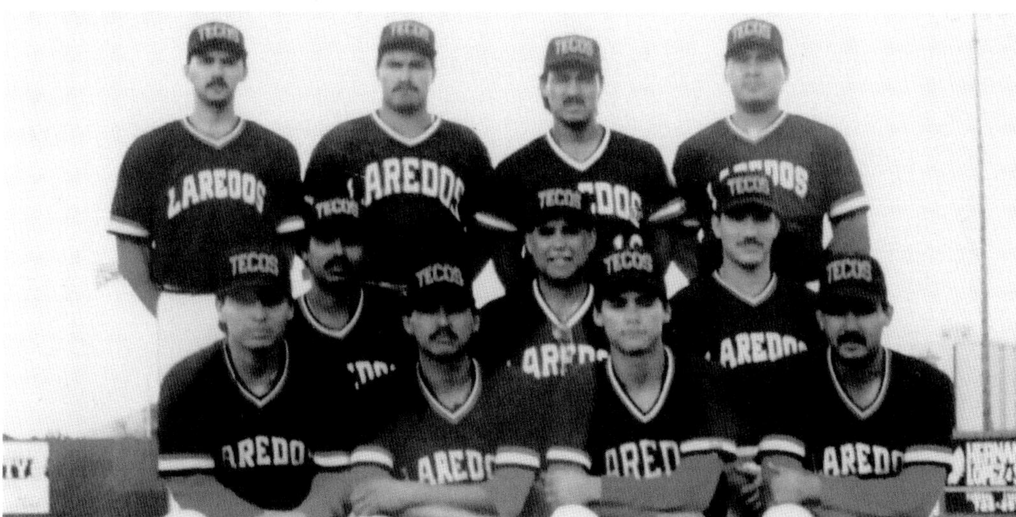

Ray Loya played in the Los Angeles Dodgers Summer League from 1959 through 1963. His teammates included Dick Nen, Joe Moeller, Nate Oliver, Bobby Cox, Norm Sherry, Dick Bogard, Al Ferrara, and Jim Barbieri. He played winter ball with the Dodgers in the Arizona Instructional League, where he was voted Comeback Player of the Year in 1960. After he retired, Loya became a very successful pitching coach. He is seen here (third row, far right) with the pitchers of the Laredo, Mexico, Tecolotes team. His protégés include Trevor Hoffman, Bobby Castillo, Esteban Loriza, Oliver Pérez, Fernando Salas, and Mike Gallegos. (Courtesy of Ray Loya.)

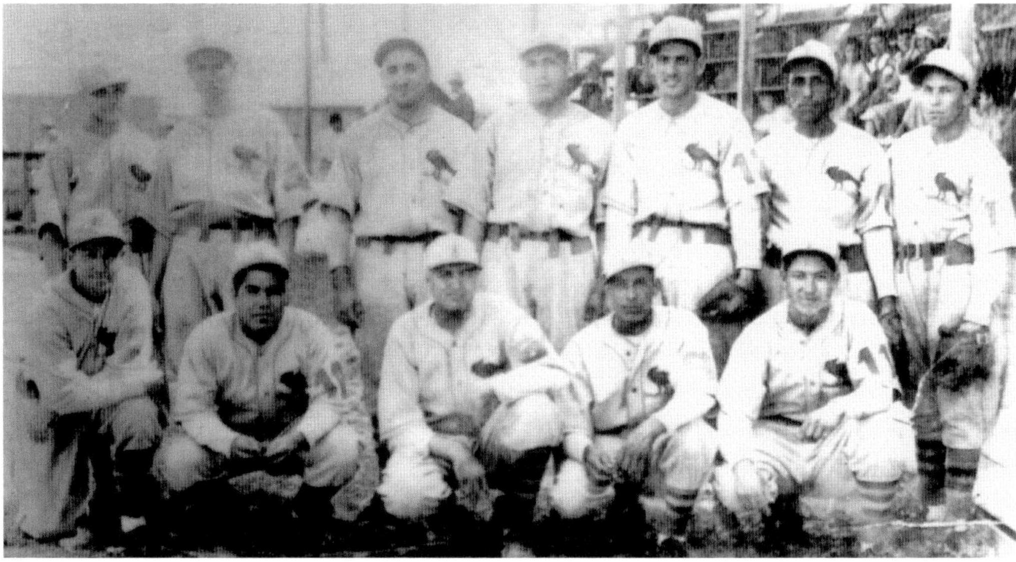

The 1936 San Diego, Texas, Redbirds dominated baseball for many years. From left to right are (first row) Rufino López, José Maria Barrera, ? Arguijo, Luís Longoria Jr., and Francisco Canas; (second row) Ernesto Labbe, Tomas H. Molina, Hank Guerra, Lefty Ramírez, ? Rodríguez, Domingo Salazar, and Bennie Solís. Tomas H. Molina was born in 1913 on a ranch north of San Diego in Duval County. Tomas's father, Teofilo, and his grandfather Regino were both working *vaqueros* on the part of the Corbett Ranch called El Flojo. Tomas moved to San Diego in 1921. (Courtesy of the Molina family.)

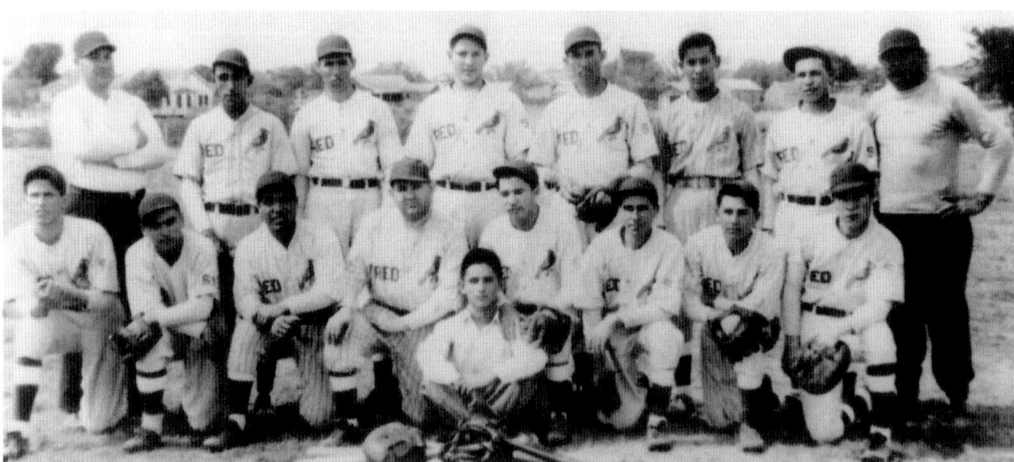

The 1930s San Diego Redbirds are, from left to right, (first row) Lefty Gonzáles, Ernesto Labb, José Maria Barrera, Armando García Jr., Rafael García (batboy), Zenon Solís, Francisco Solíz Jr., Alfredo Pérez, and Diego Navejar; (second row) E.E. Peña (manager), Domingo Salazar, Tomas H. Molina, Francisco Canas, Lauro Chapa, Luís Longoria Jr., Bennie Solís, and Willie López. Molina graduated from high school in 1932. Sometime in the mid-1920s, he discovered baseball. There were sandlot, church, and town teams in San Diego where young men could play ball year-round. (Courtesy of the Molina family.)

This 1933 handbill is promoting a game in San Diego, Texas, between the Red Birds and the Hebbronville H-99. Handbills and posters were popular methods for publicizing baseball games. Handbills were distributed throughout the Mexican American communities, especially after church services, while posters were placed on the windows of Spanish-speaking businesses. At the bottom of the handbill is an ad for the Gulf service station managed by Tomas H. Molina. Molina had been an excellent player in San Diego but had to find work in 1932, the year he graduated from high school, due to the Great Depression. He was made manager in 1935. (Courtesy of the Molina family.)

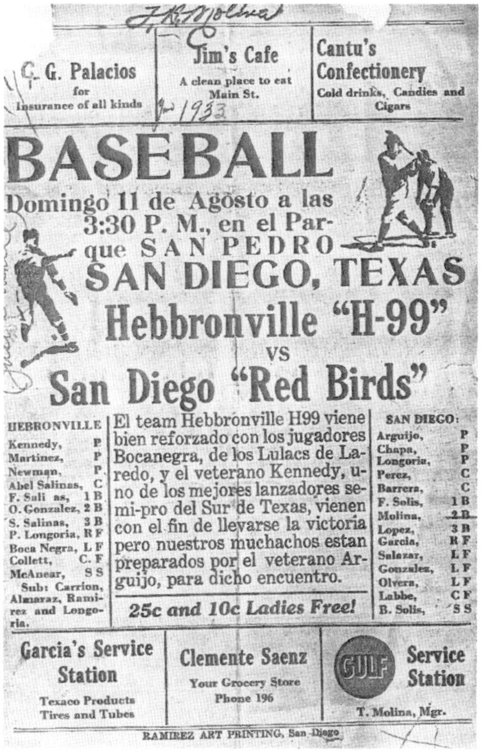

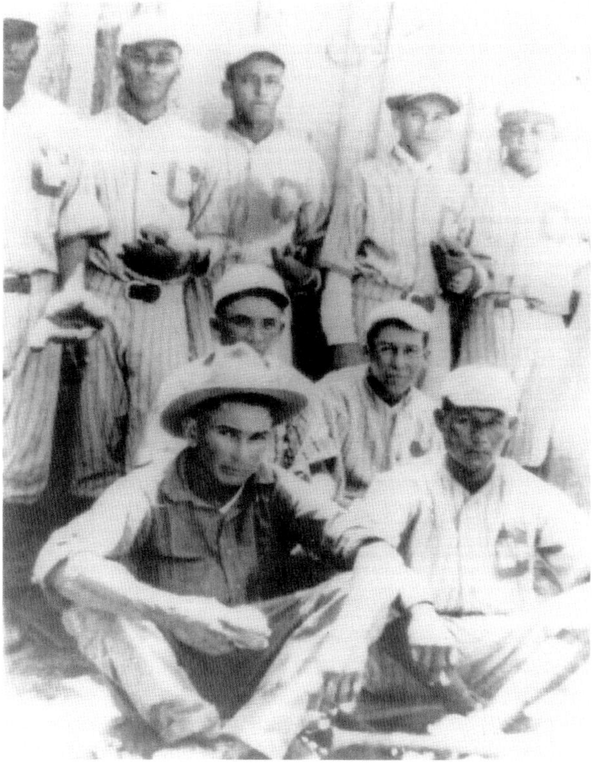

The 1920 Cotulla baseball team from LaSalle County, 70 miles north of Laredo, had a reputation for years for outstanding pitching and defense, along with speed on the base paths. From left to right are (first row) Merced Rodríguez and Jerónimo Garza; (second row) Ximo Hernández and Jesús Ayala; (third row) Delmiro Ruiz, Julián Quintanilla, Jesús Hernández, José Garza, and Carlos Peña. (Courtesy of José Garza.)

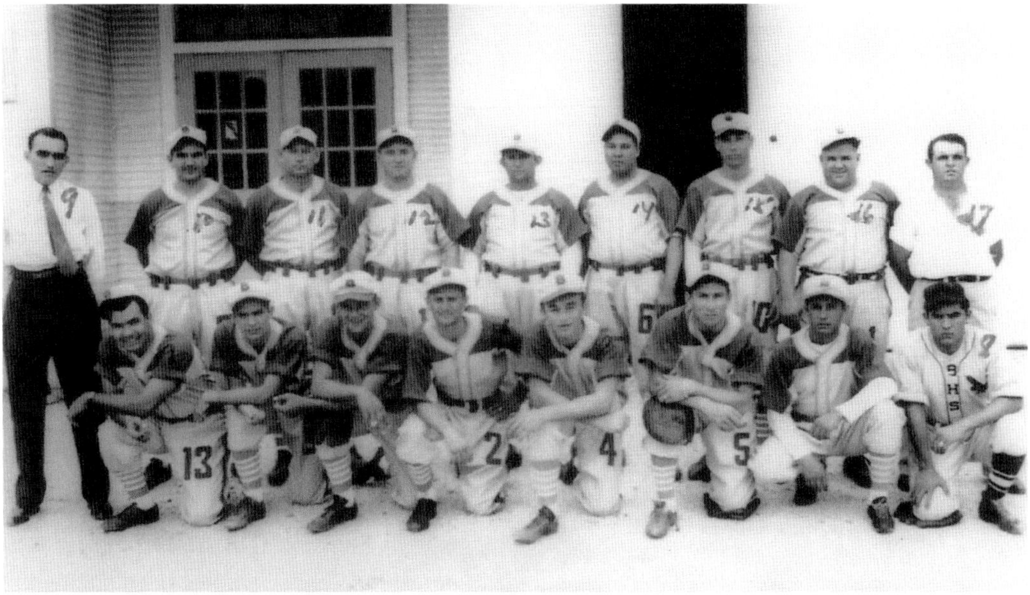

A 1940s Benavides team is pictured here. From left to right are (first row) J.M. Mel Canales, Carlos Oliveira, Gilberto "Lefty" Garza, Gilberto Hinojosa, Celso González, César Briones, Jesús "Chuy" Lozano, and Rodolfo Segura; (second row) Oscar Carrillo, E.C. Lerma, Alfredo Sáenz, Enrique "Red" Carrillo, Francisco "Pancho" Lozano, Joaquín Cavazos, Catarino García, Neme Garza, and Amando Oliveira. (Courtesy of the Molina family.)

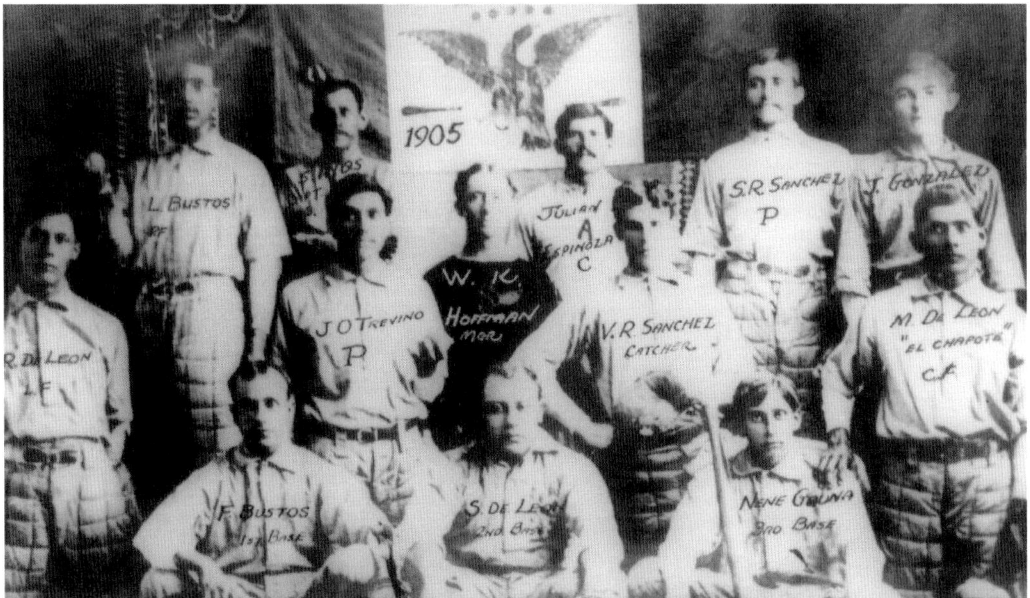

This 1905 Bruno Ríos team was sponsored by a local drugstore merchant in San Diego, Texas. He had invented and promoted a medicinal soft drink, called Brunella, "with a 'secret' formula" that some say was a precursor to Dr. Pepper. (Courtesy of the Molina family.)

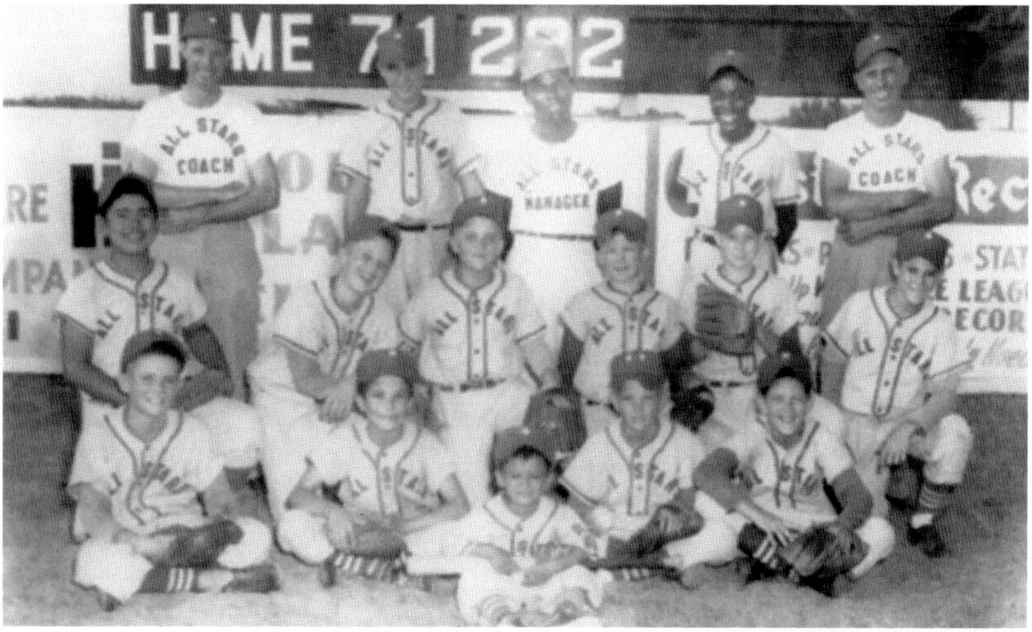

Members of the Robstown All Stars 1955 Little League team were, from left to right, (first row) unidentified, Bobby Chapa, bat boy Tony Ramirez, Joe Nemec, and Jacky "Cowboy" Reagan; (second row) Leonel Ramirez Jr., Jeff Segers, Richard Buckholt, unidentified, Sammy Ruegg, and Larry Smith; (third row) Kevin Tischendorf, Bill Keach, I.C. Hayes, unidentified, and Coach Stephen. (Courtesy of Fidencio López Jr. and the Robstown Area Historical Museum.)

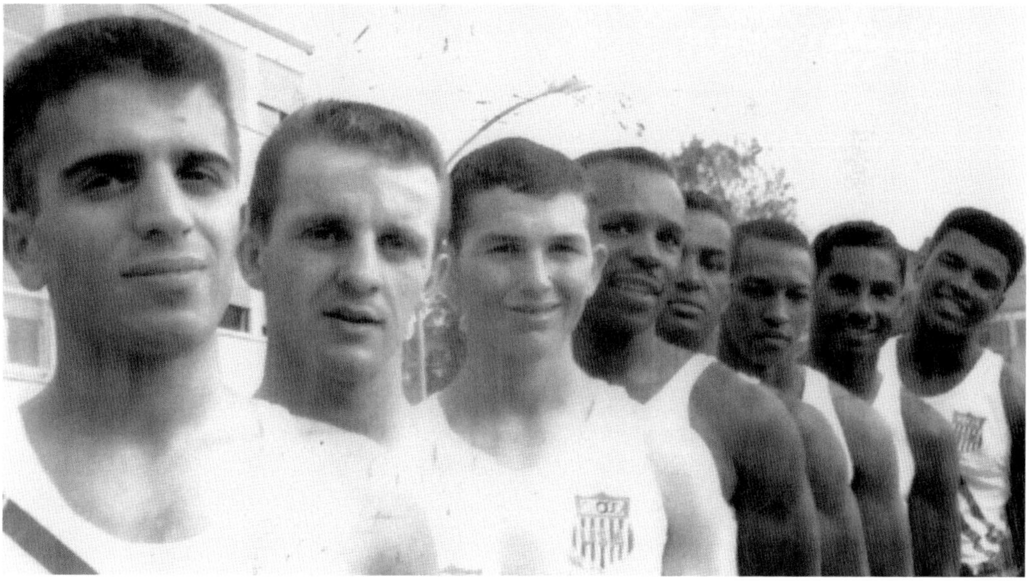

Humberto "Lefty" Barrera played Little League in Robstown, Texas, and was later an accomplished high school baseball player. He went on to become a US Olympic quarterfinalist flyweight champion boxer in 1960 in Rome. Barrera is seen here third from left. Cassius Clay (Muhammad Ali) is at far right. (Courtesy of Humberto "Lefty" Barrera and the Robstown Area Historical Museum.)

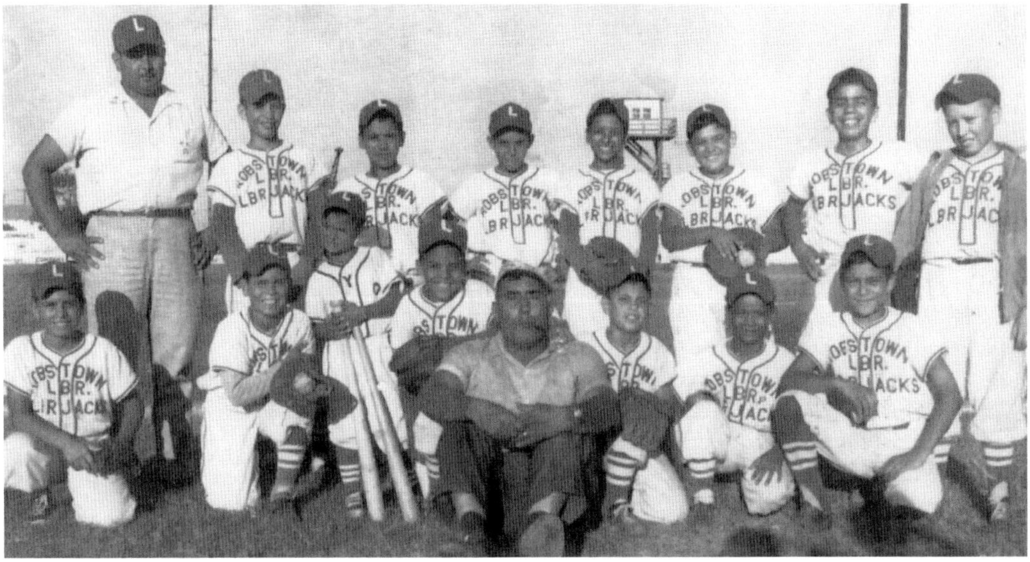

This is the 1957 Robstown, Texas, Lumberjacks Little League team. From left to right are (first row) Jesse Treviño, Rubén Wilder, batboy Tony Ramirez, Fortunato González, coach Fidencio López Sr., Joe Esquivel, Carlos García, and Oscar Treviño; (second row) coach Albino Barrera, Abel Mesa, Abraham Ramirez, Fidencio López Jr., Armando Rodríguez González, Moises Ramon, Armando Ramirez González ("el tambor"), and Joe Adame. (Courtesy of Carlos García and the Robstown Area Historical Museum.)

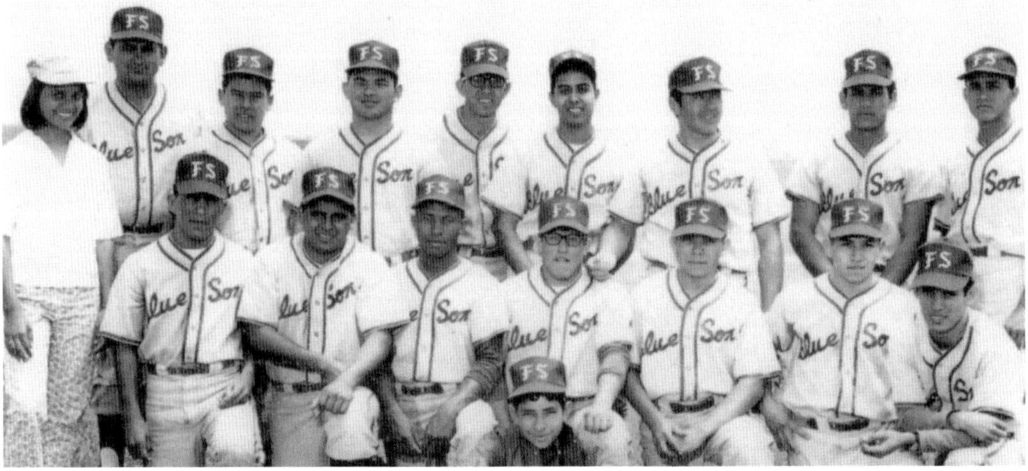

The 1967 Fort Stockton, Texas, Blue Sox semiprofessional team produced schoolteachers, administrators, and athletic directors. Pictured are, from left to right, (first row) batboy Donnie Domínguez; (second row) Salvador Duran, Junie Valenzuela, Leo Pace, Roy González, Mike Ramos, Freddy Domínguez, and Ralph Núñez; (third row) team sweetheart Freda González, general manager and coach Fred Dutchover, Baldemar Rodríguez, Manuel Lujan, Noe Franco, Oscar González, Rubén Leyva, and coach/player Fidencio López Jr. Duran was killed in Vietnam. Rodríguez was a Lone Star Conference all-star football player at Sul Ross State University. (Courtesy of Fidencio López Jr. and the Robstown Area Historical Museum.)

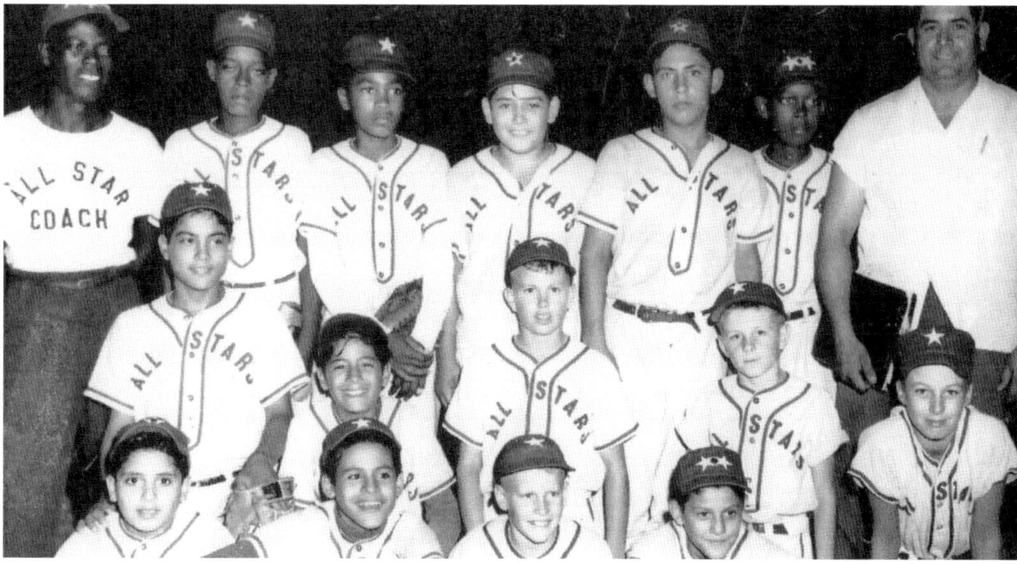

The Robstown All-Star team were the 1958 state champions. Marvin Upshaw (third row, second from left) played football for Trinity University in San Antonio, while his brother Eugene (third row, second from right), played football for Texas A&I University, now Texas A&M–Kingsville. Marvin played for the Cleveland Browns and Kansas City Chiefs. Eugene played for the Oakland Raiders and was inducted into the Pro Football Hall of Fame. He later served as the executive director of the NFL Players Association from 1983 through 2007. (Courtesy of the Robstown Area Historical Museum.)

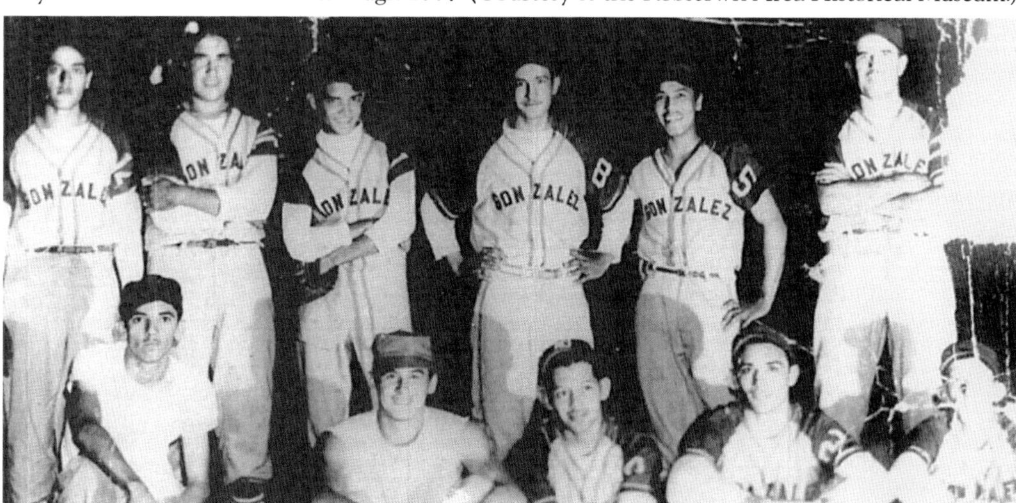

The González Grocery Store sponsored this 1950s baseball team in Robstown. Local businesses throughout Texas sponsored hometown teams. From left to right are (first row) Rodolfo Pérez, two unidentified, Lauro González, and Willie Canales; (second row) unidentified, Balo Alañiz, three unidentified, and Fred Hanson. Lauro González owned a local boxing gym and introduced a number of Robstown barrio boys to boxing who went on to successfully compete in various boxing tournaments. Humberto "Lefty" Barrera, a US Olympic boxer, was one of the young men who trained at González's Gym. (Courtesy of the Robstown Area Historical Museum.)

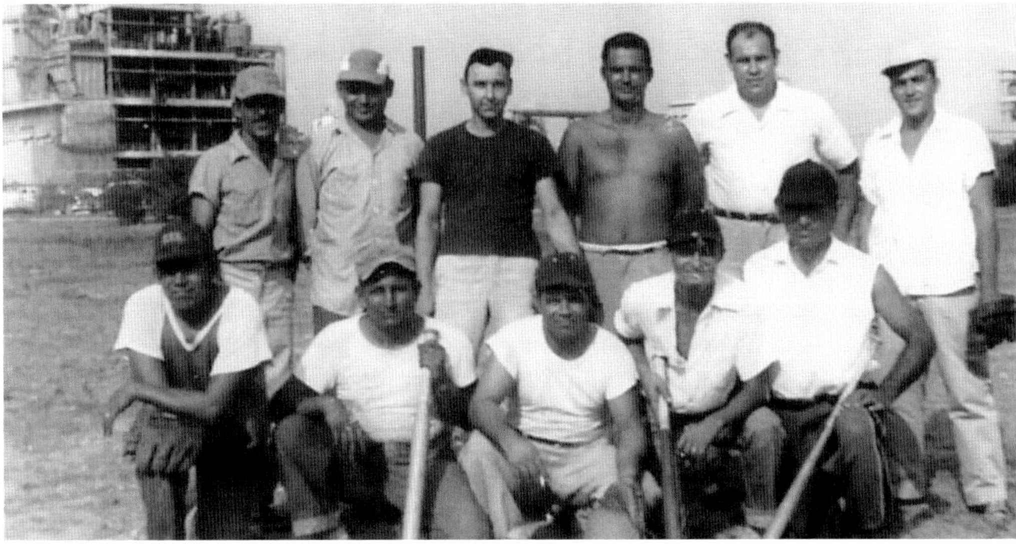

The 1955 Corn Products Milling Company baseball team had several outstanding players. The company was located at the Port of Corpus Christi and processed corn grown in the region for various products, such as corn starch. These teams were their postwork intramural entertainment. Pictured are, from left to right, (first row) unidentified, Macedonio Rodríguez, and three unidentified; (second row) Pánfilo Ayala, three unidentified, Fred Hanson, and unidentified. (Courtesy of Ernestina Ayala and the Robstown Area Historical Museum.)

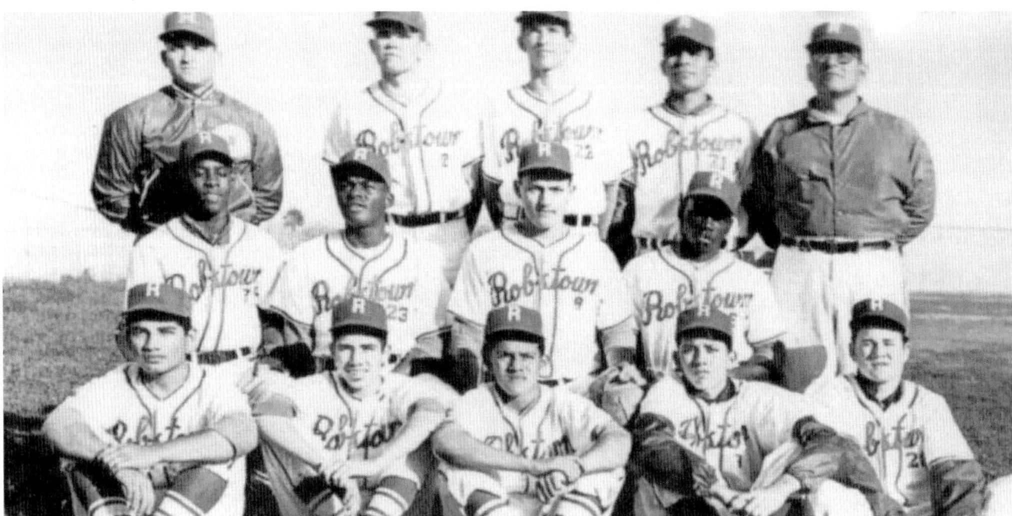

A history of Mexican American baseball in South Texas would not be complete without the accomplishments of the Robstown High School legendary baseball coach Steve Castro (first row, center). He played Little League and lettered in baseball in high school. Coach Castro went on to a successful career in college baseball and then coached at his high school alma mater for 27 years. During these years, he took his District 4A team to two state championships and a total record of 705-275-9. Coach Castro died on October 18, 2015. (Courtesy of the Robstown Area Historical Museum.)

Coach Steve Castro's winning record engendered a sense of pride in this small rural town that transcended all economic, racial, religious, and political affiliations. While his championships were notable, Castro's most cherished accomplishments were his students from the barRíos of Robstown who he helped to excel both on and off the field, including some who played Major League baseball. Coach Castro's influence was felt throughout the state of Texas, and in 2014, he was elected to the Texas High School Baseball Coaches Association Hall of Fame. (Courtesy of the Robstown Area Historical Museum and Phyllis Castro.)

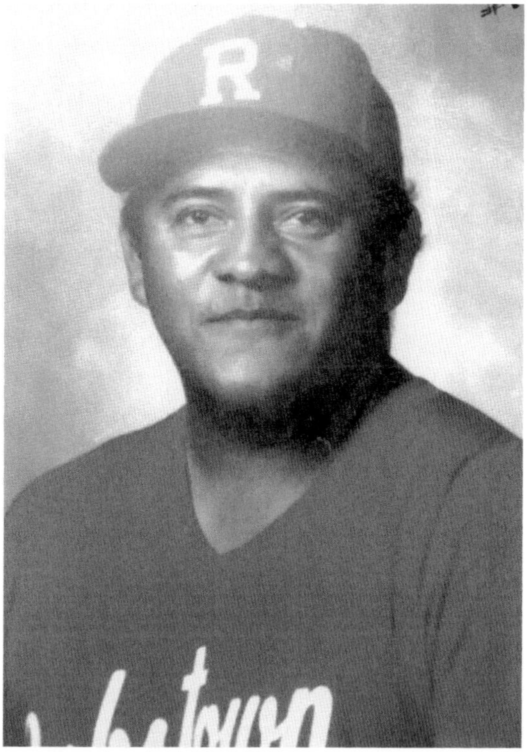

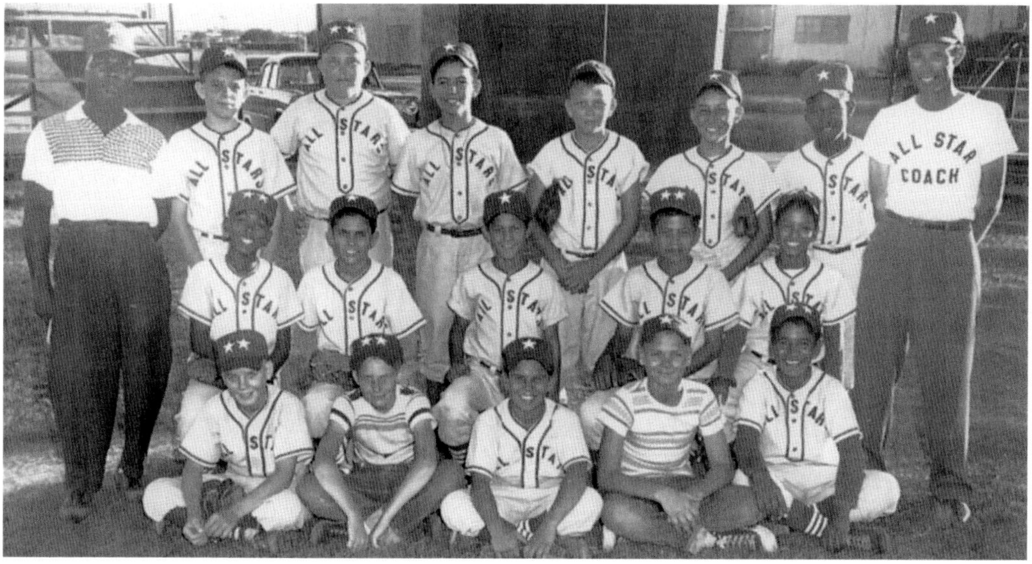

The 1957 Robstown All Star Little League team had outstanding pitching and excellent defense. From left to right are (first row) Donald Jackson, unidentified, Rubén Wilder, unidentified, and Abraham Ramirez; (second row) Melvin Parker, Fidencio López Jr., Felix Tijerina, Pete Barrera, and Armando Gonzalez; (third row) manager Isacc Hayes, Johnny Williby, Bobby Hurt, Abel Mesa, Benny Nemec, Ernest Gonzáles, Gene Upshaw, and assistant manager Calvin Teschendorf. (Courtesy of Armando Rodriguez Gonzalez and the Robstown Area Historical Museum.)

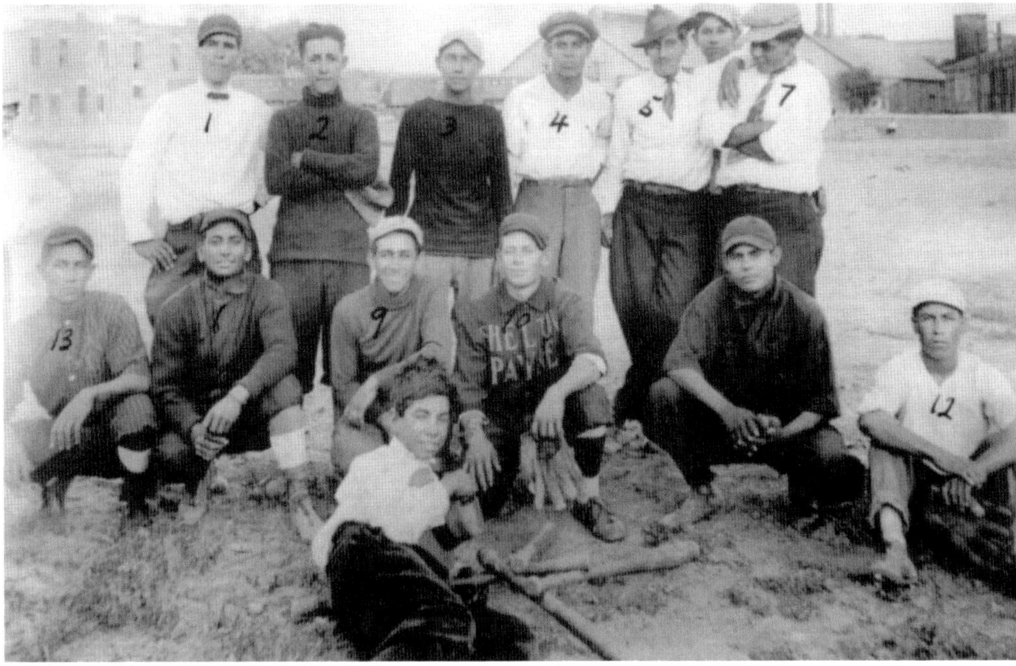

El Paso was an important city for several reasons. Many Mexicans who fled the violence of the Mexican Revolution between 1910 and 1917 passed through there. Once they entered El Paso, there were met by countless labor contractors promising them work with the railroads, steel mills, packinghouses, agriculture, auto industry, icehouses, cement factories, and salt mines throughout the United States. Baseball has been a popular sport in El Paso since before 1900. This is a pick-up team in East El Paso in 1913. (Courtesy of the Latino Baseball History Project.)

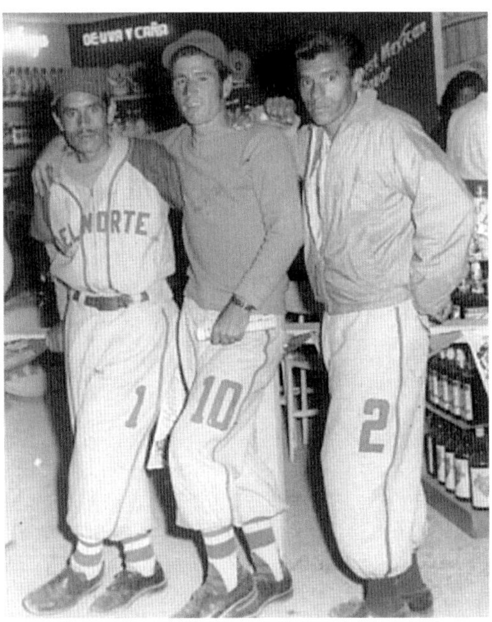

This c. 1958 photograph was taken in Ciudad Juárez, Mexico, in a liquor store after a game. The three players are members of the Del Norte team. From left to right are Gabriel Enriguez with his brother Cecilio Enriguez and an unidentified player. The Enriguez brothers were born in a ranch outside the city of Durango, Mexico. They grew up playing ball in Juárez and ultimately played for the Del Norte team sponsored by Auditorio Nacional. Gabriel pitched and played second base while Cecilio was the catcher. Gabriel continued playing ball even after moving to Los Angeles, California, with his wife, Soledad, and their two children, Gabriel Jr. and Blanca. (Courtesy of Habanero Berreteaca and Ron Cortes.)

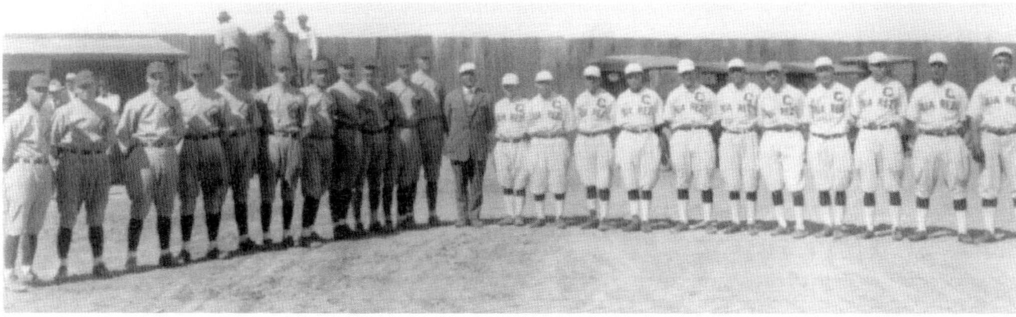

Robert Lagunas (second from right) was a significant player during the 1920s. "Lakes," the English translation of his last name, became his nickname. Before moving to Southern California during the 1930s, he played for El Paso in the Texas–New Mexico League, where he endured significant prejudice as a result of often being the only Mexican on the team. After playing an exhibition game against the St. Louis Cardinals, Baseball Hall of Famer Rogers Hornsby refused to shake Lagunas's hand because of his Mexican background. (Courtesy of Bob Lagunas.)

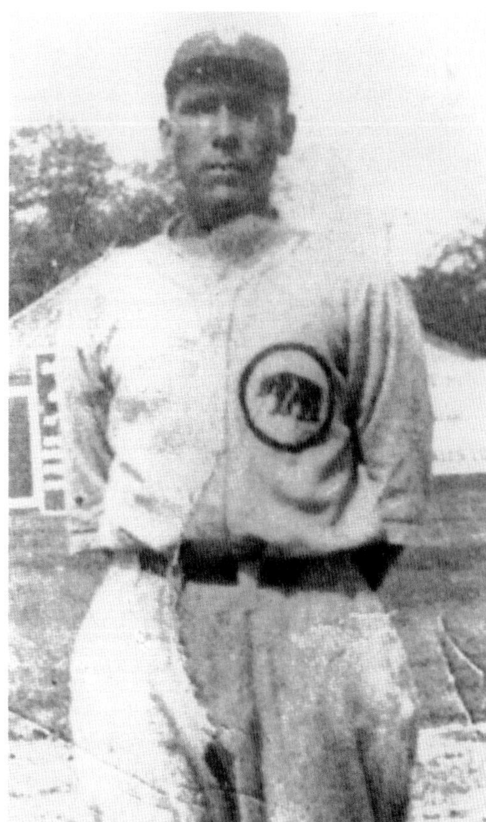

Lino Aguilar was born in 1901 and died in 1967. He started playing baseball in the 1920s as a successful pitcher for the Juárez Indios. He played for several teams along the Texas-Mexico border. He was invited for a tryout with the Washington Senators but was rejected because he was considered too old for the major leagues. After a brilliant career, he was elected to the Juárez Baseball Hall of Fame. Some of his children stayed in Juárez where they still reside, while other children moved to El Paso and to Los Angeles, California. Lino Aguilar became a cook after his playing days in Juárez and barnstorming throughout South Texas. His grandson Alfonso Aguilar Jr. said his grandfather's love of the game was passed onto him because he loved playing baseball too. Alfonso Jr. played 11 years of youth ball and high school ball, playing for the varsity team at Woodrow Wilson High School in El Sereno, and with the Mike Brito League at Evergreen Playground for two years in East Los Angeles. (Courtesy of José Cruz Aguilar.)

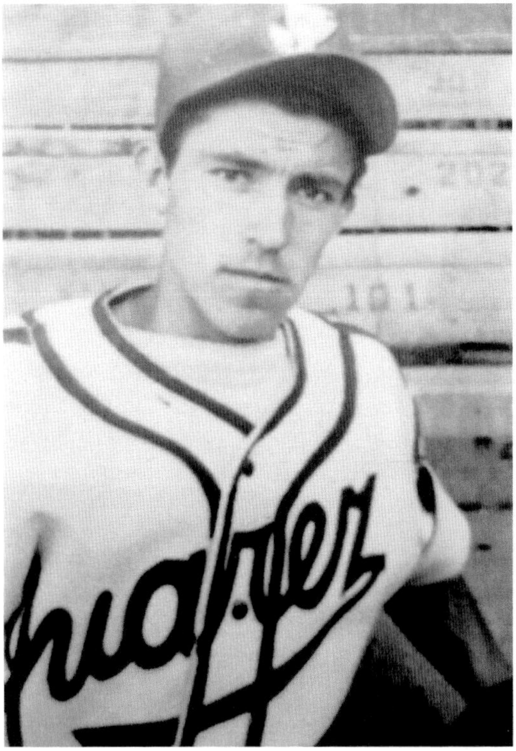

Jesús Badillo Rivera married Elvira Badillo Sánchez in 1949. They had four children, Maria Cruz, Erasto, Maria Teresa, and Jesús (Jess). He did not live long enough to meet his nine grandchildren, one of whom played football, while others played softball. He never spoke about his brilliant career while he was alive. After his wife passed away, their children found a scrapbook filled with newspaper clippings that their mother had saved for them. His children shared these clippings and a few stories with Jesús's grandchildren and great-grandchildren. (Courtesy of Jess Badillo.)

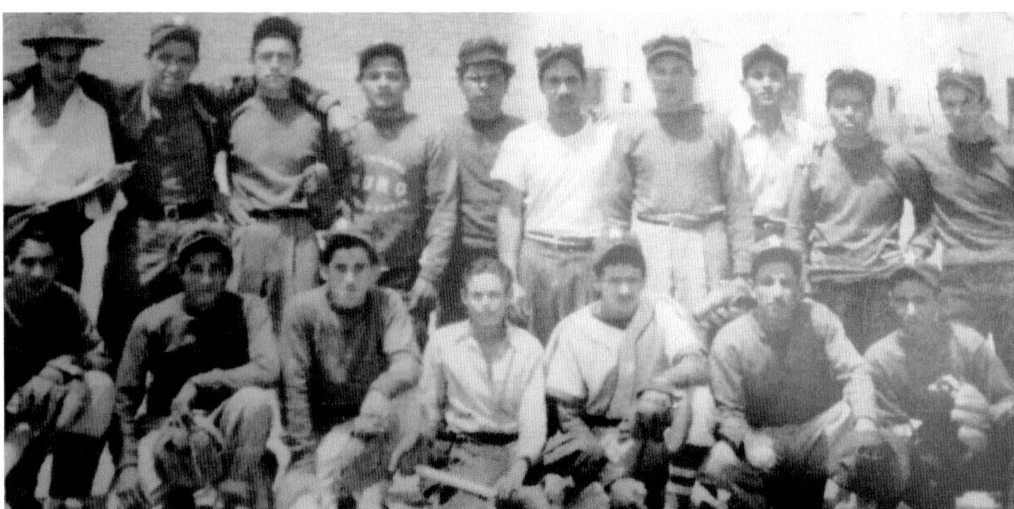

Jesús Badillo Rivera is pictured third from left in the second row. He loved the game of baseball. He pitched for Los Indios de Juárez in the Arizona-Texas League between 1948 and 1949. A local Juárez newspaper, *El Fronterizo*, wrote an article on January 4, 1975, of his passing. The story said that Rivera was a great amateur pitcher who played for several teams including Barrio Alto and Gabino Barrera. He was also the ace pitcher for the famous team Gato Negro. The article noted that after playing for Gato Negro, Rivera was scouted and advanced to the professional Arizona-Texas League. (Courtesy of Jess Badillo Jr.)

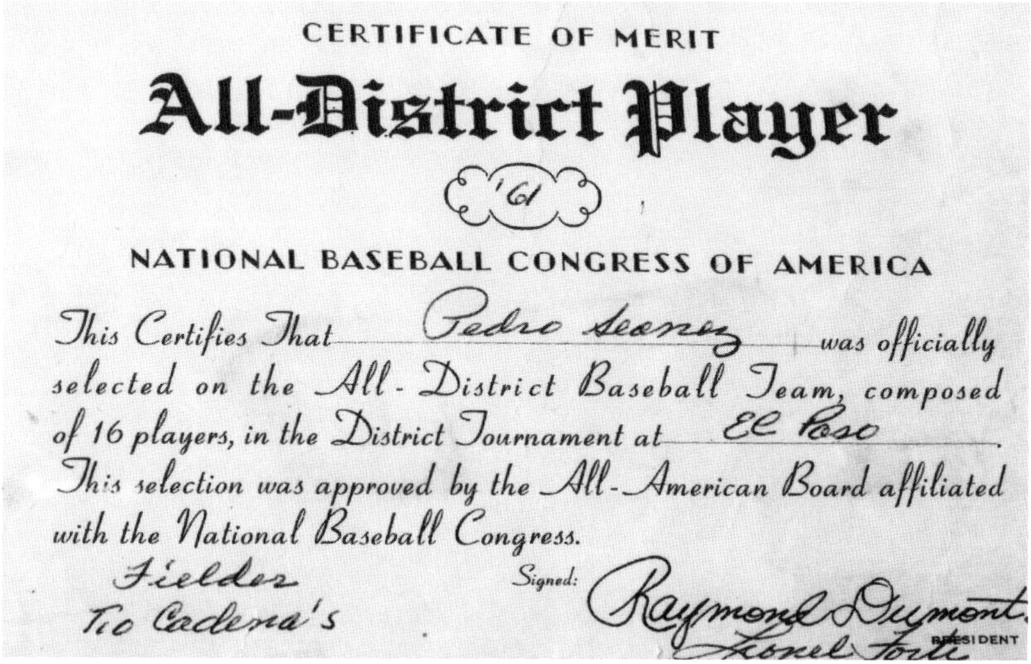
CERTIFICATE OF MERIT

All-District Player

'61

NATIONAL BASEBALL CONGRESS OF AMERICA

This Certifies That Pedro Seanez was officially selected on the All-District Baseball Team, composed of 16 players, in the District Tournament at El Paso.
This selection was approved by the All-American Board affiliated with the National Baseball Congress.

Fielder
Tio Cadena's

Signed: Raymond Dumont. PRESIDENT
Lionel Forte

Pedro Seañez was an outstanding player in Ciudad Juárez, Mexico, and El Paso, Texas. Seañez, like so many other players along the border, played on both sides. He was an excellent pitcher for baseball and softball. He played baseball in the spring and summer, and softball during the winter. He resides in the Los Angeles area. He has two sons, Richard and Greg, who remember being batboys, running the bases after each game, and being allowed to wear the gloves and use the bats of the players—a thrill they still remember to this day. (Courtesy of Pedro Seañez.)

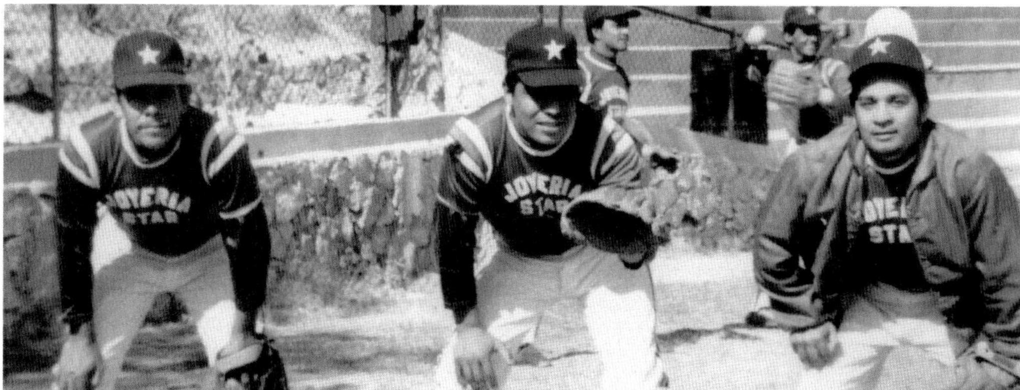

Pedro Seañez (left) is seen here around 1967 with two Juárez, Mexico, teammates, Ramón "El Bom-Bon" Gallardo and Guillermo Juárez. The team was sponsored by a local jewelry store. This is a softball team that played during the winter months. In the background are the typical cement seats for fans to sit on and watch the games. Gallardo was the catcher for Seañez. Seañez later moved his family to Los Angeles where two of his brothers-in-law, Alfredo Salazar and Felipe Adana, had found work in construction and encouraged Seañez, a carpenter, to join them. (Courtesy of Pedro Seañez.)

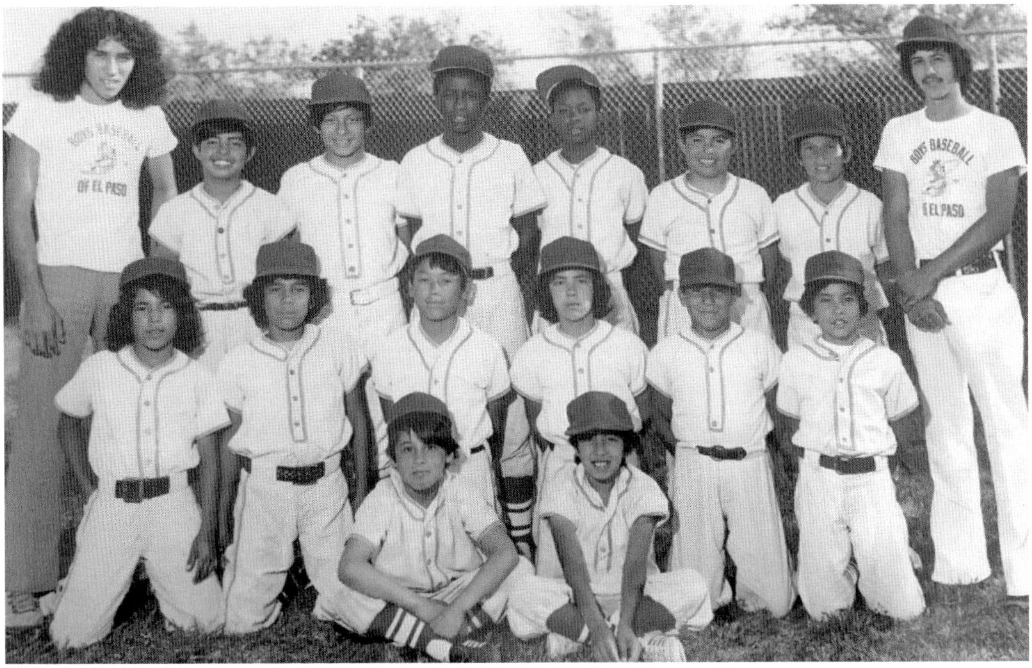

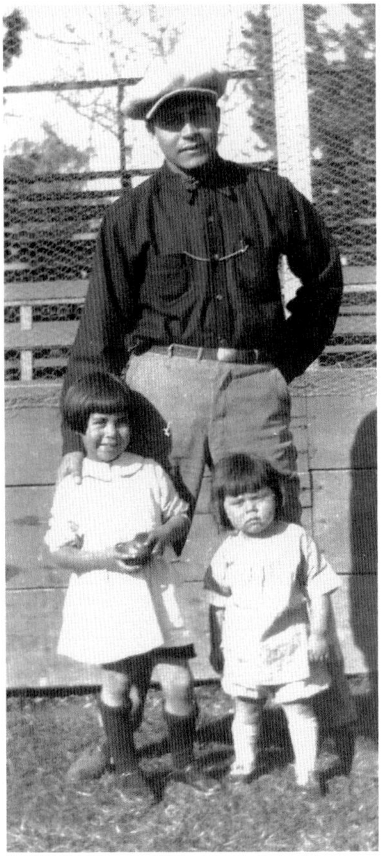

Pedro Seañez has two sons, Richard (not pictured) and Greg, who played baseball in El Paso and later baseball and football in East Los Angeles, California. Seen here on a 1970s El Paso Hawkins Rams team is Greg Seañez, second row, far right (kneeling). Other players include Alex Escalante, Richard Porras, and Albert Mendoza. Greg was a gifted athlete who played with the Rubén Salazar Park Reds in East Los Angeles and later played baseball and football at Theodore Roosevelt High School as an infielder and quarterback. (Courtesy of Greg Sienez.)

David Salazar is seen here with his two daughters Eleanor (left) and Margaret. Salazar was born in California and had a distinguished career playing on both sides of the border in Mexico and the United States, including Texas. He played for several years in Mexico and also played against Mexican teams as part of American teams. He had five children, four of whom were outstanding players. His sons David and Carlos played youth, high school, college, and community ball and later umpired for many years. His two daughters grew up to be outstanding players as well. They played in the Pasadena area for many years. (Courtesy of Carlos Salazar.)

5

Battlefields and Diamonds

Pride, responsibility, dedication, commitment, community or country, whichever one prefers, these themes are important aspects of the culture within both organized sports and the military. They became especially true for Mexican Americans in Texas, otherwise known as Tejanos.

These two theaters of the human condition, sports and the military, have been gateways to the improvement of society. They have been able to transcend the boundaries set in all other aspects of society. Many have called them social experiments when examined historically. The authors believe that it is not an experiment, but instead, an example of the genetic disposition all humans have to prove themselves worthy to others. Battlefields and baseball diamonds allowed these individuals to do just that. These were social arenas where race, religion, and economics were secondary to keeping one's fellow soldiers alive on the battlefield and turning a cohesive double play with teammates on the diamond. If one's responsibilities were fulfilled to self and team, the boundaries of society often disappeared and a brotherhood formed despite differences.

Tejanos made the most of their opportunities when they were presented. They used battlefields and baseball diamonds to demand recognition as Texans and Americans. They used these forums to show both pride in country and pride in community. The individuals featured in this chapter have used both military service and a baseball team, or two, along the way, to help define who they are as individuals. Many used the values learned in Little Leagues and Catholic Youth Organization teams, high school squads, and even amateur clubs to help them excel. Many served their countries with honor and returned to their communities as heroes.

One might have even been lucky enough to have watched these returned heroes play nine on a Sunday afternoon. The unique ability that military service and organized sports have to bring people together has created a rich history of Tejano heroes, on both battlefields and diamonds.

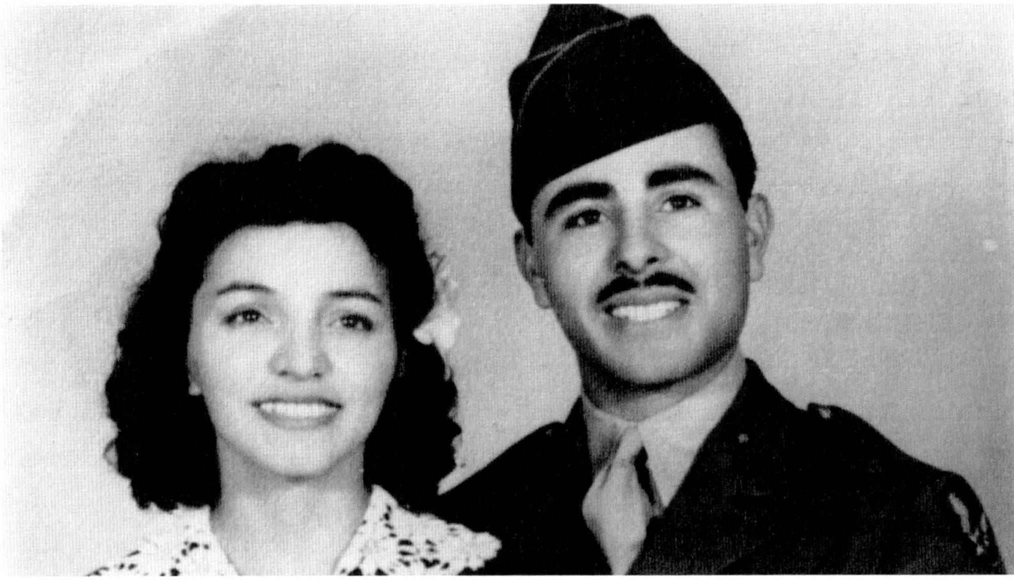

Felipe Delgado left for World War II as a young, single man. He came home to become a husband, father, and hero of the community. He also came home with a plan that would help to transform Sunday afternoons in the Tejano communities of New Braunfels. Delgado called it the West End Complex. Pictured here are Felipe Delgado and his new bride Elisa Saenz. They had two daughters, Estella and Rosalinda. (Courtesy of Estella Farias.)

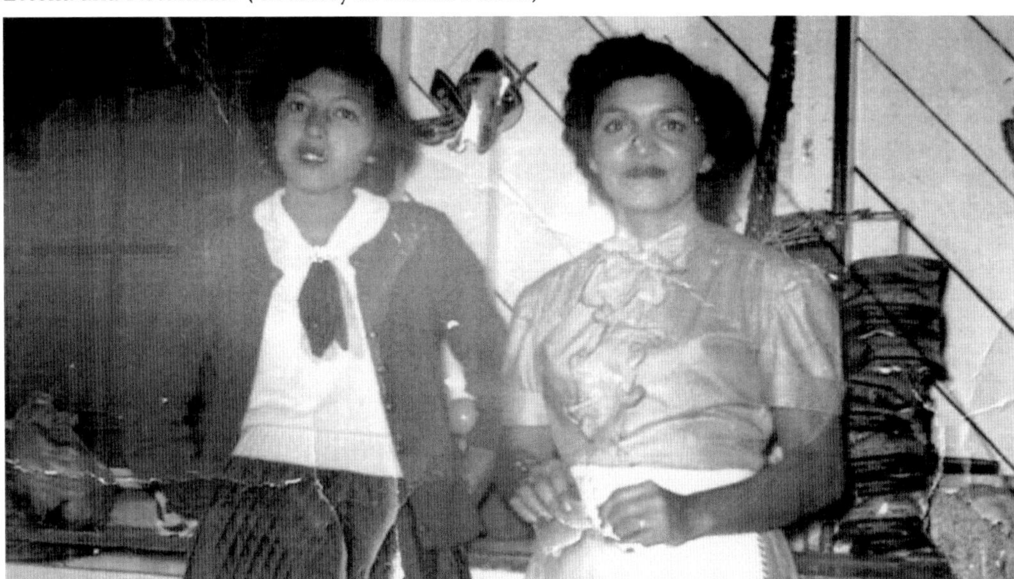

Sundays were a hive of activity down at West End Complex, and it all centered around the Lions' home games. People filled the stands, and they brought their appetites. Elisa Delgado, Felipe's wife, is pictured here at right. She ran the concessions and the small grill that fed the patrons at the ballgames. Elisa sold hamburgers, sodas, pickles, and candy, and nothing cost more than a quarter. (Courtesy of Estella Farias.)

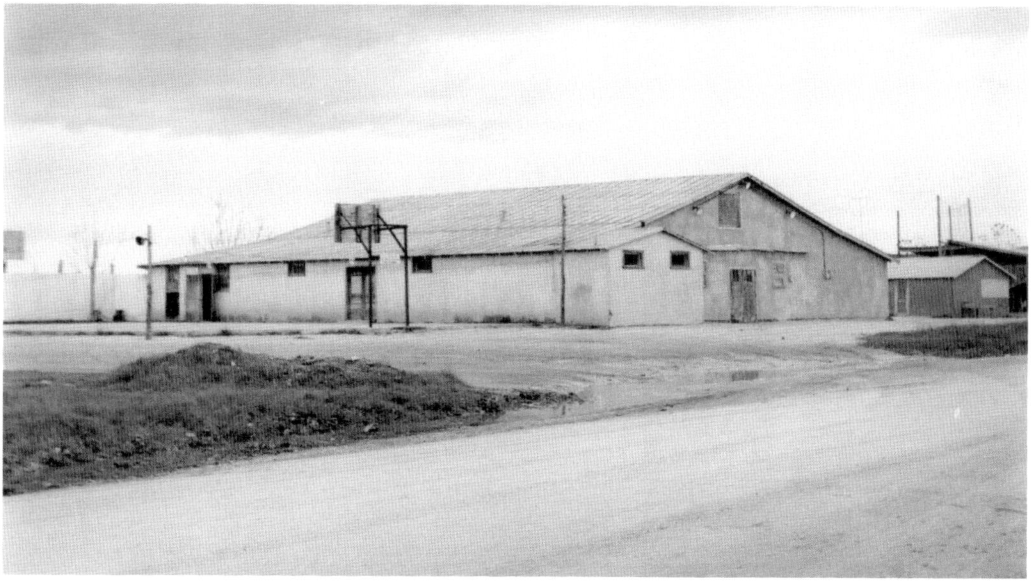

This was Felipe Delgado's vision, New Braunfels West End Complex. It consisted of a baseball field (lights can be seen in background), a dance hall, cantina, and small grill for concessions. Delgado built the field and each building with his own money, his back, and the help of individuals in the community. Men like him were able to create a social space for their communities that lacked all the social boundaries and pretenses that were the norm for the time. (Courtesy of Estella Farias.)

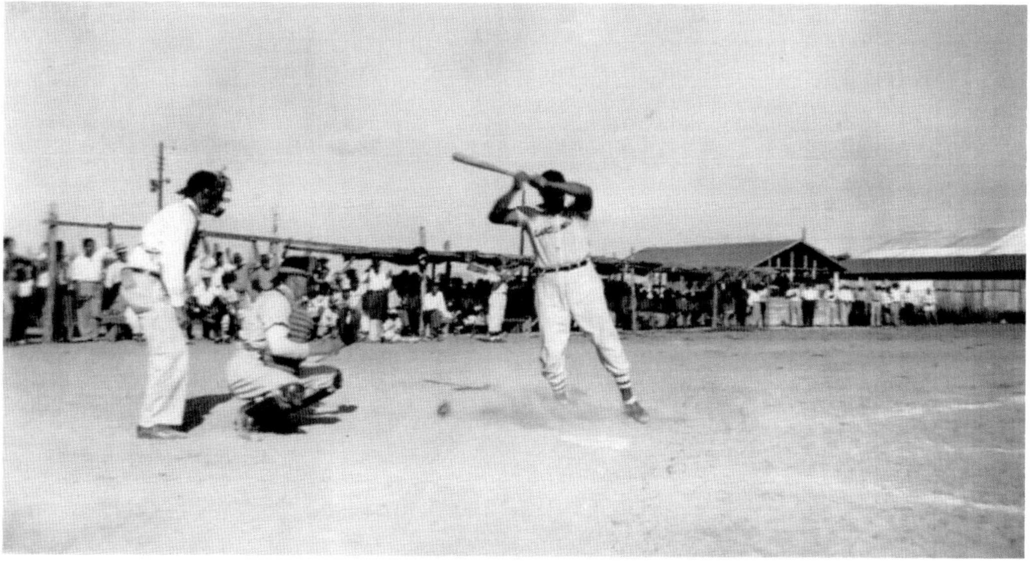

The baseball diamond is what it all revolved around. This is a shot of the West End field. Though rough around the edges, the stands were full every Sunday with screaming fans there to cheer on their Lions. It was a scene that evoked pride in one's community. Judging by several oral histories taken from those who played and frequented West End, it is a place held close to many hearts. (Courtesy of Estella Farias.)

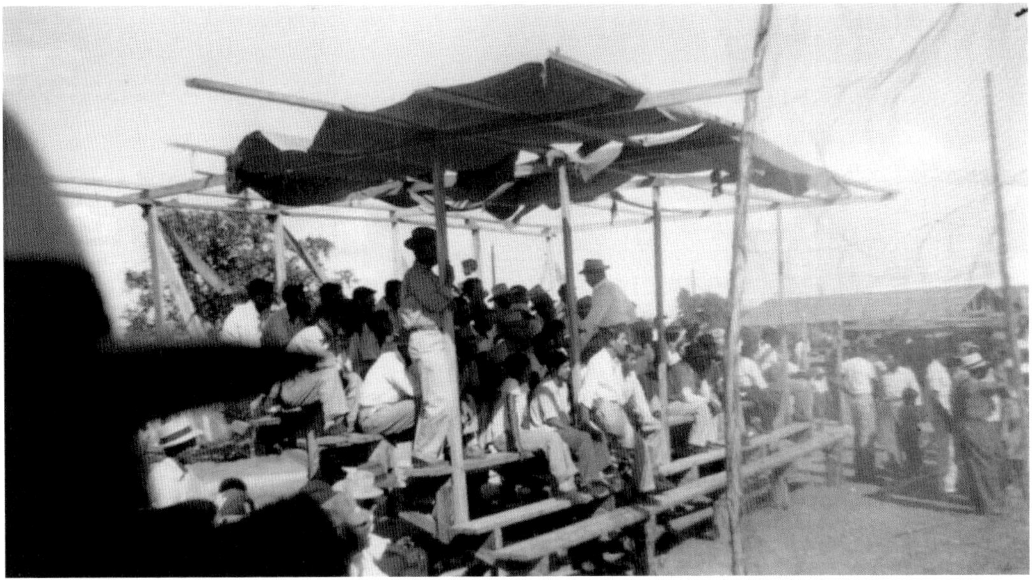

The wooden bleachers were full every Sunday, and rays of sunlight slipped through the holes in the canvas roof strung up on poles to provide the crowd shade. Cedar poles with chicken wire formed a backstop and offered the crowd protection from foul balls. This was the essence of the West End Complex. It was like many of the fields built by community leaders throughout Texas that offered the young men of their communities a place to showcase their skills. (Courtesy of Estella Farias.)

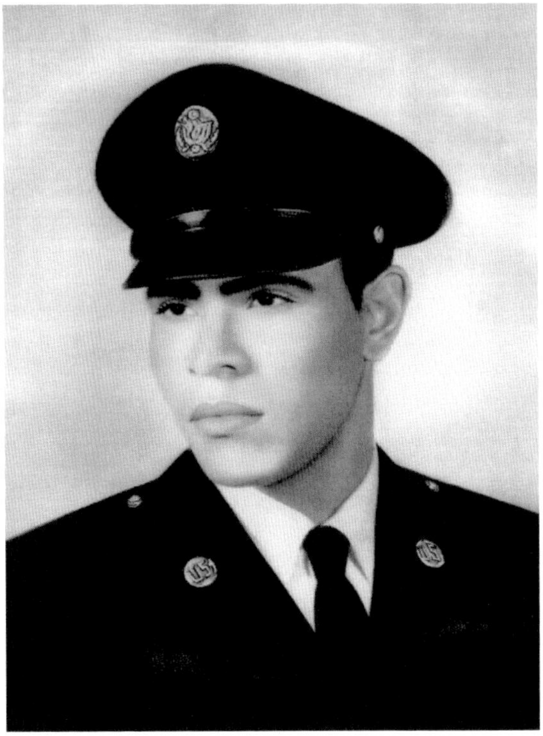

Francisco A. Baeza is a native of Alpine, Texas. He served his country with the US Army. This photograph was taken in Korea in 1960. Baeza played on military teams while serving and had a heavy dose of the diamond while a child growing up in Alpine. That entire region of border territory was a hotbed for baseball from Baeza's early childhood to the time he returned from the service. The Alpine region continues to have a strong baseball bloodline to this day. (Courtesy of Francisco A. Baeza.)

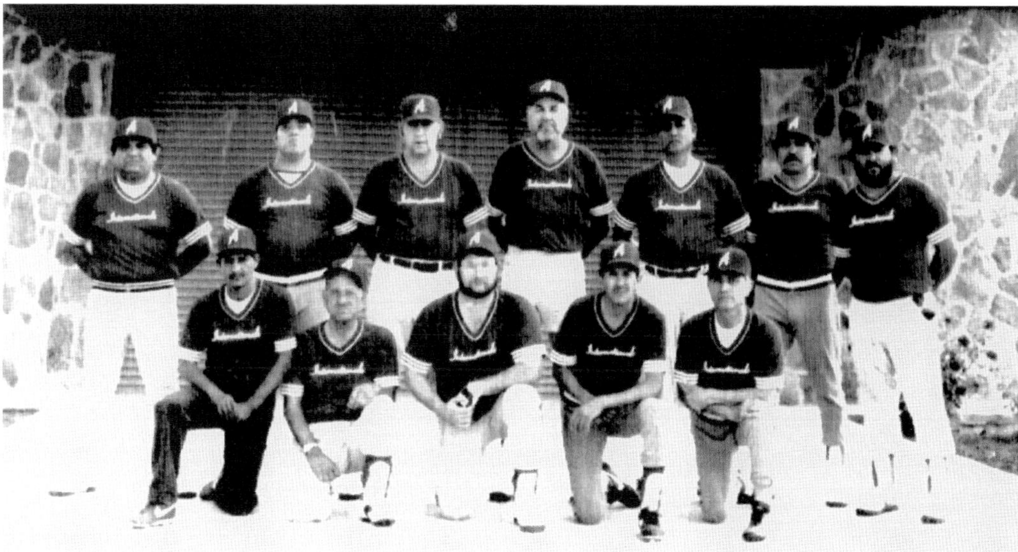

This picture was taken in Alpine, Texas, in front of Kokonut Field in 1987. It was the home of the Alpine Cowboys, a semiprofessional team that played during the 1940s through the 1960s. This is one of the softball teams that Francisco A. Baeza played on through the 1980s. He played to stay active and also to enjoy the company of friends. Baeza is standing in the second row, second from the left. (Courtesy of Francisco A. Baeza.)

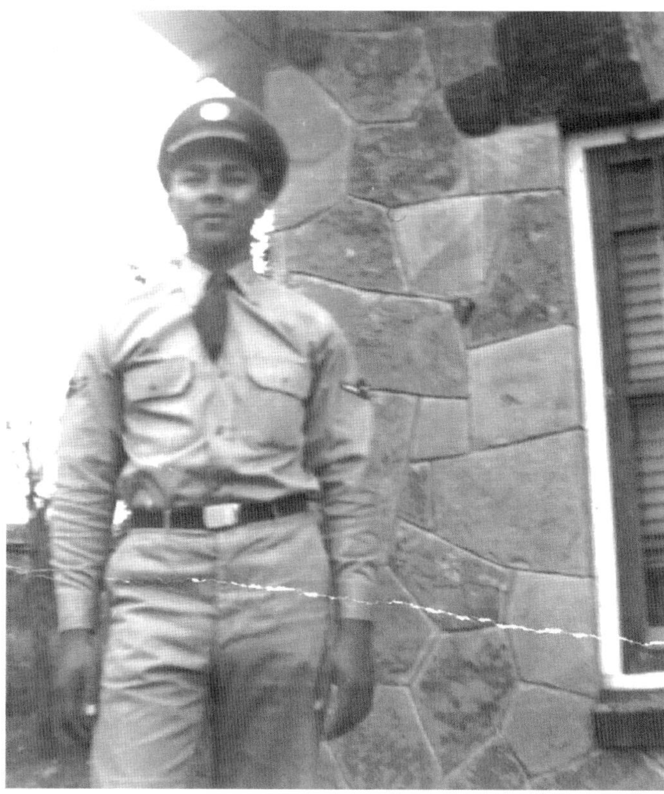

Richard Zamora was stationed at Kelly Air Force Base from 1951 to 1953 with the 76th Air Transport Squadron. Luckily, he never saw combat and stayed around his hometown of San Antonio while serving. He was able to stay in touch with his community and the baseball scene, which was a huge part of this young man's life. Zamora recalled that many of the men he signed up with went on to become coaches and teachers in San Antonio. This photograph was taken in front of the family home in South Antonio. (Courtesy of Richard Zamora.)

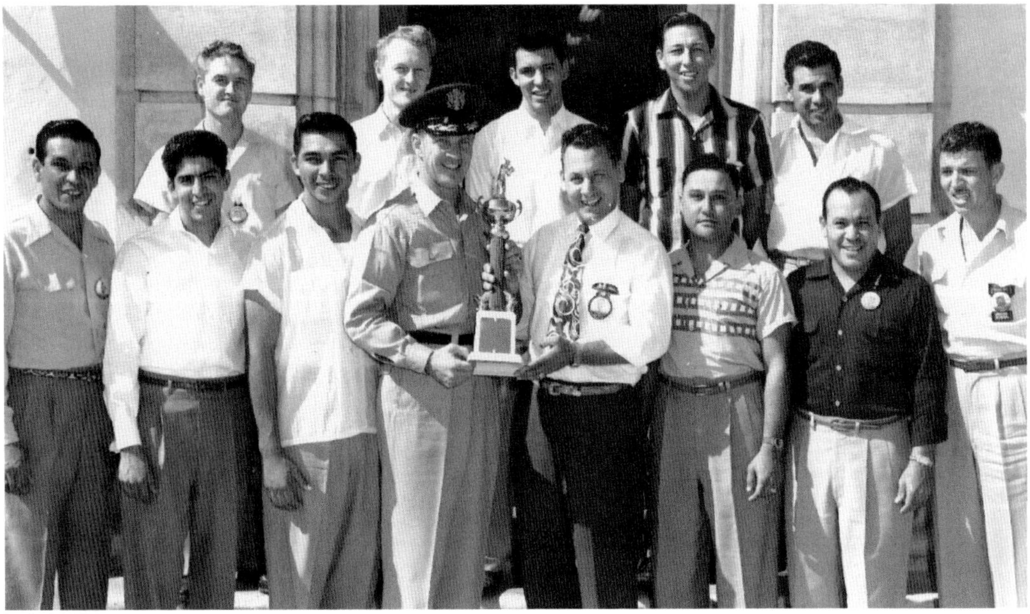

This is the Kelly Air Force Base Civilians, a softball team that played out of Kelly Air Force Base in San Antonio. From left to right are (first row) unidentified, Kino Spinoza, Richard Zamora, two unidentified, Richard Gamboa, Manny Munoz, and unidentified; (second row) two unidentified, ? Manchaca, Rudy Gonzáles, and Louie Dávila. (Courtesy of Richard Zamora.)

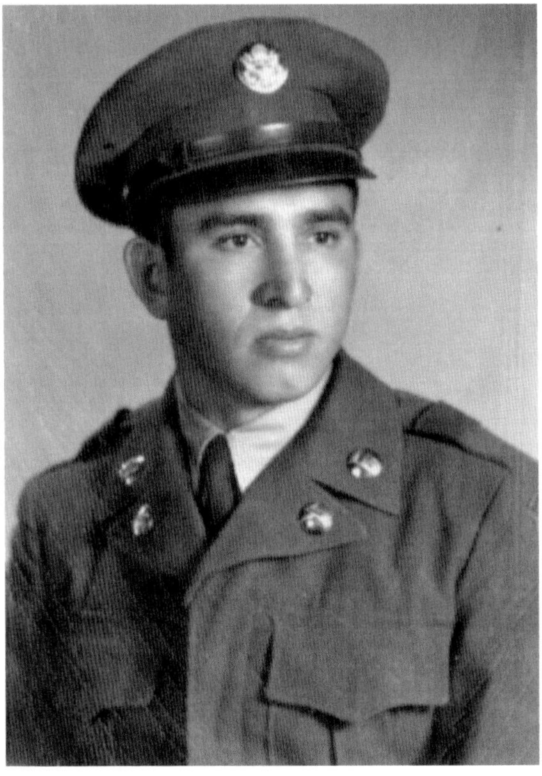

Johnny Zamora was the oldest of the Zamora clan. He made the initial waves in athletics at South San High School. Here, he is seen wearing his US Army uniform. He was assigned to Korea and also Alaska for a spell. He suffered from frostbite to his hands and feet while serving. He returned home to work as a civilian at Kelly Air Force Base. Zamora played in the Spanish-American League in San Antonio despite his war wounds. He also played on several softball teams around San Antonio. (Courtesy of Richard Zamora.)

Dr. Joe Bernal served with the US Army during World War II. He was an infantryman and saw time in the Philippines and Japan. When asked how he became a state representative, he laughingly replied, "I just stumbled into it." Though not a physically imposing man, Dr. Bernal was a giant on the West Side of San Antonio. He was known with affection in the community as "Señor Chema." Dr. Bernal would become a champion for the rights of minorities, the elderly, and the disadvantaged. (Courtesy of Dr. Joe J. Bernal.)

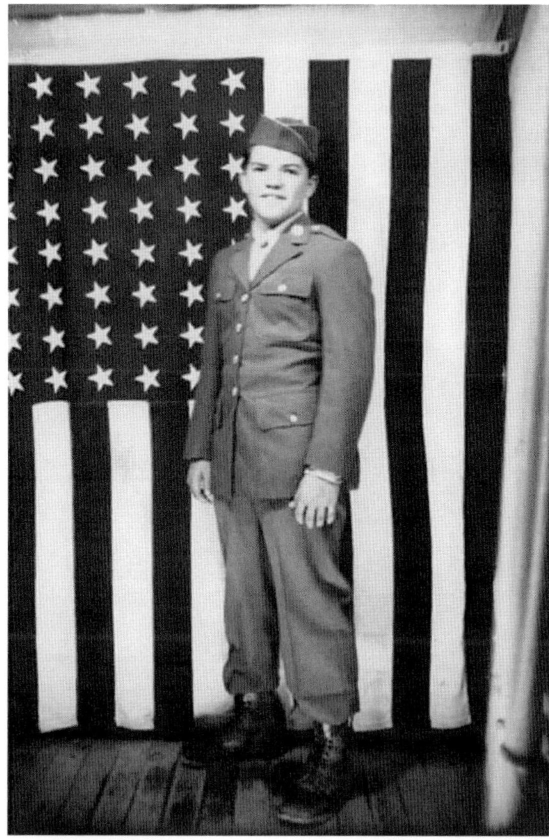

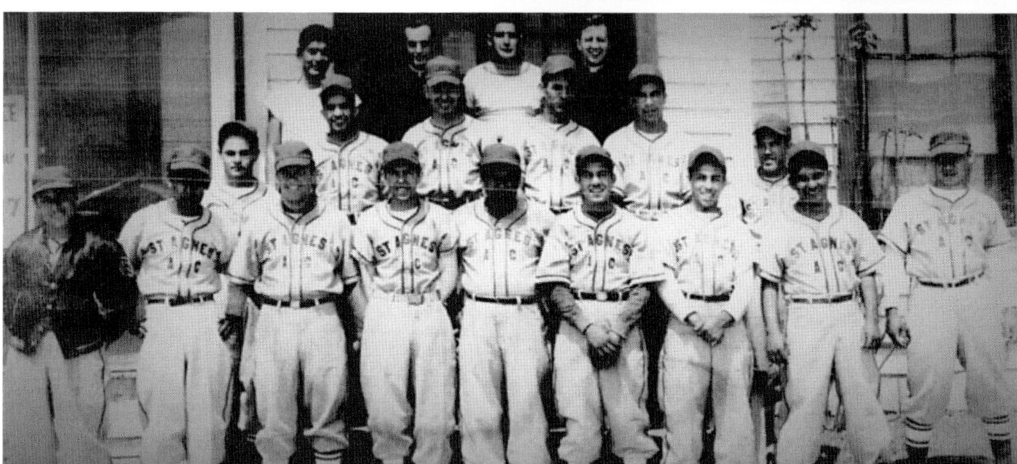

This is the adult Catholic Youth Organization team at St. Agnes in April 1950. Dr. Joe Bernal mentioned that this league was much more recreational than its counterparts in the Spanish American League. Pictured are, from left to right, (first row) Raymond Castillo, David García, Joe Bernal, Jesse Gonzáles, Johnny Castillo, unidentified, Rocky Almaraz, Bennie Ortega, and ? Rodríguez; (second row) Henry Medina, Rudy Águilar, Ralph Garza, Nick Huizar, George Rodríguez, and Chalio García (between the priests). (Courtesy of Dr. Joe J. Bernal.)

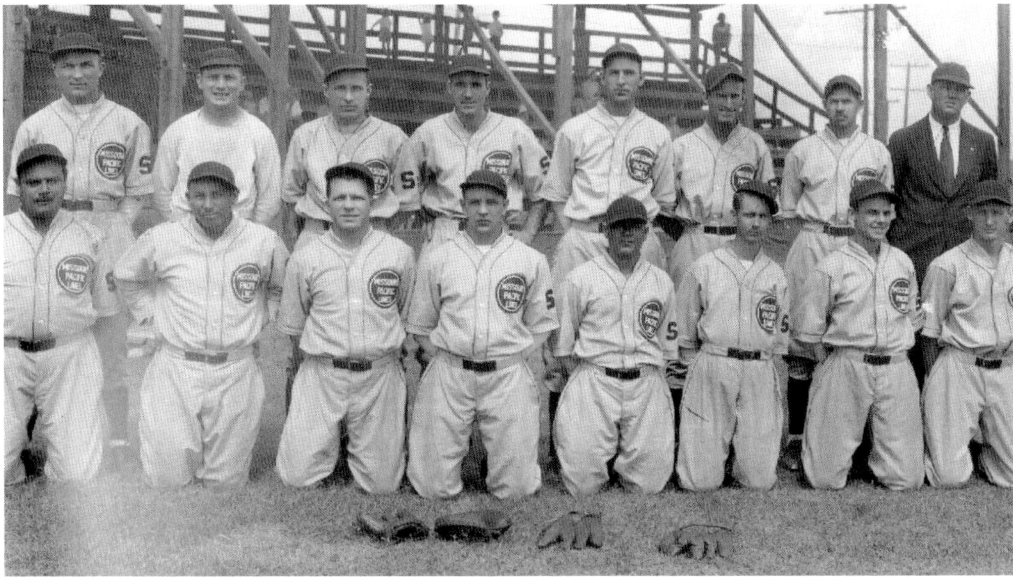

The Missouri-Pacific Railroad was an important part of the growth of baseball in the Tejano communities of Texas. Pictured here is Dr. Joe Bernal's father, Joe (second row, fourth from right), on a team sponsored by Missouri-Pacific. It is an integrated team much earlier than might be expected. Dr. Bernal's father was a great ballplayer. Dr. Bernal tried to follow in his shoes, but his mother told him early to get an education because he would never be as good as his father. (Courtesy of Dr. Joe J. Bernal.)

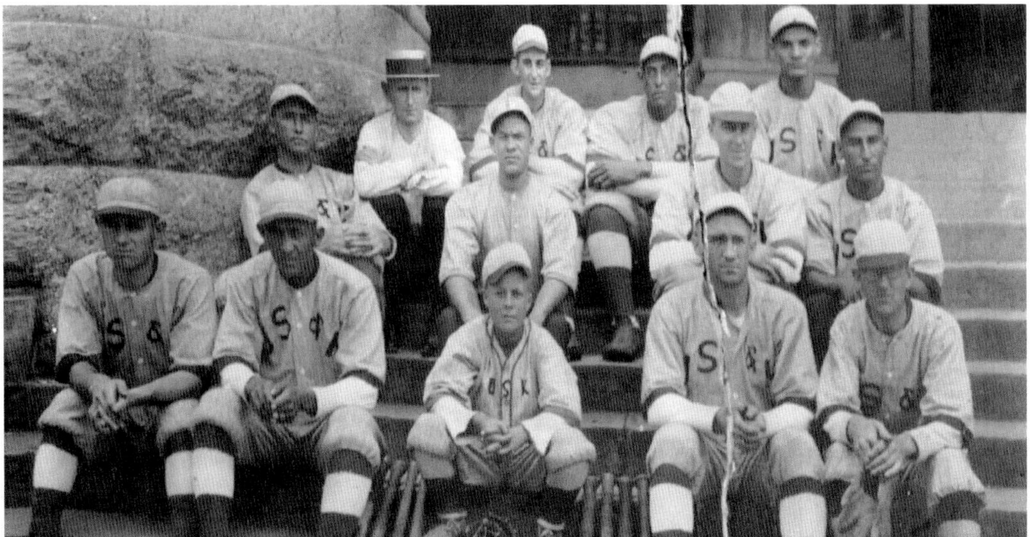

Dr. Joe Bernal's father is pictured here on one of his early teams in San Antonio in the 1920s. He is sitting in the second row, second from the left, on the steps of a downtown building. The interesting thing about this photograph is the fact that Bernal is playing on an integrated team. This was long before integration in San Antonio, and it just shows the power of the diamond to bring individuals together and break barriers. (Courtesy of Dr. Joe J. Bernal.)

This is Alvino Pacheco, who played on several teams around San Antonio during the 1920s. He played with Joe Bernal's father on the Aztecas. This team won the 1926 West Side Championship in San Antonio. Pacheco would aid his country through service with the San Antonio Air Depot. The military bases around San Antonio often brought together contests between civilian and military teams. Others like Pacheco would be civilian workers at the bases and sometimes get a taste of both worlds—a civilian playing with a base team. (Courtesy of Bobby Pacheco.)

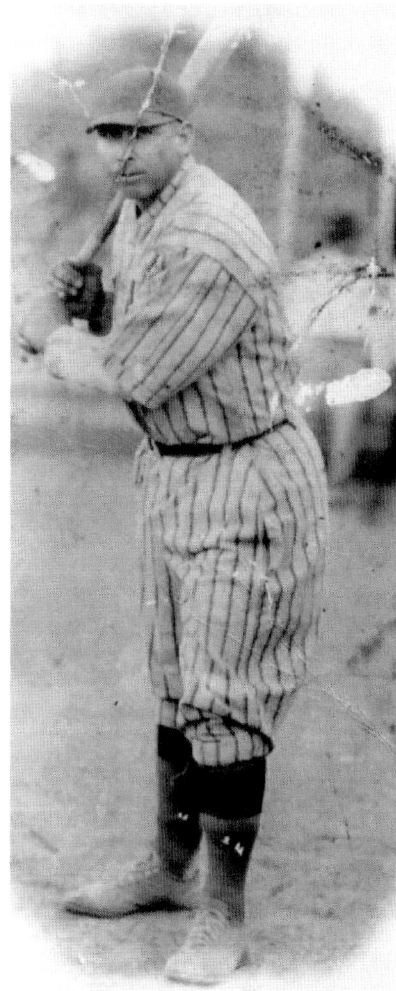

Alvino Pacheco served his country at Kelly Air Force Base in the early 1920s. Kelly was one of the few airfields that remained open after World War I. Pacheco also played with the San Antonio Air Depot team. Taken on the rickety, old bleachers at Kelly Field, this photograph shows that team. (Courtesy of Bobby Pacheco.)

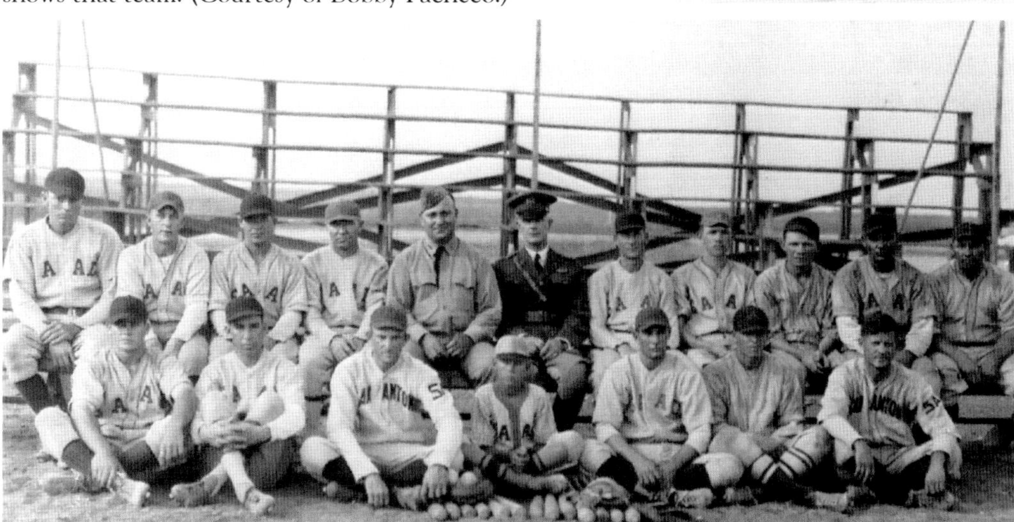

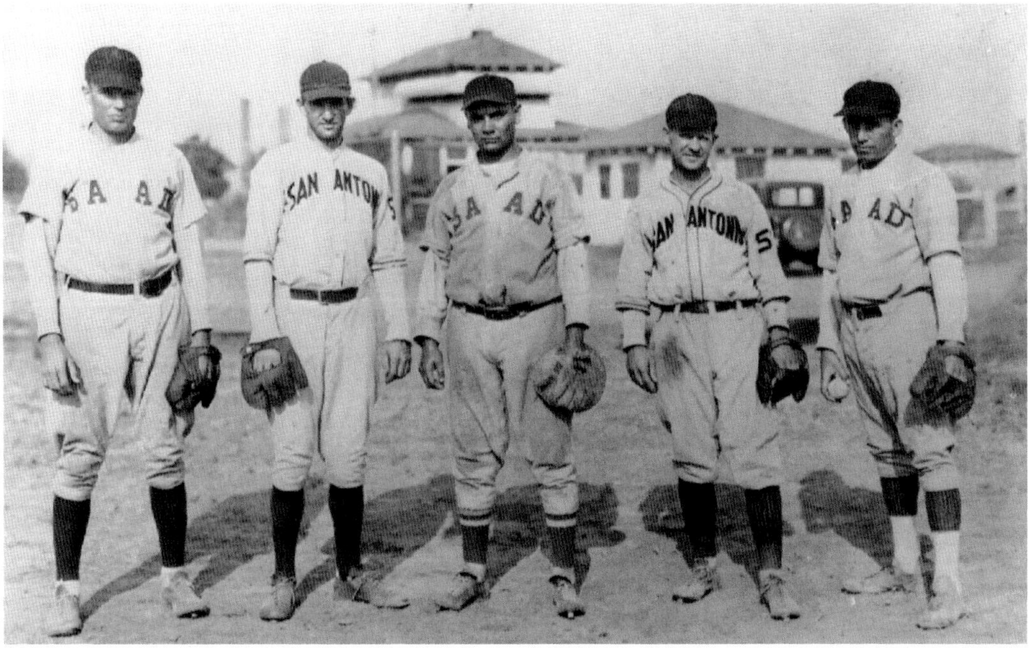

This is an image of some of Alvino's teammates. Unfortunately, the names of these individuals have been lost to time. It is possible to determine the era by looking at the gloves and the old car in the background. This was also taken at Kelly Field in the early 1920s, long before integration. (Courtesy of Bobby Pacheco.)

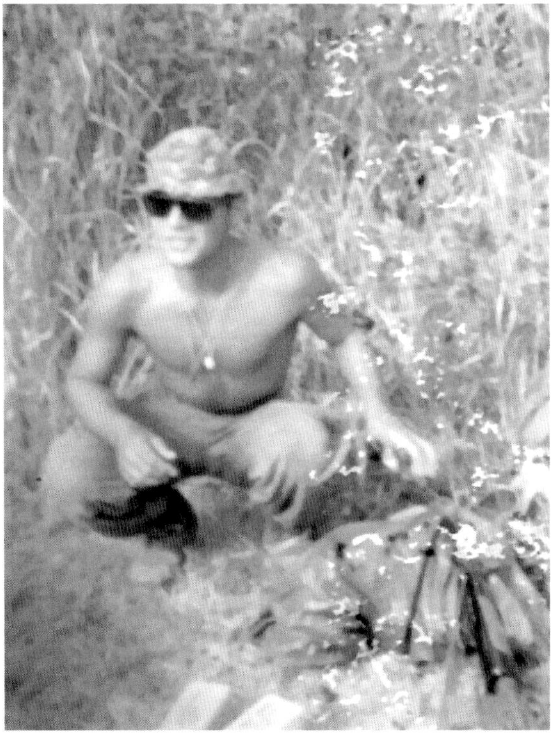

This is Sgt. Val Estrello Jr. while serving in Vietnam in 1967. Estrello was part of the 173rd Airborne Brigade. He had been an avid baseball player growing up in San Antonio. His 1964 Edgewood High School baseball team won the state championship. Estrello would return to San Antonio a hero and continue to serve his community with pride and faithfulness. (Courtesy of Charlie Calderon.)

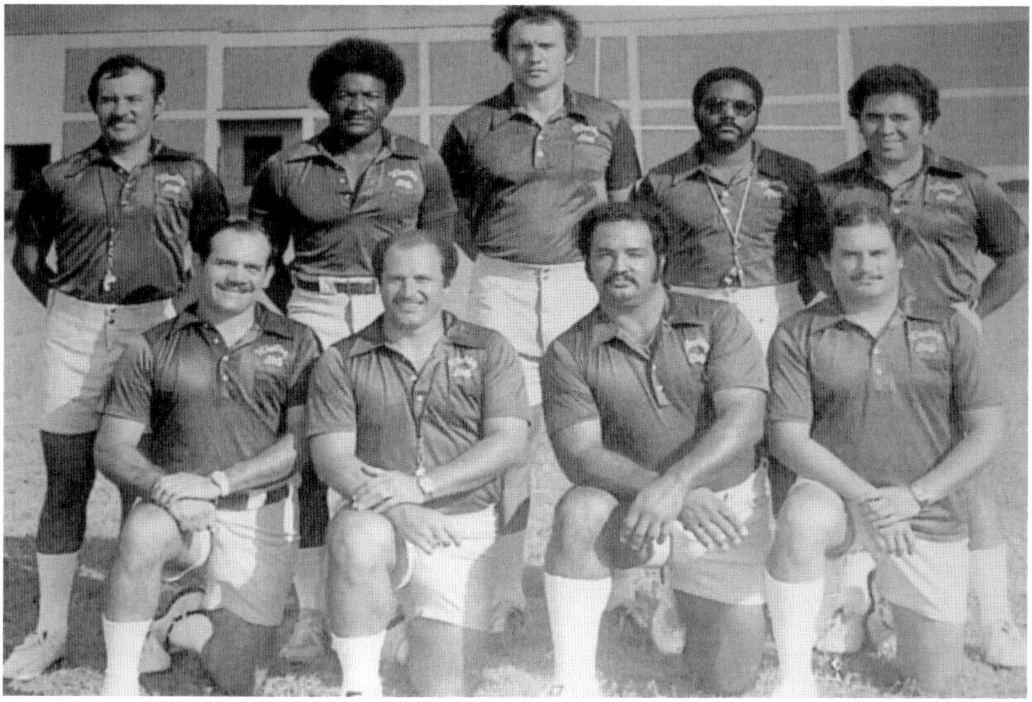

One of Val Estrello's stops as a contributing member of his San Antonio community was as a coach at Wheatley High School in San Antonio. He was on the staff at Wheatley from 1978 to 1985. During this period, he was able to have a positive effect on the young men of the community through sports. He is standing on the far left. (Courtesy of Charlie Calderon.)

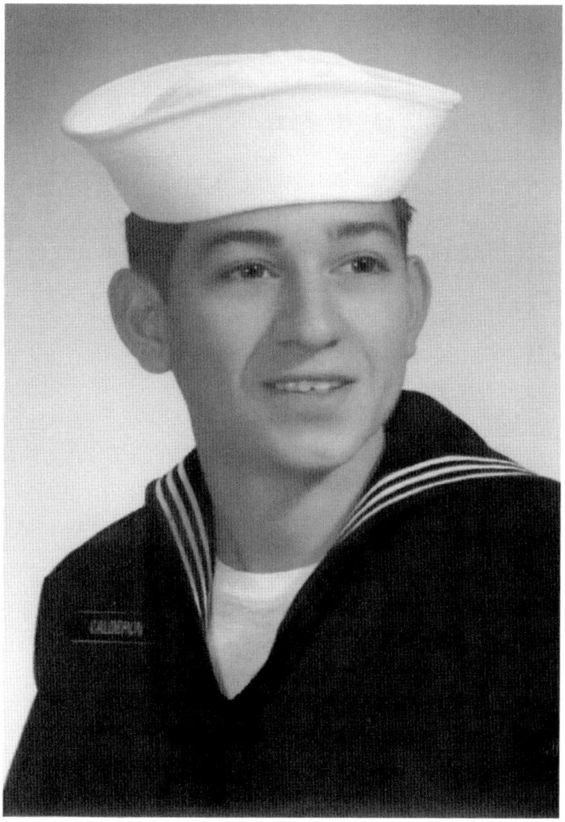

Charlie Calderon served in the Navy from 1964 to 1968. He was aboard the USS *John H. Weeks* from 1966 to 1968. Petty Officer 3rd Class Calderon played a little baseball growing up in San Antonio. He and Val Estrello played on some Little League teams together. Today, the two men are close friends. Calderon continues to honor his brothers and sisters in the military with extensive work in the community. (Courtesy of Charlie Calderon.)

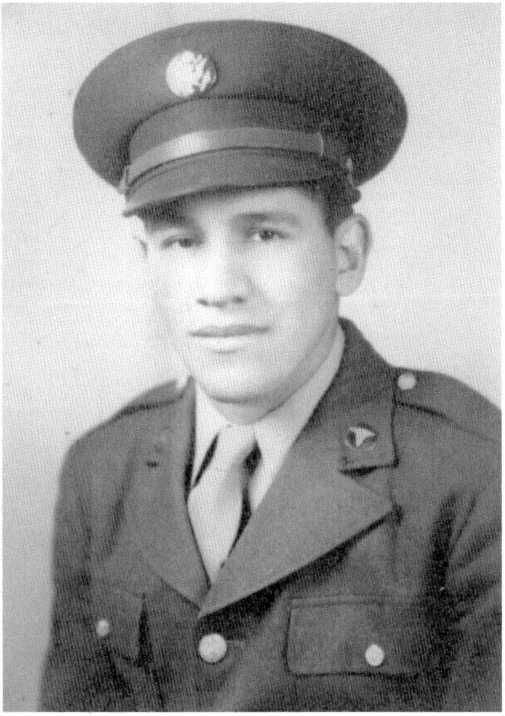

Francisco "Frank" Maldonado proudly served in the Pacific Theatre during World War II. The Brownsville native was stationed in the Philippines until 1946. Maldonado was present at Leyte Gulf, the site of the largest naval battle of World War II. After serving his country, Maldonado returned to play semi-pro baseball in South Texas and then enrolled at the University of Colorado on a baseball scholarship, playing first base. (Courtesy of Francisco "Frank" Maldonado)

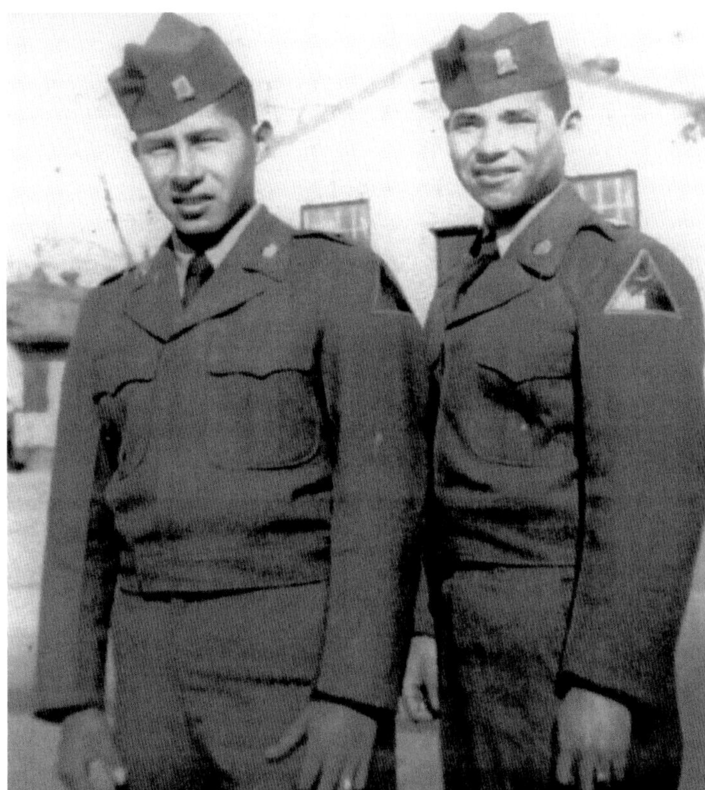

Pictured are Francisco Estevís (left) and Guadalupe Abrego during the Korean War. Estevís, a native of Edinburg, Texas, was a pitcher for Pan American College. He was drafted and served his country toward the end of the Korean War. Estevís continued to play baseball on his return home from serving. (Courtesy of Vicente and Francisco Estevís.)

This is Adolfo Arguijo, who served his country during World War I. Arguijo was stationed in Europe and was able to pitch for a military team during his service. Unfortunately, any image of his team has been lost to time. Arguijo returned home to become a legend of South Texas baseball during the 1920s. (Courtesy of Judy Everett Ramos.)

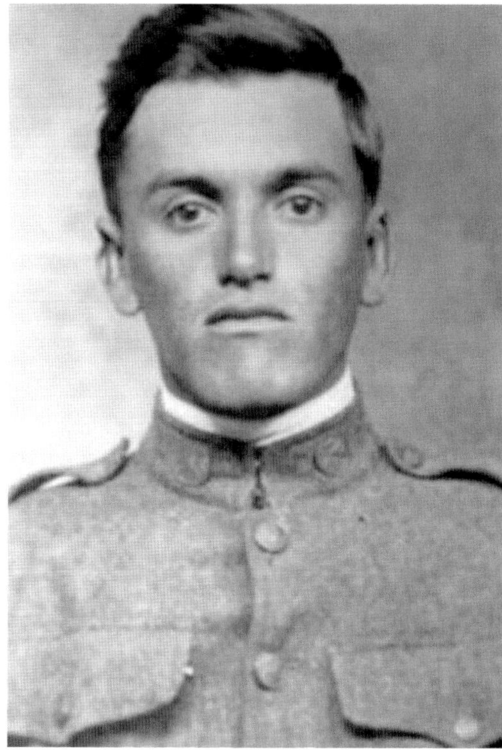

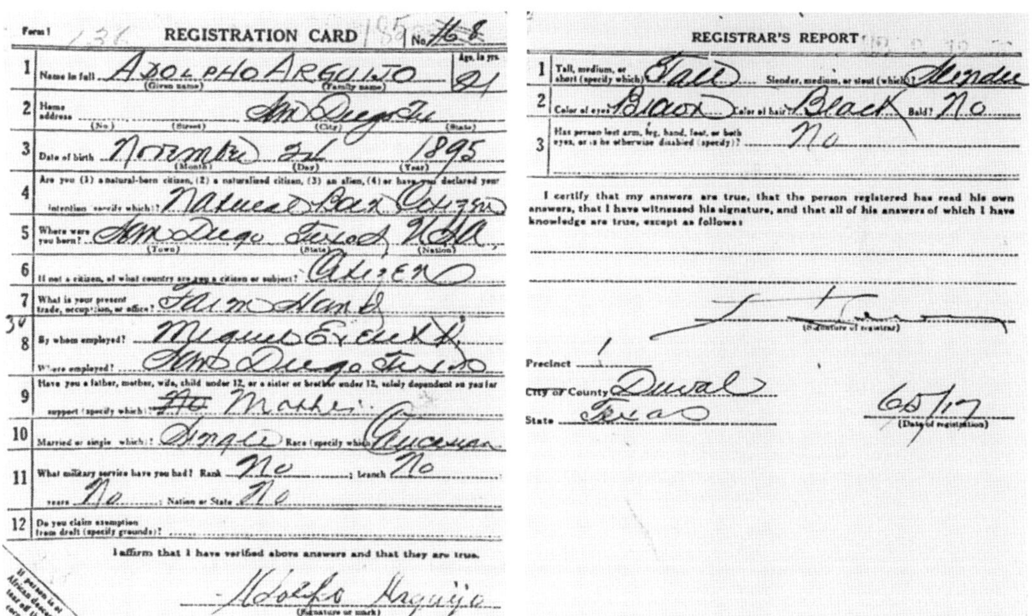

REGISTRATION CARD No. 168

1. Name in full: Adolpho Arguijo (Given name) (Family name) — Age, in yrs.: 21
2. Home address: San Diego Tex (No.) (Street) (City) (State)
3. Date of birth: November 21 1895 (Month) (Day) (Year)
4. Are you (1) a natural-born citizen, (2) a naturalized citizen, (3) an alien, (4) or have you declared your intention (specify which)? Natural Born Citizen
5. Where were you born? San Diego Texas USA (Town) (State) (Nation)
6. If not a citizen, of what country are you a citizen or subject? Citizen
7. What is your present trade, occupation, or office? Farm Hand
8. By whom employed? Miguel Everett. Where employed? San Diego Texas
9. Have you a father, mother, wife, child under 12, or a sister or brother under 12, solely dependent on you for support (specify which)? No Mother
10. Married or single (which)? Single. Race (specify which)? Caucasian
11. What military service have you had? Rank: No; branch: No; years: No; Nation or State: No
12. Do you claim exemption from draft (specify grounds)?

I affirm that I have verified above answers and that they are true.

Adolfo Arguijo (Signature or mark)

If person is of African descent, tear off this corner.

REGISTRAR'S REPORT

1. Tall, medium, or short (specify which)? Tall. Slender, medium, or stout (which)? Slender
2. Color of eyes? Brown. Color of hair? Black. Bald? No
3. Has person lost arm, leg, hand, foot, or both eyes, or is he otherwise disabled (specify)? No

I certify that my answers are true, that the person registered has read his own answers, that I have witnessed his signature, and that all of his answers of which I have knowledge are true, except as follows:

(Signature of registrar)

Precinct: 1
City or County: Duval
State: Texas
6/5/17 (Date of registration)

As a young man growing up Tejano in South Texas, Adolfo Arguijo, like many, saw World War I as an opportunity to prove that he too was a patriotic American. Arguijo left the South Texas community of San Diego at the age of 22 and signed his name on the dotted line. Pictured here is Adolfo's World War I registration card. (Courtesy of Helen Wallace.)

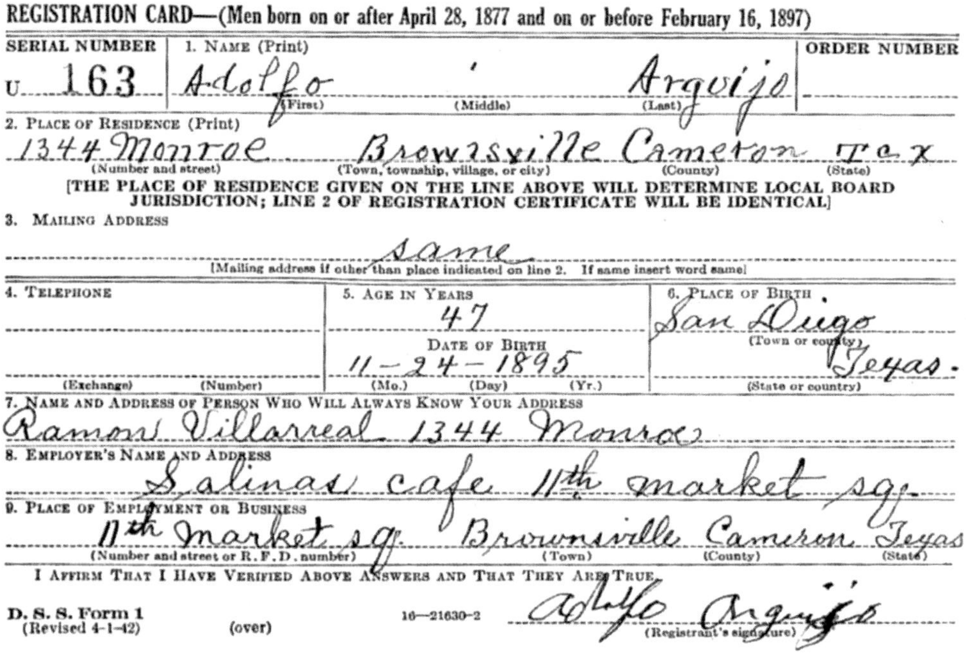
REGISTRATION CARD—(Men born on or after April 28, 1877 and on or before February 16, 1897)

SERIAL NUMBER	1. NAME (Print)			ORDER NUMBER
U 163	Adolfo (First)	(Middle)	Arguijo (Last)	

2. PLACE OF RESIDENCE (Print)
1344 Monroe (Number and street) Brownsville (Town, township, village, or city) Cameron (County) Tex (State)
[THE PLACE OF RESIDENCE GIVEN ON THE LINE ABOVE WILL DETERMINE LOCAL BOARD JURISDICTION; LINE 2 OF REGISTRATION CERTIFICATE WILL BE IDENTICAL]

3. MAILING ADDRESS
same
[Mailing address if other than place indicated on line 2. If same insert word same]

4. TELEPHONE	5. AGE IN YEARS	6. PLACE OF BIRTH
	47	San Diego (Town or county)
(Exchange) (Number)	DATE OF BIRTH 11 – 24 – 1895 (Mo.) (Day) (Yr.)	Texas (State or country)

7. NAME AND ADDRESS OF PERSON WHO WILL ALWAYS KNOW YOUR ADDRESS
Ramon Villarreal 1344 Monroe

8. EMPLOYER'S NAME AND ADDRESS
Salinas cafe 11th market sq.

9. PLACE OF EMPLOYMENT OR BUSINESS
11th market sq. (Number and street or R. F. D. number) Brownsville (Town) Cameron (County) Texas (State)

I AFFIRM THAT I HAVE VERIFIED ABOVE ANSWERS AND THAT THEY ARE TRUE.

D. S. S. Form 1
(Revised 4-1-42) (over) 16—21630-2 Adolfo Arguijo (Registrant's signature)

Adolfo Arguijo dedicated his entire adult life to baseball in South Texas. Whether he was playing, managing, or just setting up games, he was a lifer. That is, until World War II came along. Arguijo loved his country as much as he loved baseball. He did not hesitate, at the age of 47, to register for World War II. He was prepared to leave his job at the Salinas Café in Brownsville, Texas, to once again serve. (Courtesy of Helen Wallace.)

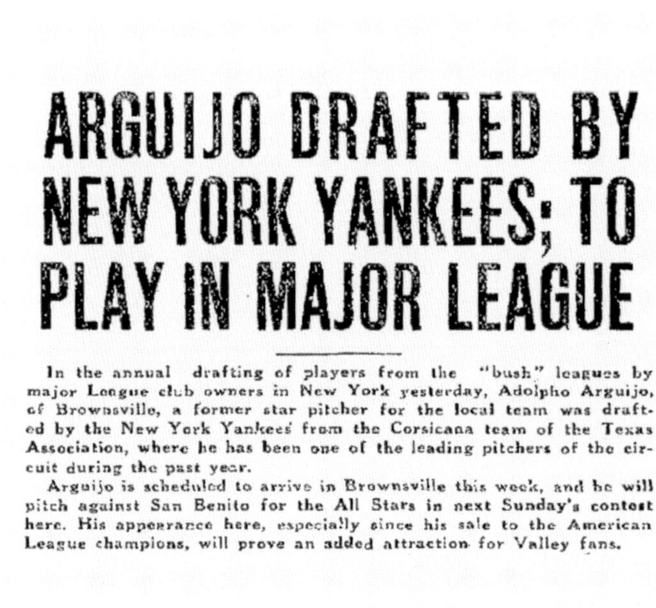
ARGUIJO DRAFTED BY NEW YORK YANKEES; TO PLAY IN MAJOR LEAGUE

In the annual drafting of players from the "bush" leagues by major League club owners in New York yesterday, Adolpho Arguijo, of Brownsville, a former star pitcher for the local team was drafted by the New York Yankees from the Corsicana team of the Texas Association, where he has been one of the leading pitchers of the circuit during the past year.

Arguijo is scheduled to arrive in Brownsville this week, and he will pitch against San Benito for the All Stars in next Sunday's contest here. His appearance here, especially since his sale to the American League champions, will prove an added attraction for Valley fans.

This headline is proof of Arguijo's accomplishments in the early 1920s. He was drafted by the New York Yankees after playing a year with the Corsicana Gumbo Busters. Arguijo would go onto spring training with the Yankees in New Orleans that year. He did not make the squad but was well aware of the stars the team had. Despite not making the show, he did have the opportunity to strike out Babe Ruth. (Courtesy of Helen Wallace.)

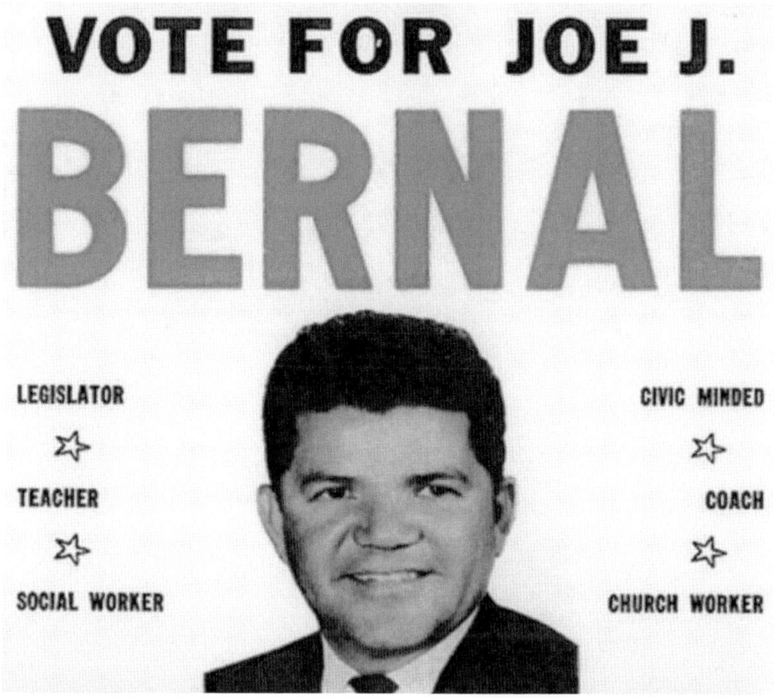

This is a campaign poster for Representative Bernal's successful run for the Texas legislature. Politics grew out of his love for the community—kids, ball teams, and the Guadalupe Cultural Center. His home was San Antonio, and he dedicated himself to a life serving the people of that community. (Courtesy of Dr. Joe Bernal.)

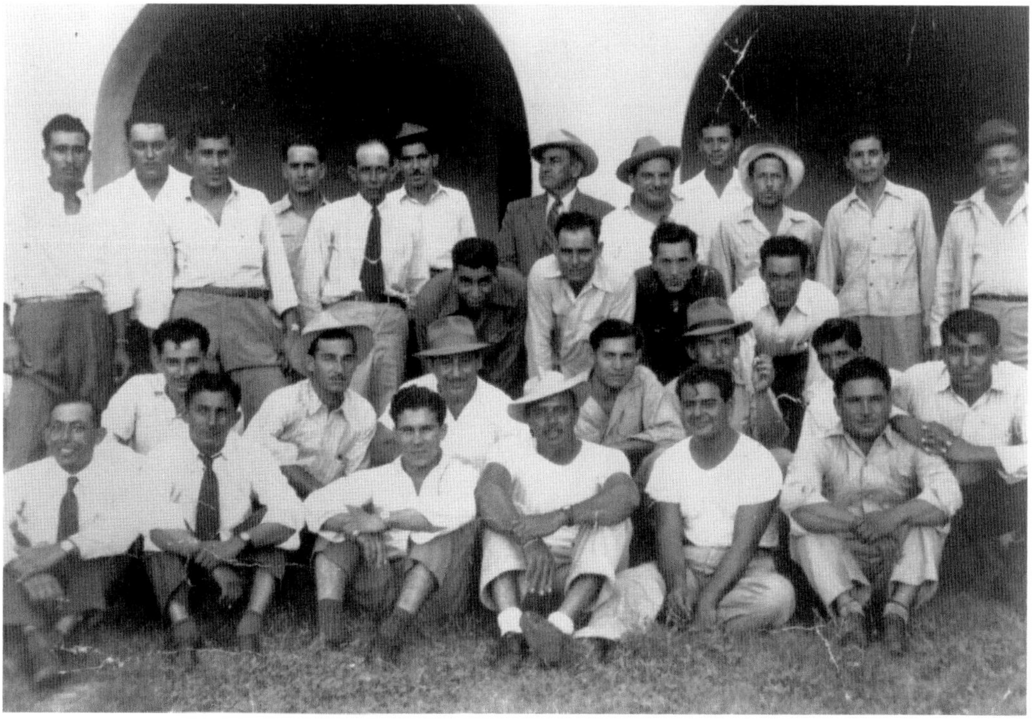

These are members of the Goliad Baseball Club, mostly veterans of World War II. The picture was taken around 1946 outside of the Spanish Mission in Goliad, Texas, known as Mission Espiritu Santo. (Courtesy of University of Texas Special Collections.)

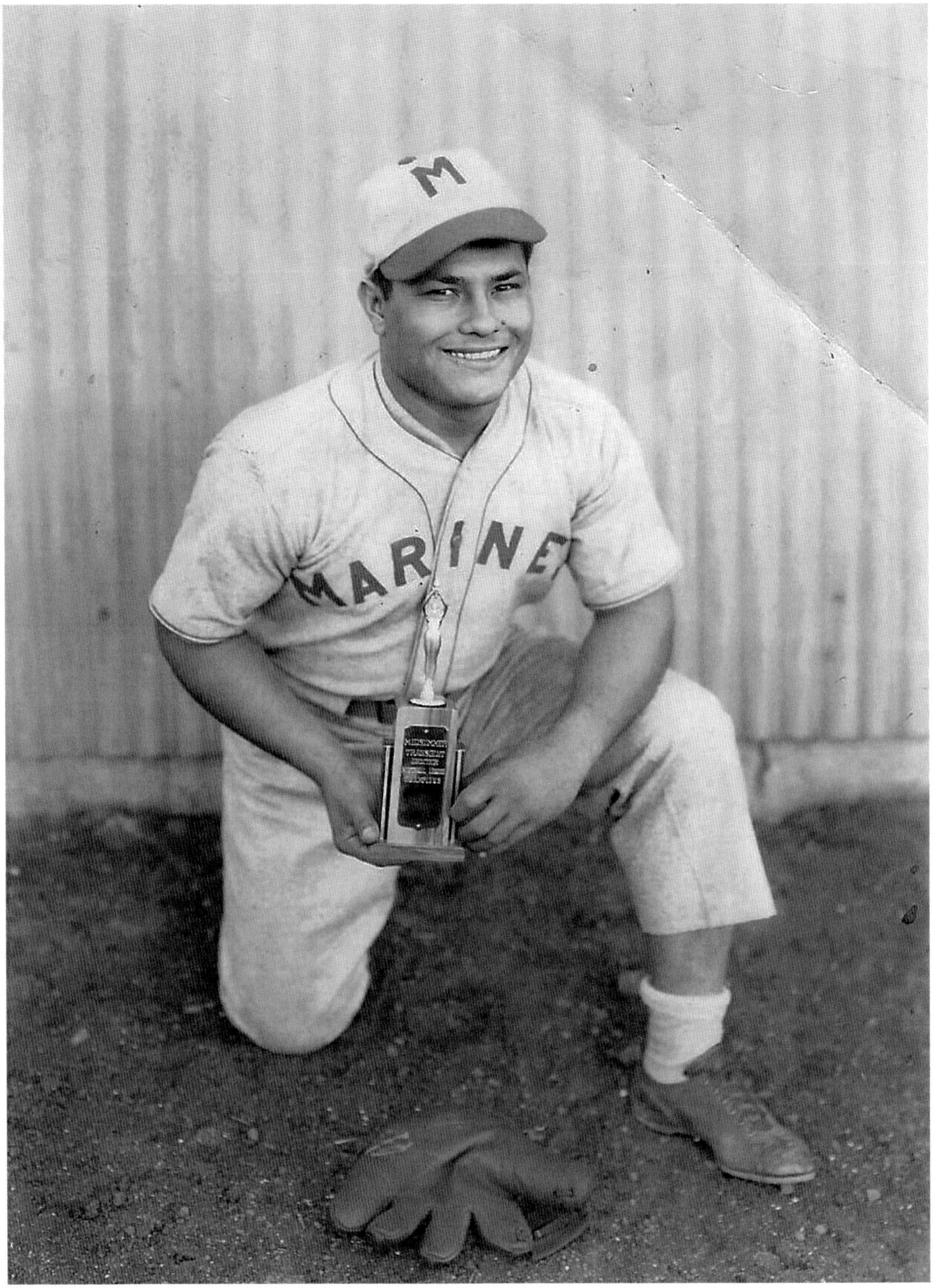

This is Mauro García Sr., who served with the Marines and is shown wearing the uniform of the US Marines team he played on while on active duty from 1941 to 1945. García was a catcher who played in San Diego, Texas. (Courtesy of Betty García.)

6

Coast to Coast

Mexican migration to the United States, especially between the 1890s and 1930s, is striking because immigrants settled in nearly every state outside the traditional Southwest region. Mexicans moved to New York, Pennsylvania, Ohio, Indiana, Wisconsin, Minnesota, Michigan, Nebraska, Kansas, Iowa, Missouri, Oklahoma, Wyoming, Louisiana, Arkansas, Idaho, Washington, and Oregon. They formed distinct communities in large cities like New York City, Philadelphia, Pittsburgh, Cleveland, Detroit, Lansing, Gary, East Chicago, Chicago, South Chicago, Milwaukee, St. Paul, Omaha, Lincoln, Des Moines, Wichita, Topeka, and Kansas City. And they settled in other communities like Allentown, Palmerton, Hershey, Lorain, Adrian, Flint, Waukesha, Racine, Kenosha, Albert Lea, Mason City, Fort Madison, Silvis, Moline, Bettendorf, Davenport, Sterling, Aurora, Elgin, Rockford, Joliet, South Bend, Fort Wayne, Emporia, Chanute, Newton, Liberal, Dodge City, Hutchinson, Garden City, Parsons, Wellington, Freedonia, Scottsbluff, Mitchell, and Bayard.

They gave colorful names to their communities based largely on the type of industry near their neighborhoods. The originality of these names indicated whether they worked at a sand or cement company, a railroad yard, steel mill, water plant or mine, the city pound, or in agriculture. These names also suggested whether their housing was located on a hill or ravine, or near a river. Thus, they promoted vivid names for their residences such as the Flats, Smelter Hill, Las Lomas, Silver City, Cement Row, Las Casitas, El Jardin, West Bottoms, Goat Hill, the Y, the Strand, La Hoyita, Holy City, Barrio Dogtown, Sandtown, El Pozo, La Polvosa, the Bush, Steeltown, and El Palomar. These clever names clearly informed others that Mexican Americans lived in the less desirable parts of these cities and had low-paying jobs when they arrived.

By the early 1920s, many of these communities had formed athletic clubs that promoted a host of sports, especially baseball. After World War II, civil rights organizations such as the G.I. Forum, the League of United Latin American Citizens, Latin American Social Clubs, Mexican American Veterans Association, Mexican G.I. Club, and Latin Americans Veterans sponsored baseball and softball teams. This chapter takes a snapshot view of Mexican American teams from the Pacific Ocean to the Atlantic coast.

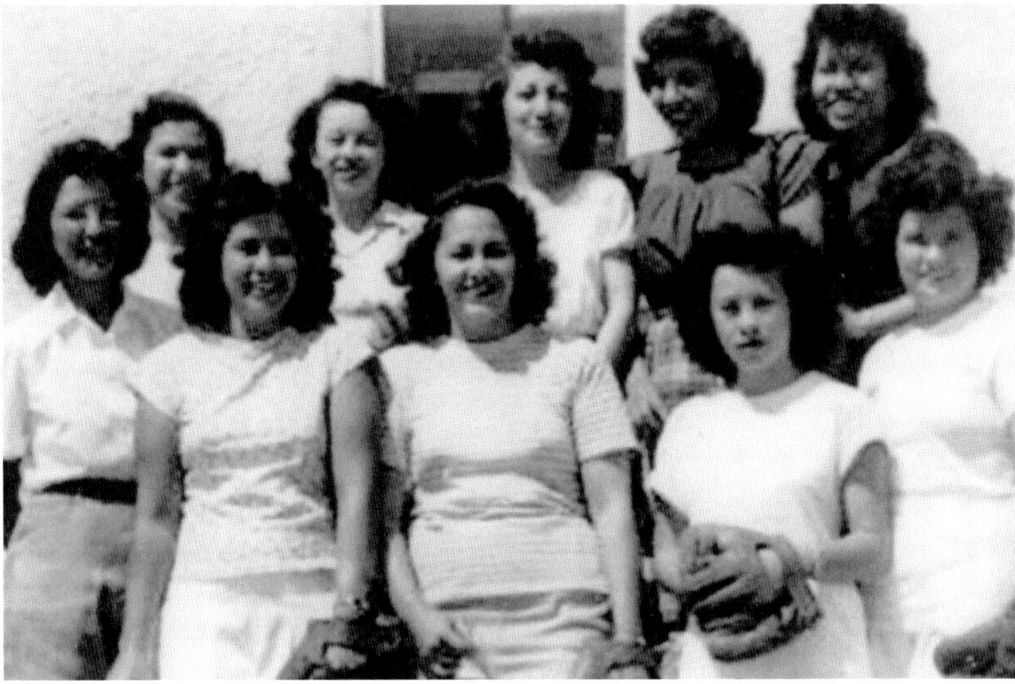

Tombstone, Arizona, was founded in 1879, less than 30 miles from the Mexican border. The silver and gold mines attracted countless Mexicans, especially from Sonora, to work in the mines. Mexicans were paid less for doing the same work as white workers and were barred from higher-paying occupations. Mexicans and Chinese were segregated in housing facilities. During their days off, Mexicans formed baseball and softball teams, including this women's team. None of the players are identified. Today, nearly 30 percent of Tombstone's population have Spanish surnames. (Courtesy of Darcy Meyer.)

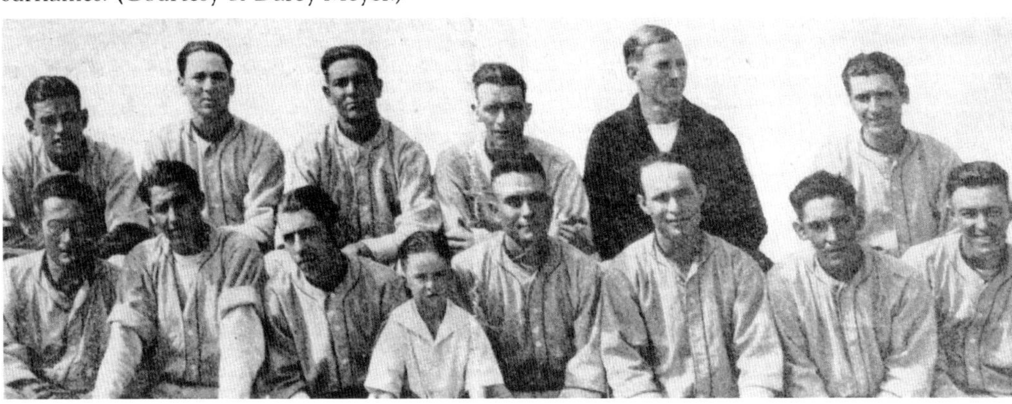

Several railroad companies sponsored baseball teams. Being an outstanding player nearly guaranteed full-time employment. The Southern Pacific Railroad Company in Arizona formed several teams throughout the state. This team won the 1928 Tucson City Championship. Many Mexican Americans were on this powerhouse team, including Diego Carrillo, Fito Aros, Jake Peralta, Charlie Pellón, Al Orozco, Carlos Carrillo, and Jimmy Oliva. Mike Robles managed the team. (Courtesy of Darcy Meyer.)

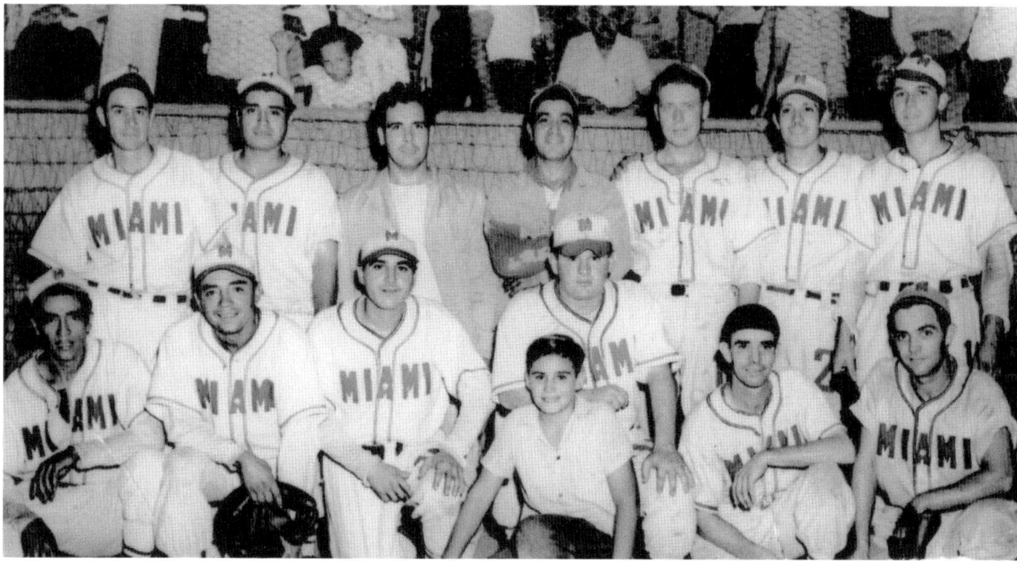

The 1946 Miami, Arizona, Miners team was sponsored by the Inspiration Consolidated Copper Company. Opposing baseball clubs from Miami and Globe were sponsored by local business merchants and civic organizations. The season lasted about six months. From left to right are (first row) Félix García, centerfield; "Lally" García, second base; unidentified; Wade Sawaia, outfield; and three unidentified; (second row) Ray Franco, manager; Lupe Trujillo Marín, third base; Jimmie Casillas, third base; Isaac García, pitcher; Benny Wilkin, pitcher; Mike Medina, catcher; and Martín Sertich, utility man. (Courtesy of Christine Marín.)

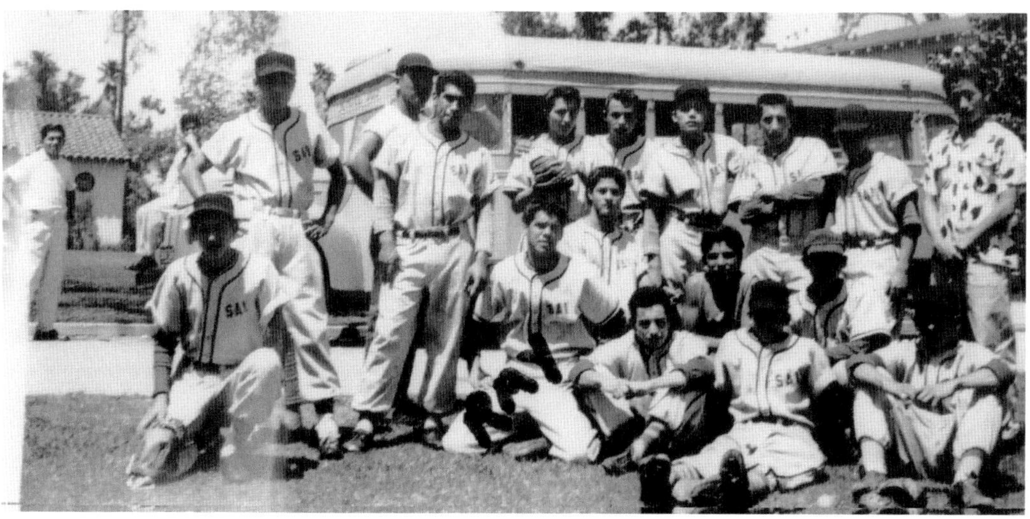

This 1955 Spanish American Institute team from Gardena, California, was sponsored by a Catholic church. Ray Loya is kneeling at center. He played outfield and third base, and practiced pitching against the church walls. His team beat the Catalina Island team at Wrigley Field in Los Angeles for the championship. Loya also played on the institute's basketball team. He was an outstanding athlete at Gardena High School, lettering four times in football. At the Spanish American Institute, he milked cows at 5:00 a.m. as part of his chores. (Courtesy of Ray Loya.)

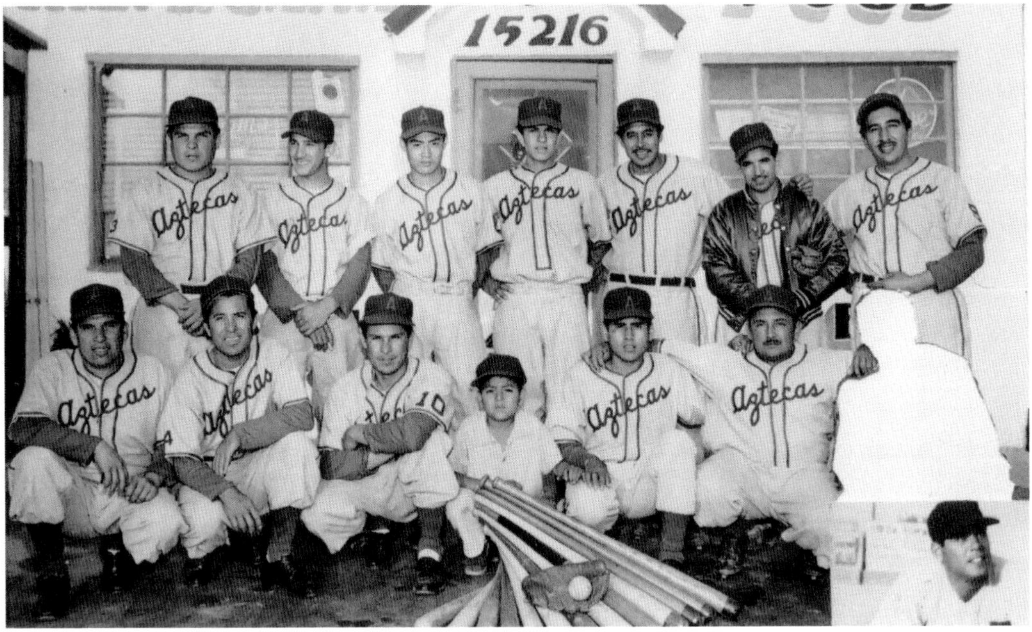

This 1956 photograph was taken in Gardena, California. The owner of La Fiesta Café sponsored the team. Ray Loya (inset, lower right) was a ward at the boys' correctional school nearby. He would sneak out of the school to practice and play for the team. Loya pitched for the Aztecas for three years. Kenny Meyers, a Dodgers scout, wanted to sign Loya, but he said no because he did not want to reveal his association with the school, and was too young to legally sign a contract. Seven years later, he signed with the Dodgers. (Courtesy of Ray Loya.)

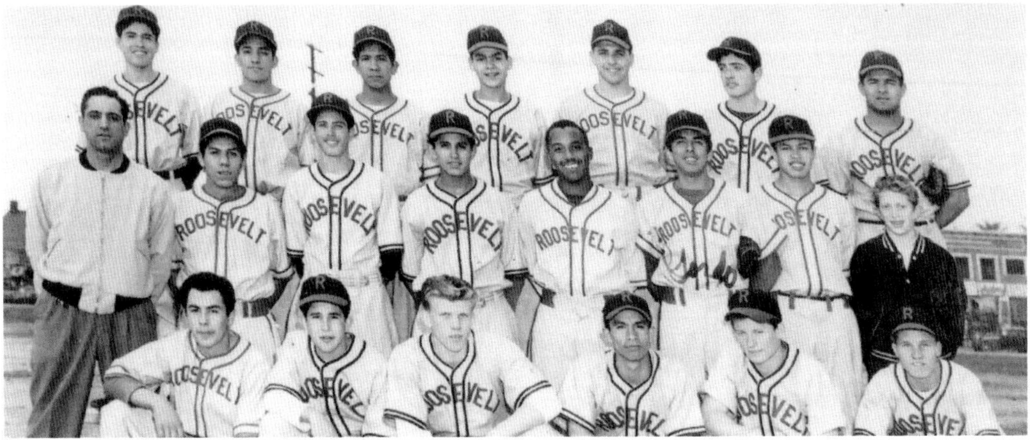

The 1953 Roosevelt High School Roughriders from East Los Angeles played their home games at Evergreen Park, across the street from the campus. This team had lost several stars and was rebuilding. Pictured are, from left to right, (first row) Bob Morales, Tommy Martínez, Louie Mills, Manny Arellanos, Bill, and Alex Novakoff; (second row) coach Dominck Campallo, Art Malanez, Bobby Recendez, Fernando Farfan, Donald Watson, Joe Herrera, unidentified, and ? Miller; (third row) Joe Muñatones, Art Velarde, Tinker De La Rosa, Ray Terrones, ? Miller, Conrad Muñatones, and Mark Urqiti. (Courtesy of Bobby Recendez.)

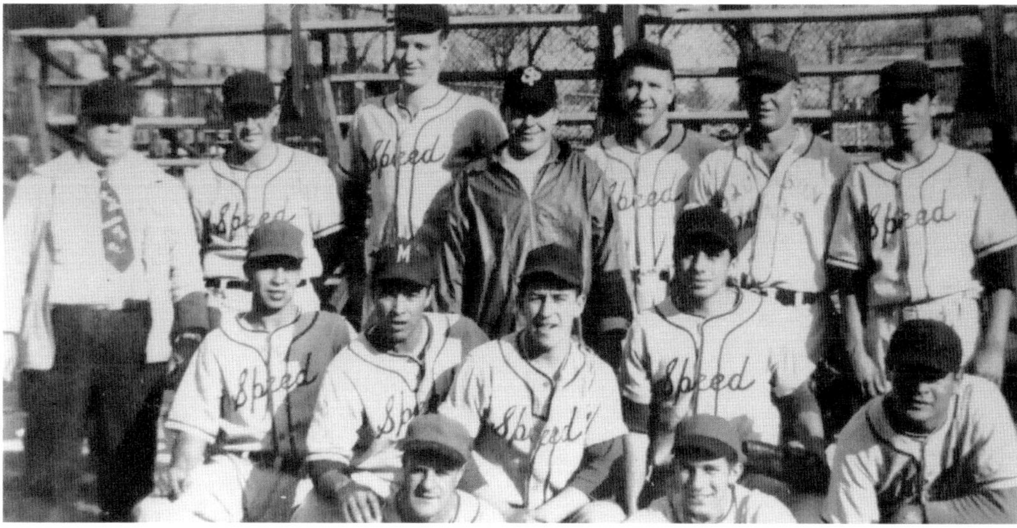

The Speed Liquor store sponsored this team around 1953 at Griffith Park in Los Angeles. Speed Liquor was a farm team for the Carmelita Chorizeros. Several members of the Chorizeros saw action during the Korean War, which gave several of the Speed players an opportunity to play for the Chorizeros. From left to right are (first row) manager Gordy Leach and ? Morton; (second row) Joe and Chano Gaitan, Ernie and Mando Rodríguez, and Greg Regalado; (third row) scorekeeper ? Leach, three unidentified, Sy Vernal, Chuck Sarni, and Bobby Recendez. (Courtesy of Bobby Recendez.)

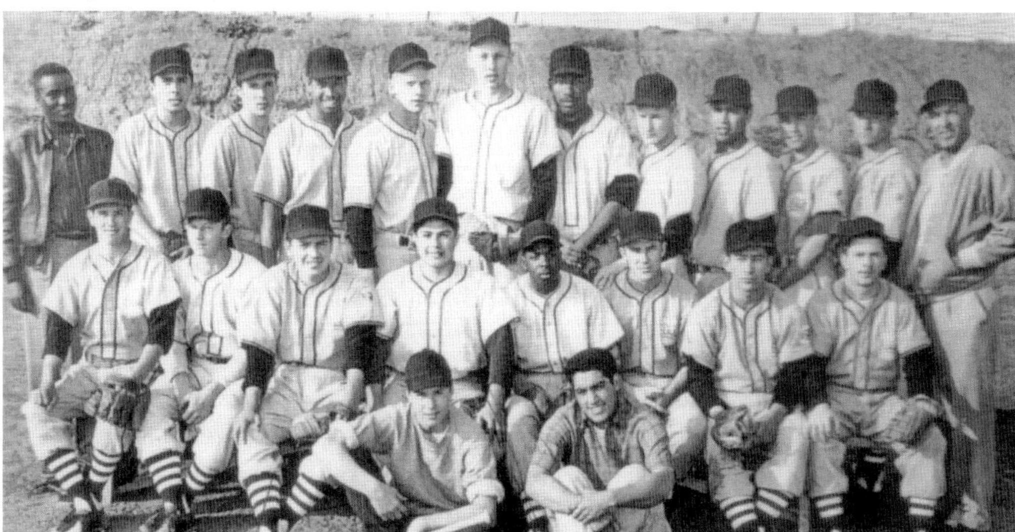

The 1956 East Los Angeles College team had several outstanding players, including Art Velarde (first row, far right), Ernie Rodríguez (second row, second from right), Bobby Recendez (second row, far left), Rubén Rodríguez (second row, third from left), Mando Pérez (third row, second from left), Ray Gutiérrez (third row, fourth from right), and ? Maldonado. Chink Duln (third row, far right) was their outstanding manager. This team broke Long Beach City College's 20-game winning streak. Recendez went five-for-five in that game. (Courtesy of Bobby Recendez.)

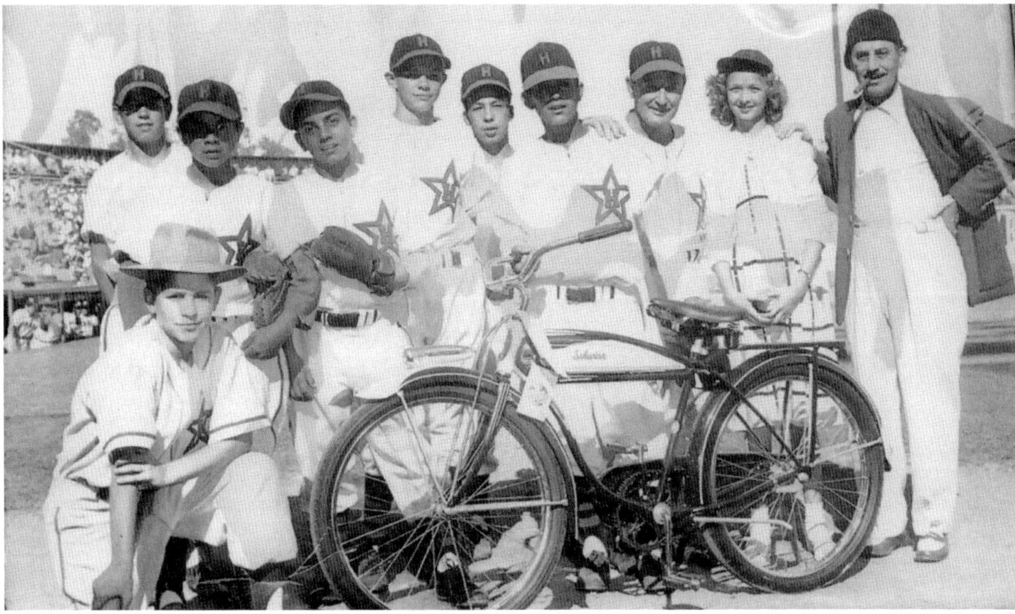

The Hollywood Stars sponsored an event at Gilmore Field called the Infield of the Future, where neighborhood teams were invited to take infield practice. Fresno and Evergreen Parks from East Angeles participated around 1950. The players wore borrowed youth Stars uniforms. From left to right are Bobby Recendez, Tom Robles, Richard Casares, Don Dangleis, Joe Gaitan, Fernando Farfan, Fred Haney, Haney's niece, and Groucho Marx. The batboy kneeling at left is wearing Groucho's hat. Farfan won the bike. Coach Lunetta (not shown) knew Billy Martin and Casey Stengal and arranged for Eastside teams to be invited. (Courtesy of Bobby Recendez.)

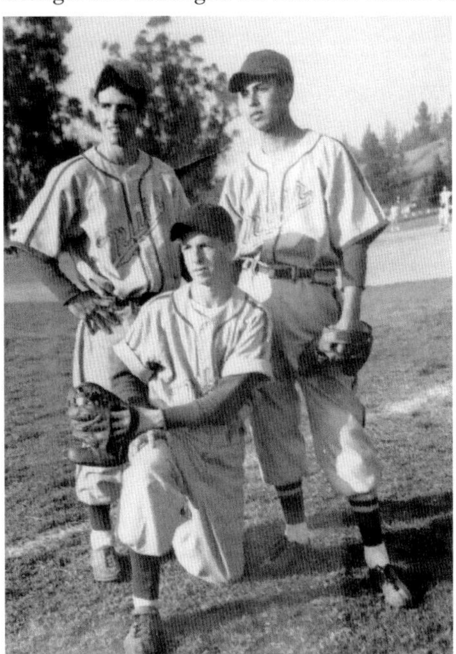

David Salazar (standing, right) is pictured with his high school teammates in 1949. Salazar made the All Coast second team at John Muir High School in Pasadena, California. His All Coast teammates included future Major Leaguers Lee Wall and Jim Marshall. Salazar played two years ar John Muir Junior College, joined the National Guard, served in Korea, played military ball in Japan, and came back to play at Cal State Los Angeles. He began umpiring Little League and Babe Ruth baseball in the Pasadena area with his younger bother Carlos. After David retired from the Los Angeles Post Office, he began umpiring high school softball from 2000 to 2014, retiring at the age of 84. (Courtesy of Carlos Salazar.)

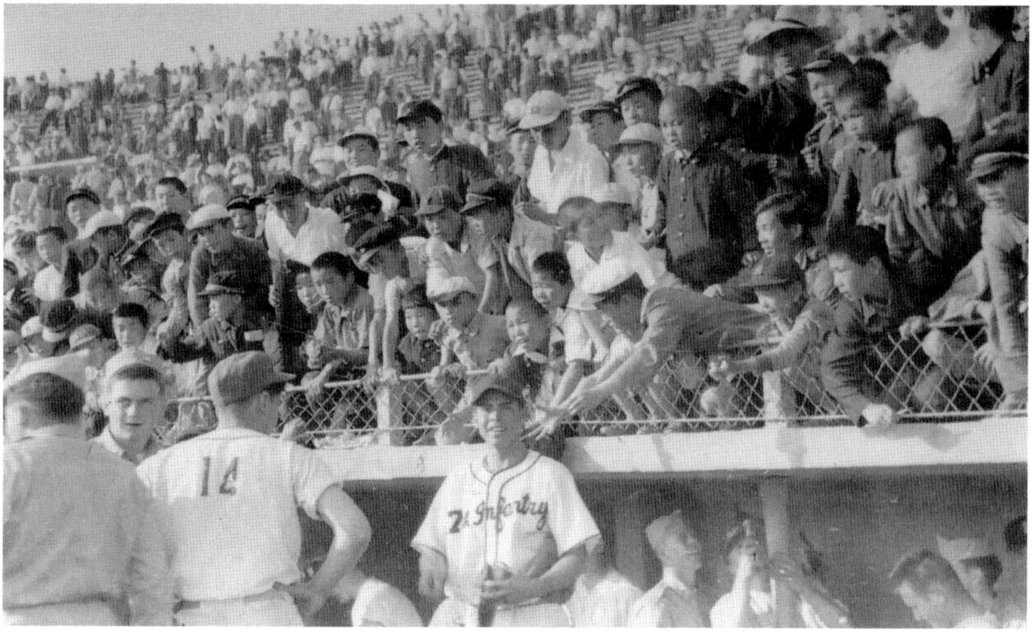

David Salazar played military ball for the Army in Sendai, Japan, for the 40th Division 225th Regiment against the Japanese All-Star team. Nearly 35,000 Japanese fans attended the game. Here, a few are trying to get a ball from David Salazar, who is standing near the US dugout. Salazar served in Japan during the Korean War. He came home and played ball at Cal State Los Angeles from 1953 to 1954. (Courtesy of David and Mike Salazar.)

Pete Powell (left) and Carlos Salazar are seen here at Brookside Park in Pasadena, California, in 1955. Brookside Park was the former spring training camp for the Chicago White Sox from the 1940s through 1952. Powell and Salazar made the Babe Ruth All-Star team and were in play-off games at Wrigley Field in Los Angeles, but lost the chance to play for the championship game in Austin, Texas, by losing to Oakland at Gilmore Field in Los Angeles. They beat Fresno 2-0 at Brookside Park; the game featured Dick Ellsworth and Chuck Lampier, both of whom later pitched in the Major Leagues. (Courtesy of Carlos Salazar.)

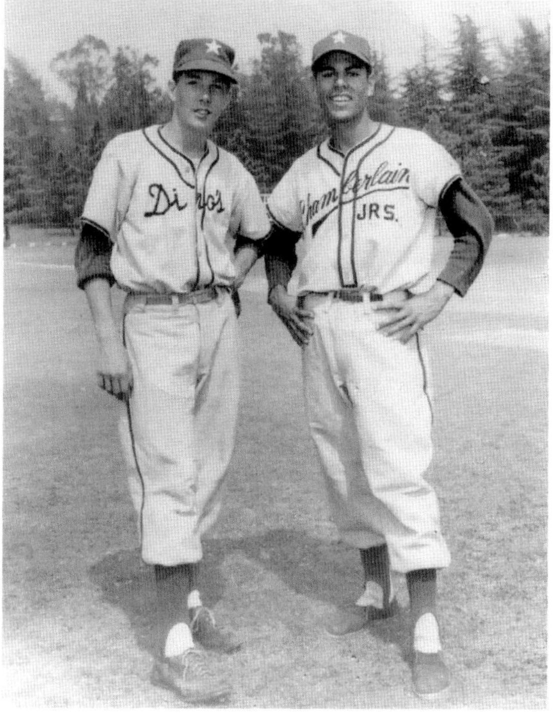

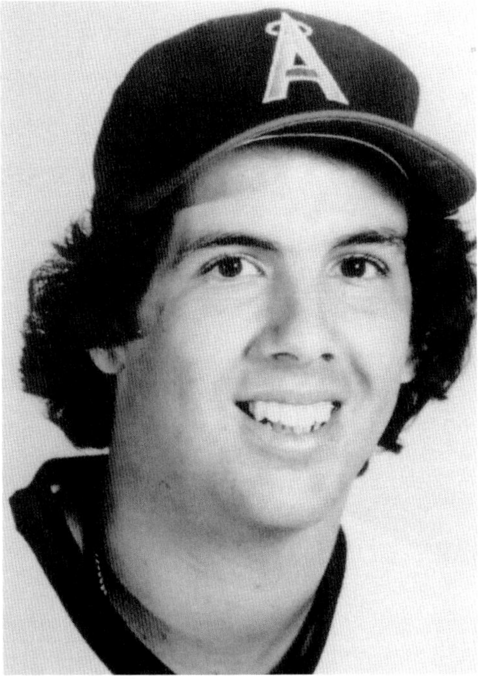

Fred Martínez grew up in Lincoln Heights and played ball at Downey playground for Dan Alessi. He is proud to be a Downey playground "gremlin." He pitched and played first base at Lincoln High School in the 1970s, and played for Whittier College, East Los Angeles Junior College, and Cal State Los Angeles. Martínez was drafted by the New York Mets in 1977, playing in their minor league system for three years. His contract was purchased by the California Angels in 1979. In 1980, Martínez started 23 games for the Halos and was named Angel Rookie of the Year. His manager was Jim Fergosi and his pitching coach was Larry Sherry. He is currently a Los Angeles fireman. (Courtesy of Fred Martínez.)

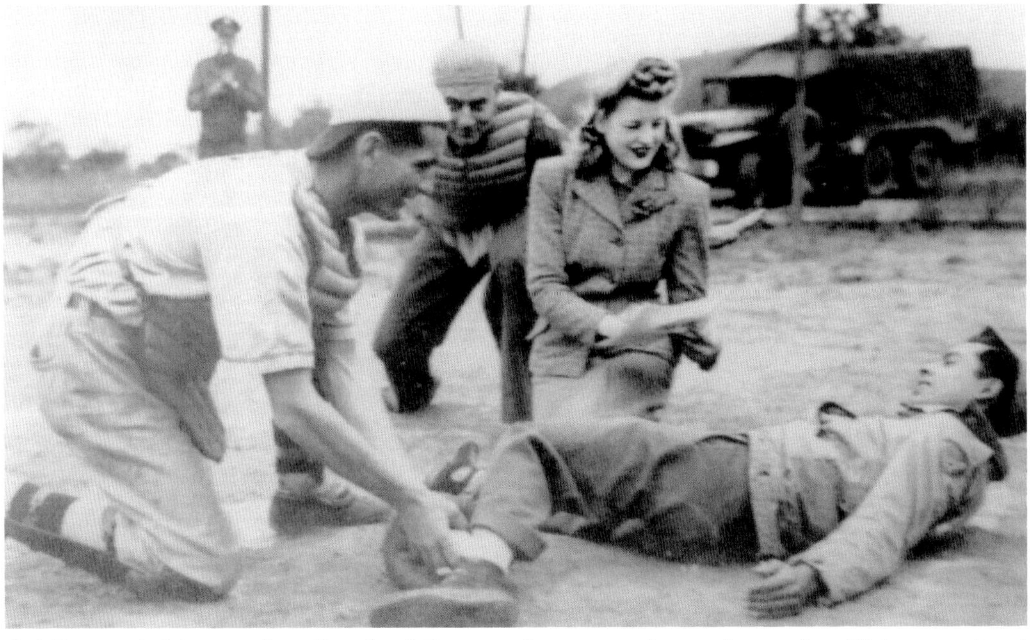

Cpl. Ramón A. Martínez from Copeland, Kansas, is being tagged out at home plate. This promotional photograph was taken after a game at Royal Air Force Station Wattisham in England on August 9, 1944. The young lady is supposed to be selling a war bond to Corporal Martínez. When the Americans of the 479th Fighter Group arrived at the base, the lower-ranking minority men were cruelly segregated into "nissen huts" near the base at Great Bricett. These huts still stand today and are part of a small business park. (Courtesy of Rod Martínez.)

One of the most famous East Los Angeles families was the Peña family with nine boys, who all played ball. Six of the brothers were trained as catchers like their father, who was their manager. Gabe Peña, one of the brothers, seen here on the right, played ball in Germany in 1954. Colonel Edwards is throwing out the ceremonial first pitch to start the new season. Peña was assigned to the 22nd Infantry Regiment and also played on the football team. (Courtesy of the Gabe Peña family.)

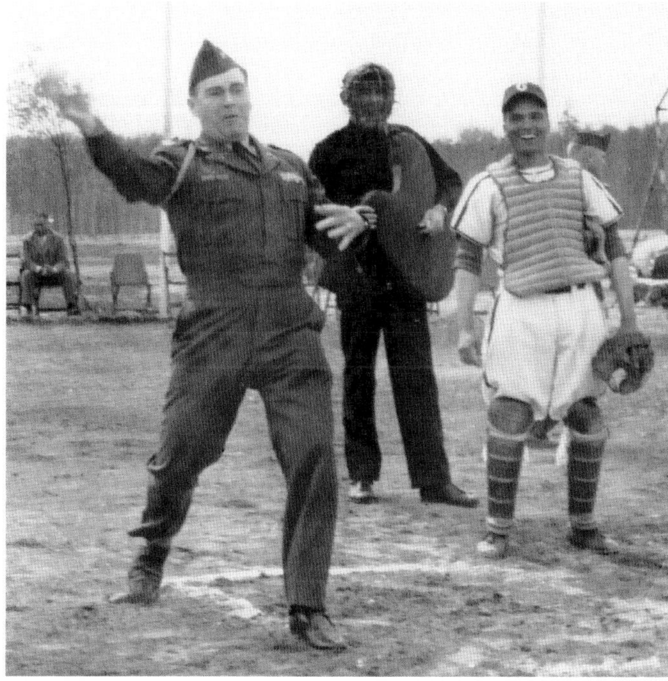

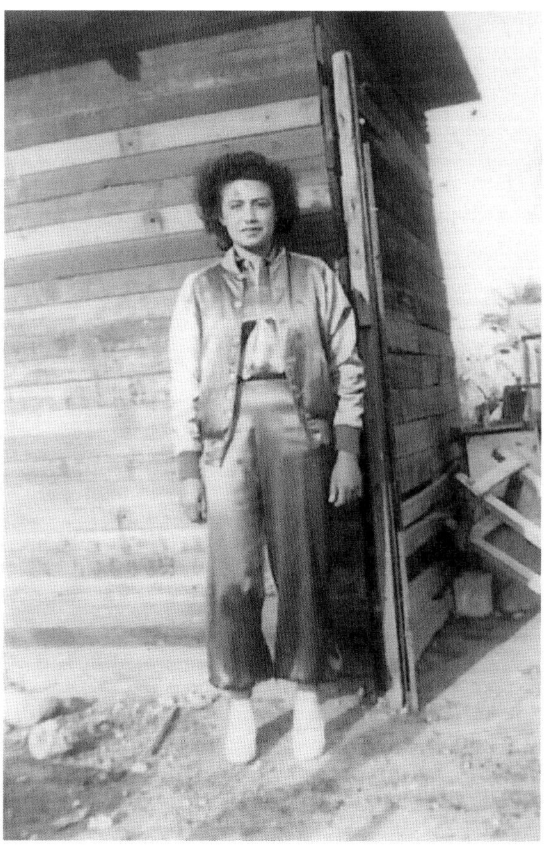

Maggie (Salazar) Guzmán was born in 1931 and raised in Irwindale, California. Her father, Julián, worked for the railroad and her mother, Irene, raised eight children. Maggie was the last of seven daughters. She loved sports and started playing catcher at the age of 14. Maggie's coach Luís Ruelas was a former catcher himself and mentored her. She was recruited by the Baldwin Park Royals, a semiprofessional team. Maggie had eight children and retired as a nurse. She serves on the Irwindale Senior Citizen Commission and is extremely proud that all of her grandchildren and great-grandchildren played ball. (Courtesy of Maggie Salazar Guzmán.)

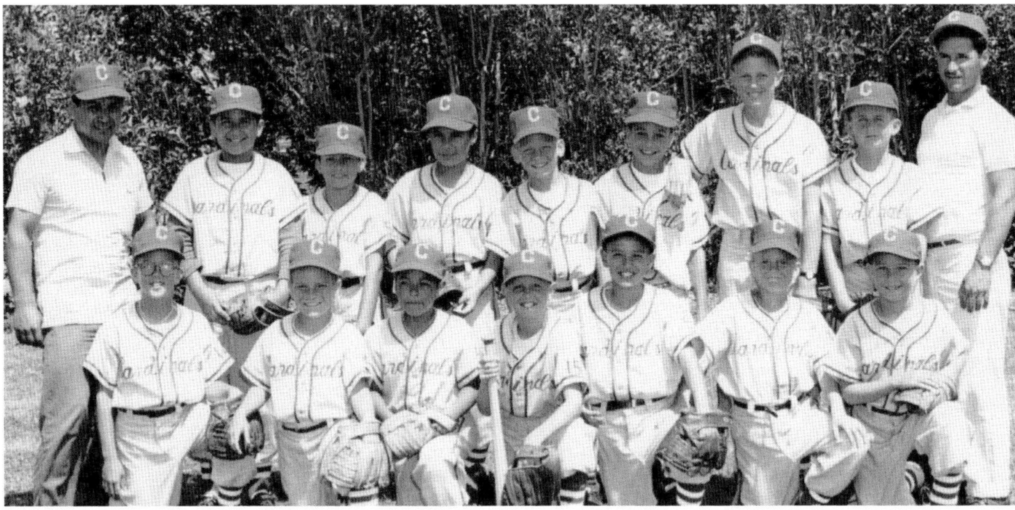

Brothers-in-law Cleo LaFarga, standing far left, and Daniel Gonzáles, standing far right, coached the 1959 Cardinals at Peck Park in San Pedro, California, with players from Holy Trinity School. Players included Larry Gonzáles (Coach Gonzáles's son), George Morones, and Cleo LaFarga (Coach LaFarga's son). Kneeling third from left is Carlos LaFarga, also Coach LaFarga's son, and kneeling fifth from left is Bobby Núñez. The four were Larry Gonzáles's cousins. Cleo LaFarga grew up in the now-gone Mexican neighborhood known as Hollywood, on San Pedro's waterfront. Daniel Gonzáles, a veteran, grew up in the town's la Rambla *colonia*. (Courtesy of Daniel Gonzáles.)

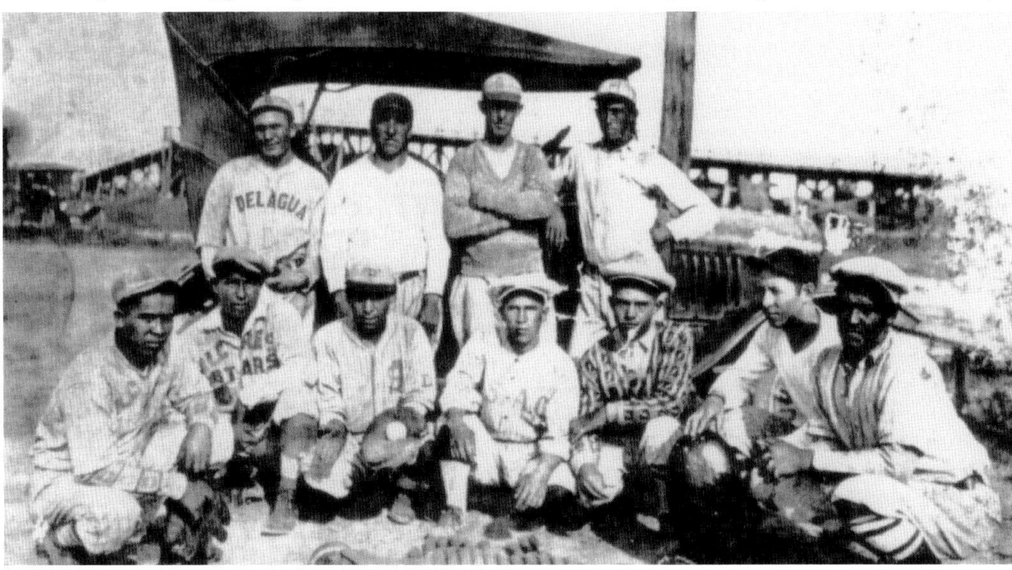

These players of the 1927 Gilcrest, Colorado, Aztecs are unidentified. Mexicans came to work in four factories between Eaton and Brighton for the Great Western Sugar Company. Men, women, and children who were old enough to work were in the fields. Their cheapest form of entertainment was baseball. Two of the team's early managers were Fastino Lemon and John López. The Aztecs played against teams from Fort Collins, Greeley, Ault, Milliken, Wattenberg, and Cheyenne. (Courtesy of Gabriel and Jody López.)

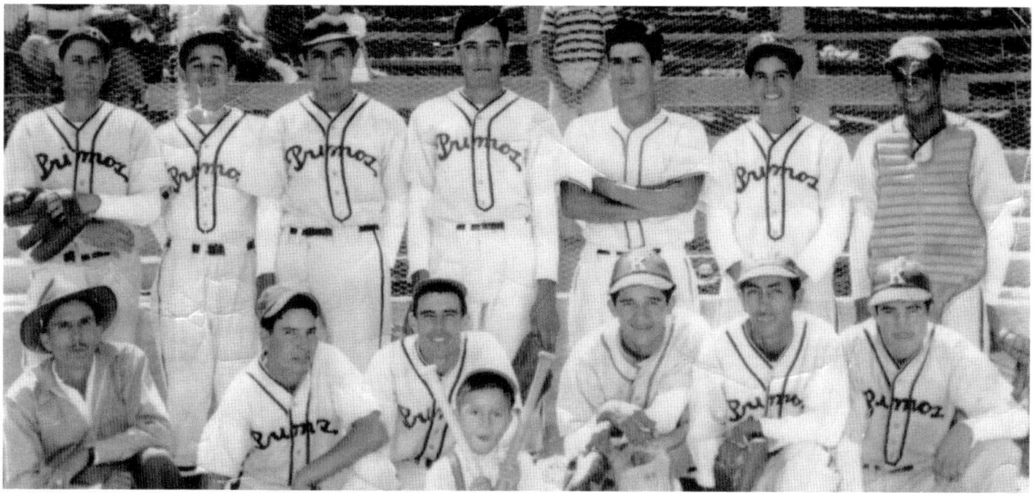

The Kersey, Colorado, Primos (Cousins) began in 1946 with none of the players having played ball before. The Great Western Sugar Company, which had once been used as a prisoner-of-war camp, owned the ballfield. The uniforms were purchased from a Montgomery Ward's catalog for $12. From left to right are (first row) manager Richard Archuleta, Leroy Vigil, Joe Archuleta, Pete Archuleta, batboy Tony Salazar, Ben Córdova, and Sal Salazar; (second row) John Bedan, Fiberto Salazar, George Córdova, Ernie García, Archie Batrez, Paul Salazar, and Rudy García. (Courtesy of Gabriel and Jody López.)

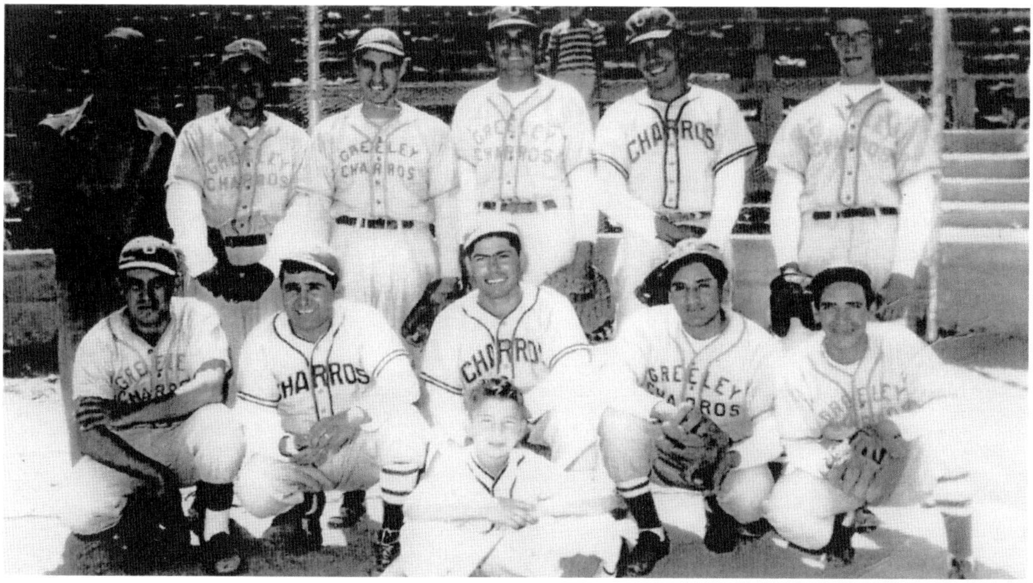

The 1946 Greeley Charros would often thin sugar beets and then play ball in their work clothes. No spikes and no uniforms, they just wore regular work clothes with tennis shoes when playing baseball. Eventually, they had money to buy uniforms. Pictured are, from left to right, (first row) batboy Birdie Carabajal; (second row) John Juárez, Ray Villa, Mike Esquibel, Dan Solíz, and Manuel Bajarano; (third row) coach Fred Olivas, Paul Soro, Julio Mendoza, Albert Muñoz, Ángel Alcarez, and Gunsi García. (Courtesy of Gabriel and Jody López.)

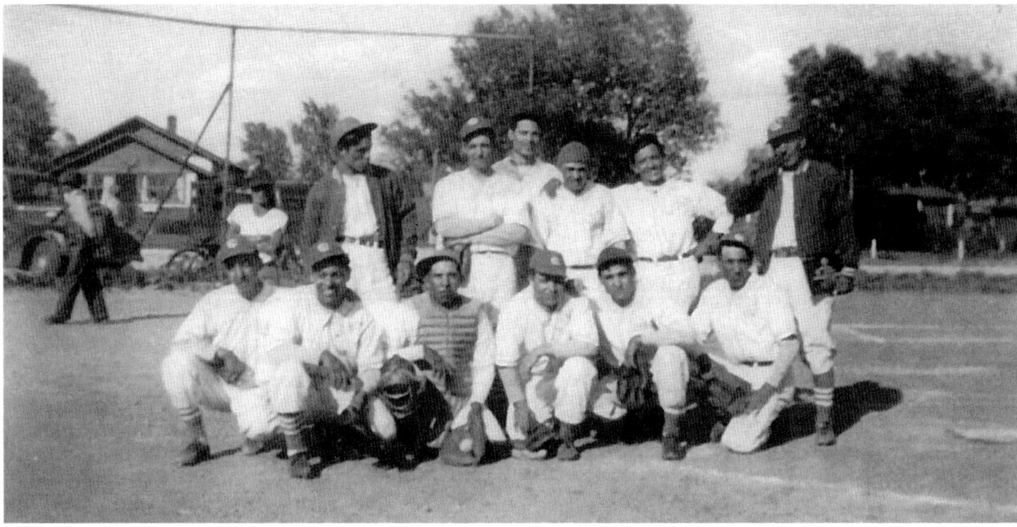

The 1947 Cheyenne, Wyoming, Lobos team was formed with about 20 players during the late 1930s and early 1940s. They played teams from throughout Colorado, Nebraska, and Wyoming. In Nebraska, they played against Scottsbluff and Mitchell and against Warren Air Force Base in Cheyenne. The Lobos were chartered in 1953. From left to right are (first row) Paul García, Phil Mercado, Eddie Montoya, Roy Salazar, Joe Bustos, and Joe Abeyta; (second row) unidentified, George Armijo, Tony Sánchez, Dan Padilla, unidentified, and Joe Borrego. (Courtesy of Gabriel and Jody López.)

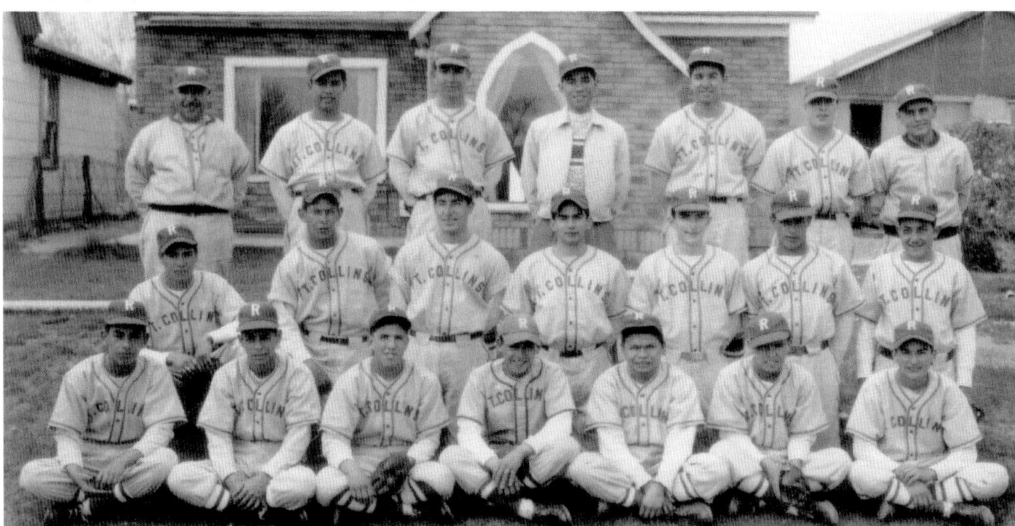

The Fort Collins, Colorado, Rebels team was formed by Pat and Al Chavez to help under-privileged boys. There were no heroes; everyone gave their best effort in every game. The 1950 Rebels are, from left to right, (first row) G. Mosqueda, T. Baca, L. Sánchez, J. Escobeda, H. Martínez, S. Mosqueda, and R. Moore; (second row) G. Córdova, S. Córdova, W. Arrellano, A. Chávez, T. Vigil, S. Meléndrez, and N. Martínez; (third row) H. Chávez, J. Sánchez, coach Al Chávez, manager Pat Chávez, C. Montoya, D. Pino, and treasurer S. García. (Courtesy of Gabriel and Jody López.)

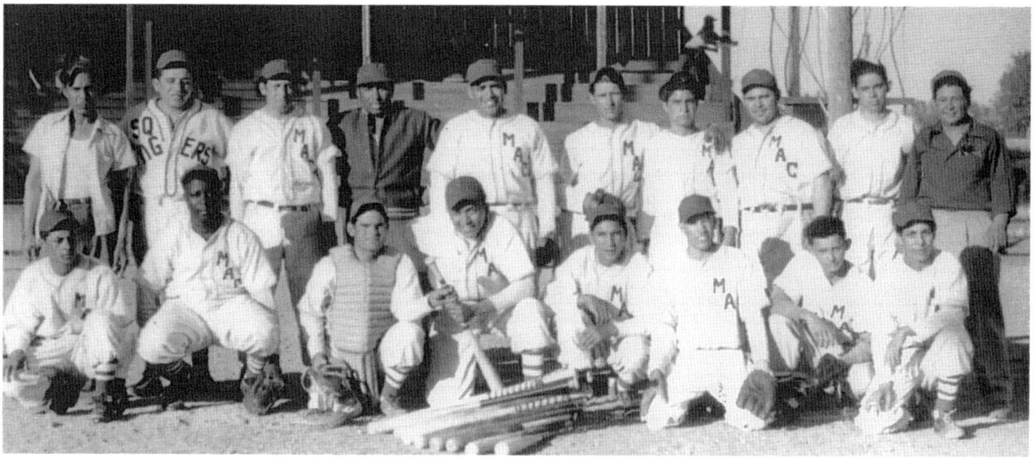

Dolores Gonzáles was known affectionately as "Kid Coke" because his sponsor was Coca-Cola when he boxed. Gonzáles founded the Cheyenne Mexican Athletics Club in the early 1930s. While working with the Union Pacific Railroad Company, he convinced them to donate land by Crow Creek to build a park for the children and a baseball diamond. This 1952 team includes, from left to right, (first row) Rudy Apodaca, Tony Carter, Joe Tofoya, unidentified, Robert Martínez, Louie Ojeda, unidentified, and Manuel Muñoz; (second row) Jesse González, Wesley Bocanegra, Paul Rodríguez, manager Dolores González, Joe Ramírez, Tacho Ortega, unidentified, Louis Yordanti, Alex Tenario, and unidentified. (Courtesy of Gabriel and Jody López.)

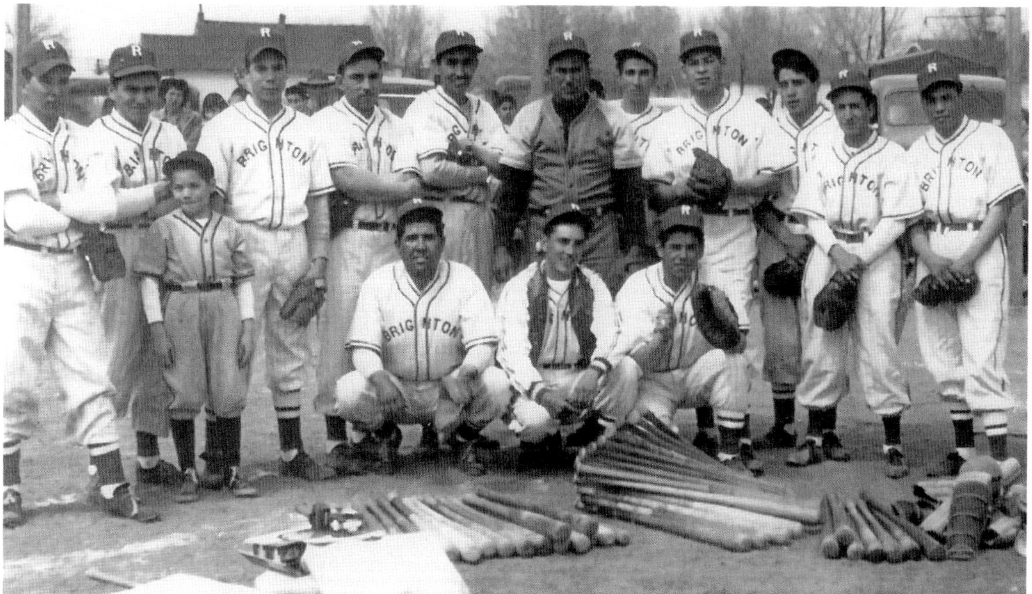

The Brighton, Colorado, Rams first played from 1952 to 1955 and then resumed playing from 1962 through 1969. From left to right are (squatting) Tony Alatorre, Frank Sandoval, and Jesse Rodríguez; (standing) Leroy Vigil, Max Sandoval, batboy Joe Sandoval, John Rael, Alberto Rodríguez, Tony Stone, Joe Moreleon, Paul Olivas, John Ramírez, Phil Rodríguez, Junior Fernández, and Dave Fernández. (Courtesy of Gabriel and Jody López.)

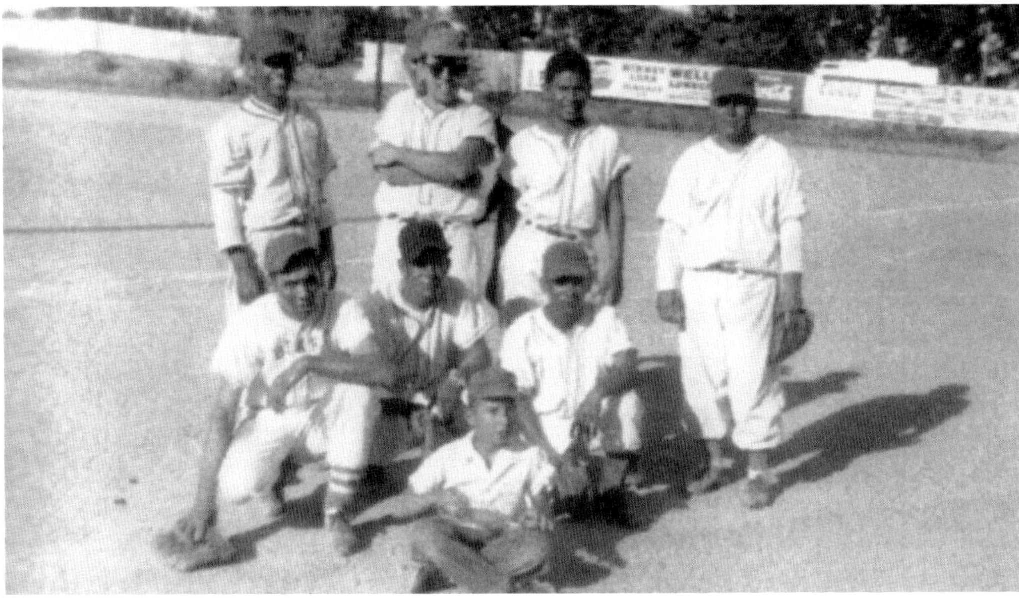

Before each game, players prepared the field by dragging the infield and securing the bases, which were often sacks of dirt or sand or both. For many young boys, especially the batboys, summer was one endless game of fun. The 1954 Greeley Bears are, from left to right, (first row) batboy Pete Archuleta; (second row) Ernie García, Paul Soria, and Ben Córdova; (third row) Rudy García, unidentified, George Córdova, Paul Salazar, and Leroy Vigil. (Courtesy of Gabriel and Jody López.)

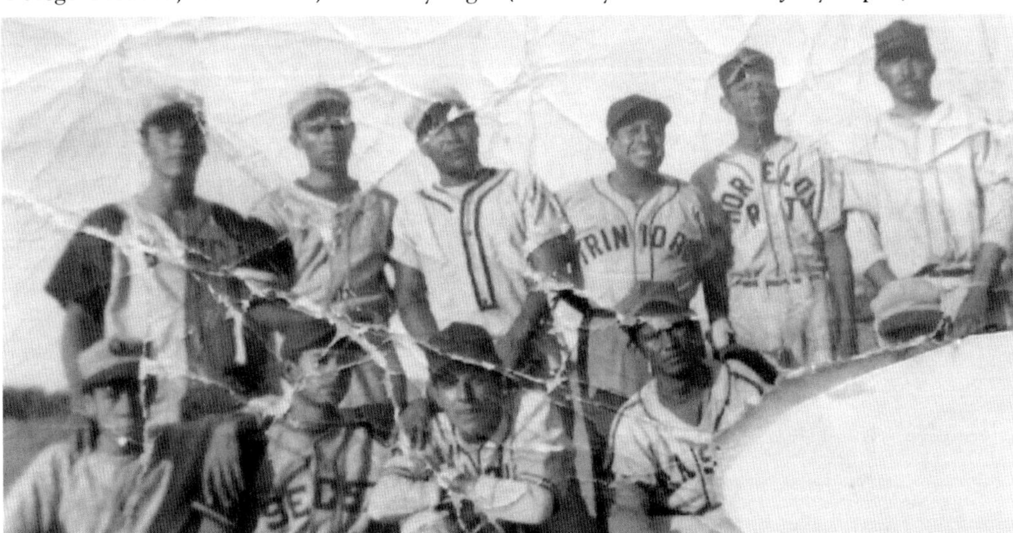

Pedro "Lefty" López-Torres (second row, far right) was in his early 20s when he played first base for this 1950s semiprofessional team for a minor league in Greeley, Colorado. He gives tremendous credit to the Cuban players he played with in Juárez, Chihuahua, Mexico, during the winter league seasons. They were pivotal in helping develop and nurture his fundamental understanding and love and passion for the game. His fondest memory was being selected to the all-star game in Greeley at first base. (Courtesy of the López-Torres family.)

This photograph was taken in Julesburg, Colorado, in 1938. From left to right are Isaac Estrada, Andensio "Lencho" Ortiz, and Ralph Guerra. Like many Mexicans in Colorado and Nebraska, they worked in the sugar beet industry and formed baseball teams traveling from town to town to play on Sundays. Estrada was born in Winfield, Kansas, and served in World War II in Italy. He played on several teams, including the Chestnut All-Stars in the Negro League. Ortiz was born in Mexico in 1914 and worked for the Pacific Union Railroad. Guerra was born in Parsons, Kansas, in 1918 and served with the Marine Corps during World War II. (Courtesy of Phyllis Pérez.)

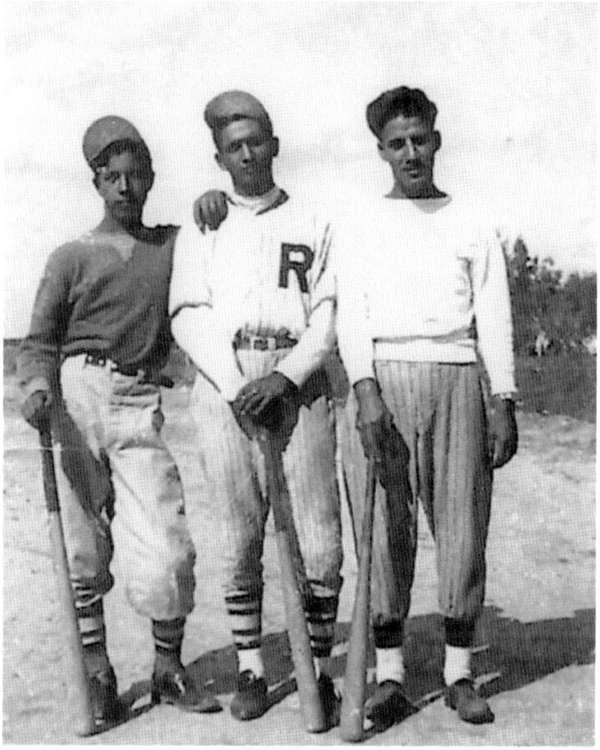

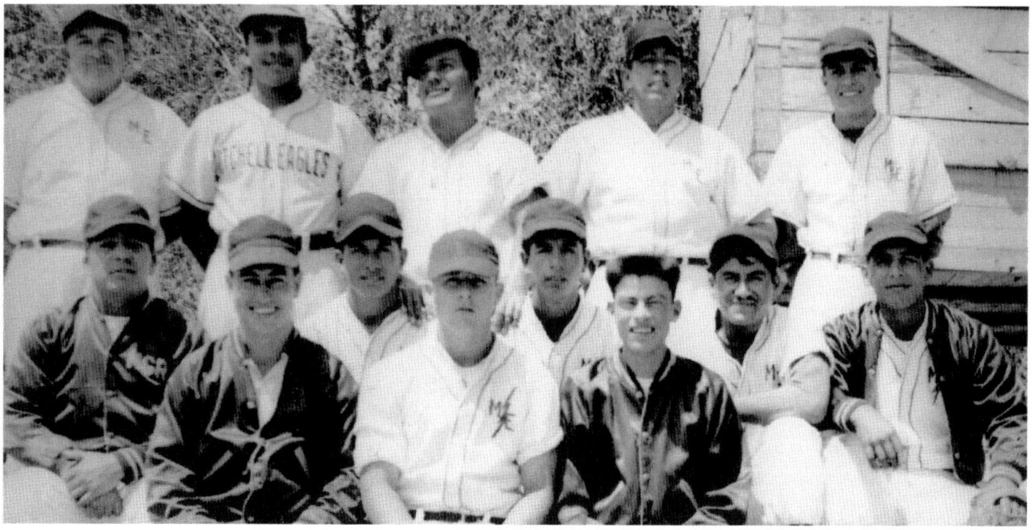

This 1950s Mitchell, Nebraska, Eagles team was part of the Mission League. The league ceased after several years, but was reactivated as the North Platte Valley Baseball League and survived for a few more years. From left to right are (first row) unidentified, Isabel Ramírez, and Phillip Huerta; (second row) Harry Guzmán, Carmelo Reyes, Marshall Reyes, Conrad Huerta, and unidentified; (third row) Senovio Reyes, Eddie Guzmán, Louis Velásquez, Ralph Miranda, and Pasqual Huerta. Many Mexican Americans worked in the sugar beet industry in western Nebraska. (Courtesy of Isabel Ramírez.)

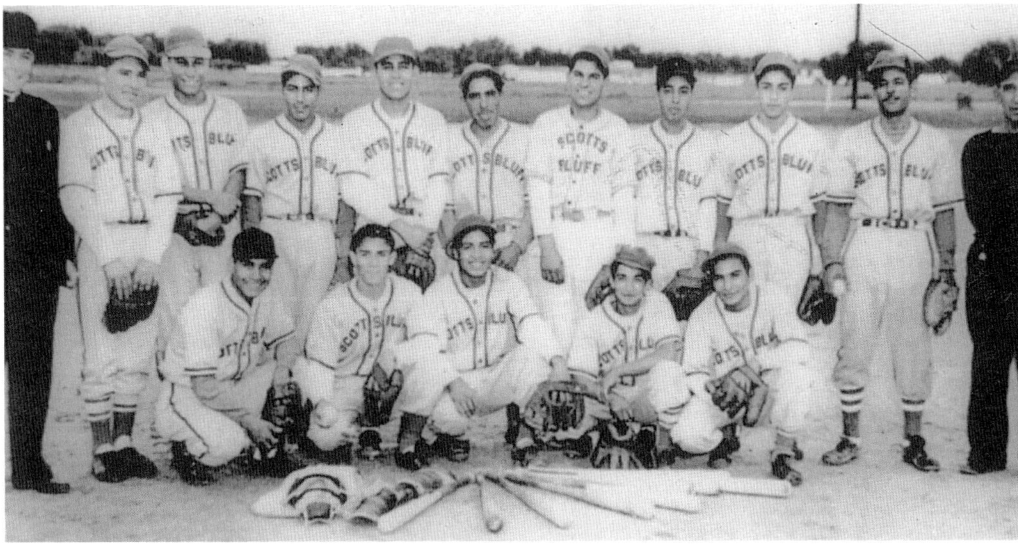

This 1948 Scottsbluff, Nebraska, team was sponsored by the Southeast Recreation Center. From left to right are (first row) Jesse Romero, Rodney Rentería, Jesse Espinoza, Ramón Cortes, and Johnny Olmos; (second row) Fr. Lawrence Portrey, Pete Perales, Andy Saucedo, Fermín Lozoya, Jim Flores, Albert Ramírez, Julián Flores, Joe Delgado, Joe Rentería, Bennie Treviño, and manager Paul Payer. (Courtesy of Isabel Ramírez.)

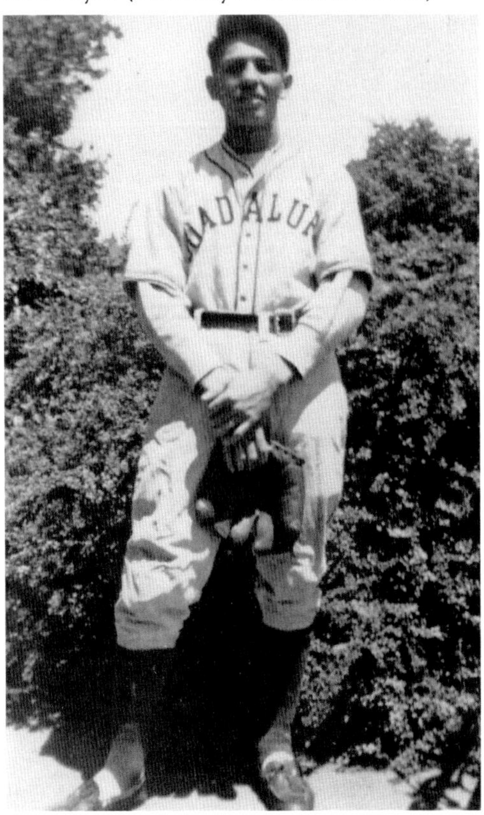

Lano Oropeza organized social, civic, and sporting events in Omaha, Nebraska, since the 1930s. He was a member of the Our Lady of Guadalupe baseball teams and later coached baseball and softball teams. He founded the Aztecs, Omaha's first Mexican American basketball team, in 1938 and started the Mexican American Basketball Team Tournament in 1955. Oropeza was a member of the American G.I. Forum, the Disabled American Veterans, Mexican Veterans, Knights of Columbus, and Casa de America. He has twice served as grand marshal of the Cinco de Mayo parade. He worked at Cudahy Packing Company for 18 years and retired from the US Postal Service. At 96 years old, Oropeza resides in Omaha. (Courtesy of Isabel Ramírez.)

Phillip Gutiérrez was considered one of the great Mexican American players to come out of Kansas. He played for the Chanute Aguilas during the early 1930s. Like so many of his generation, Gutiérrez enlisted during World War II. Mexican American ballplayers throughout the United States enlisted in the military to defend their country despite the discrimination directed against them at home. Several played ball in the military. Mexican Americans were highly decorated for their bravery, including the Medal of Honor. Tragically, Gutiérrez was killed in action. (Courtesy of Andy Gutiérrez.)

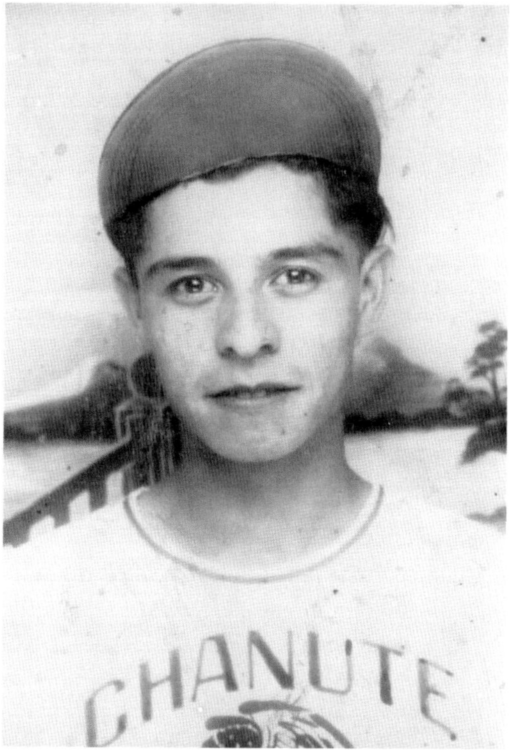

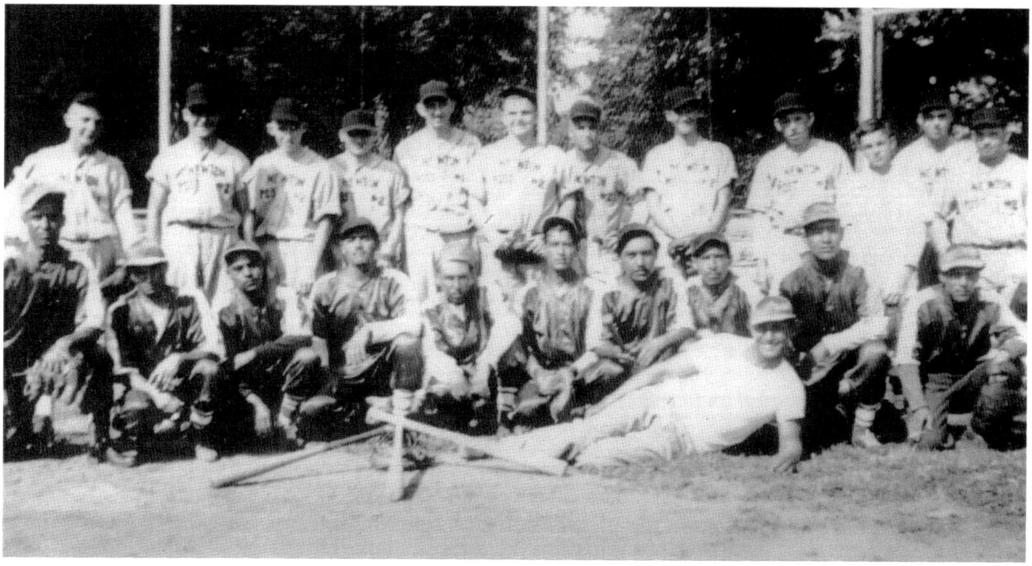

During World War II, the United States and Mexico signed an agreement that brought thousands of Mexican workers to help with the war effort. These workers, known as *braceros*, worked in a variety of industries including agriculture and the railroads from coast to coast. Their contributions were significant in helping win the war. On Sundays, braceros formed baseball teams and played other camps and local teams. This 1943 photograph from Newton, Kansas, shows Mexican braceros (first row) playing a white team (second row). (Courtesy of Ray Oláis.)

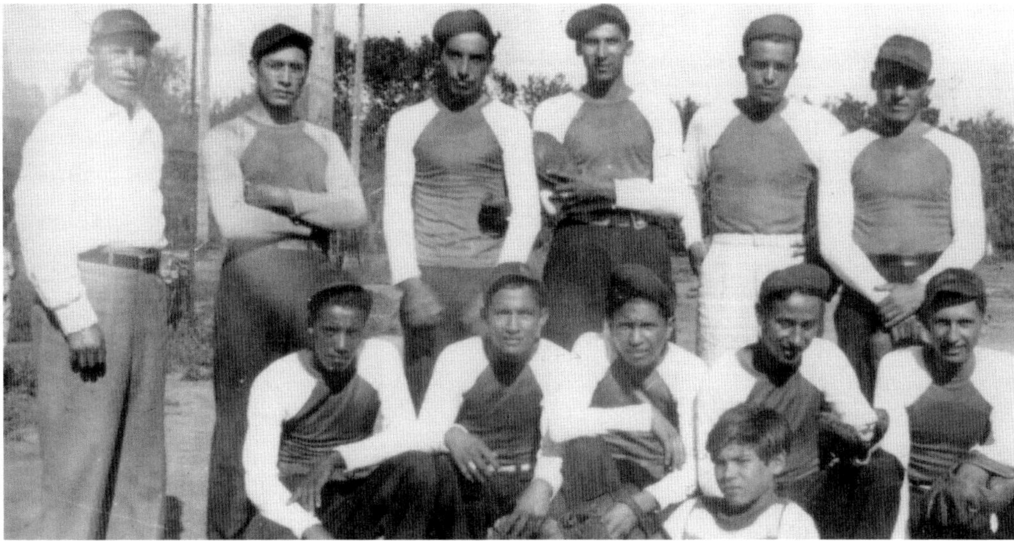

Throughout the United States, Catholic churches sponsored teams in Mexican American communities. This 1946 Newton, Kansas, team was known as the Catholics. From left to right are (first row) Curly Rodríguez, Nick Jaso, Maggie Gomes, Bill Lujano, and John Florez; (second row) coach Raymundo Jaso, Frank Florez, Ángel Rodríguez, Elmer Vega, Lalo Viramontes, and Frank Lujano. The batboy is Lee Peña. (Courtesy of Ray Oláis.)

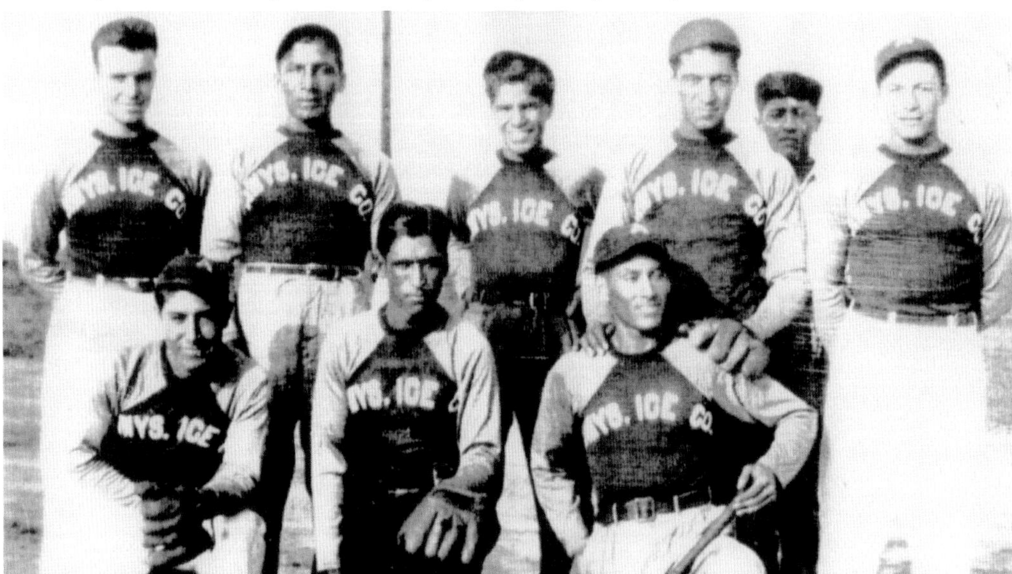

The Kansas City Ice Company team started in the 1930s. The players were the sons of immigrants. Los Hieleros (Ice Workers) worked long hours packing ice cars for meat and produce but still found time to play the game they loved. They have passed on their passion to several generations of players. They helped establish the Eagles Vet's Club after World War II. From left to right are (first row) Fred Sauceda, James Santillán, and Paul Sauceda; (second row) Jess Rodríguez, Leanord Mejia, Tony Jamie, Mack Quiroga, Vince Sauceda, and Lupe Rodríguez. (Courtesy of Vince Sauceda.)

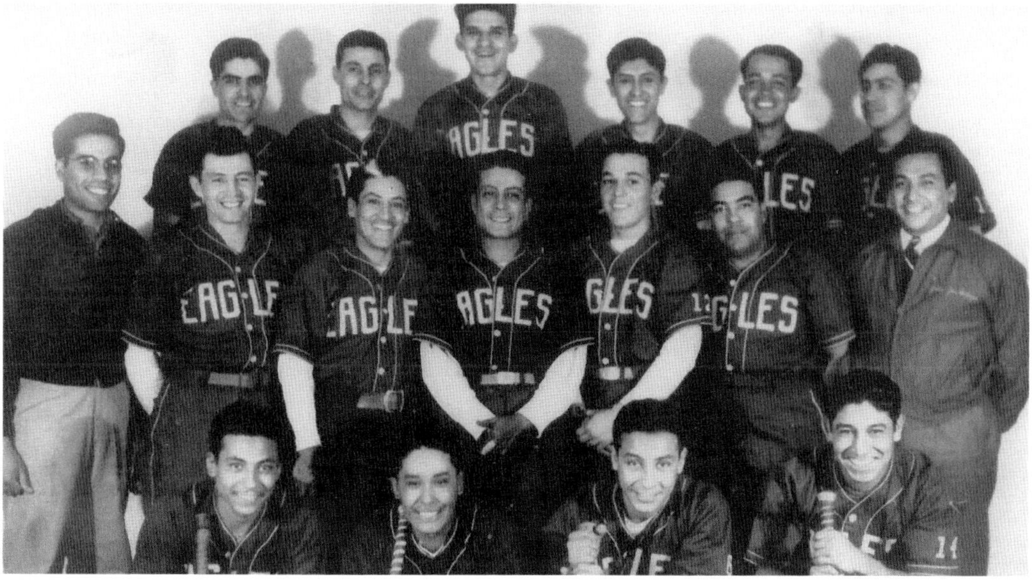

The Kansas City, Kansas, Argentine Eagles Vet's Club formed after World War II when they experienced blatant discrimination in public accommodations. Especially hurtful was their rejection as members of the local veterans' club in Argentine. The new post was dubbed The Eagles Nest. From left to right are (first row) Andy Medellian, Stanley Castañeda, Froylan Hernández, and Fred Sauceda; (second row) Joe Jaime, Lupe Rodríguez, Paul Sauceda, Jerry Hernández, Jesse Castro, Joe Marrón, and John Joe Salazar; (third row) Tony Jaime, Manuel Pérez, Bing Méndez, Vince Sauceda, Juan Pacheco, and Paul Contreras. (Courtesy of Patricia Castro.)

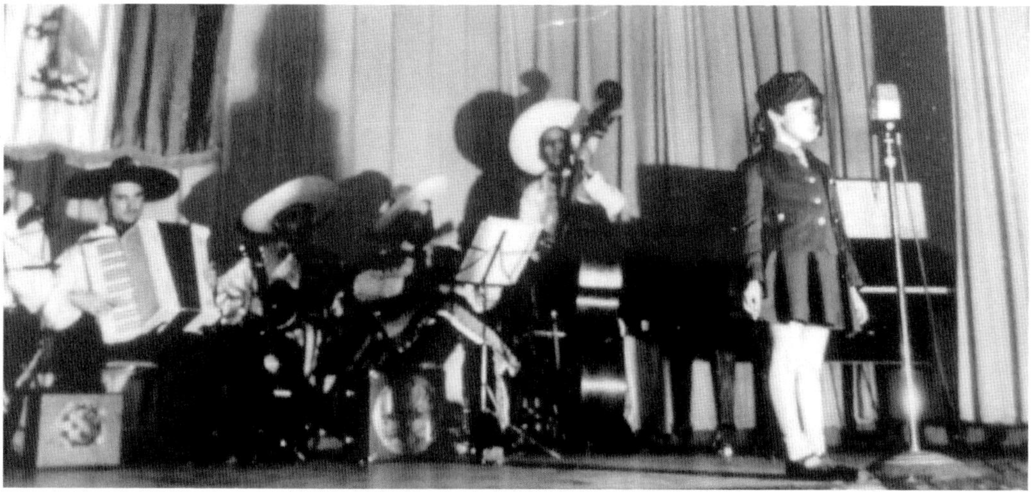

This Shirley Temple lookalike is a young Mexican American girl singing at a war bond rally in St. Louis, Missouri, around 1943. The community event was sponsored by the Benito Juárez Mutual Aid Society at the St. Louis Auditorium and drew Mexican people from the nearby communities of East St. Louis, Granite City, and Fairmont City. Mexicans had come to this part of the country in the early 1900s to work in the steel mills, cement plants, oil refineries, textile mills, and railroads. Many of these communities had baseball teams. (Courtesy of José Inez Santa Cruz.)

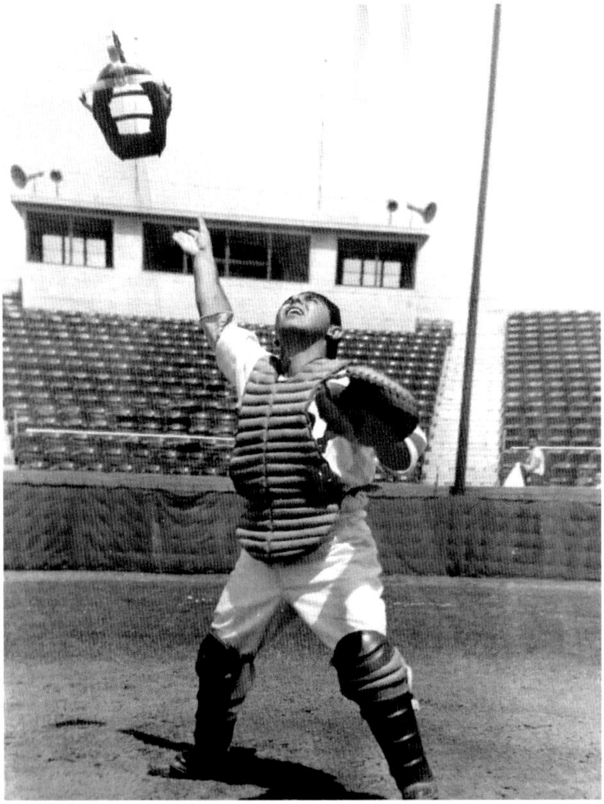

Arnold "Chappo" Riesgo was born in 1923 and raised in Tucson, Arizona, along with his four sibilings by Enrique and Emilia Riesgo. Enrique worked for the Southern Pacific Railroad. Arnold started playing ball in the 1930s as a catcher with the Tucson Junior Legion Baseballers, and starred at Tuscon High School. He played on the Cowboys city softball championship team in 1937, and played ball at the University of Arizona in 1940, eventually serving in World War II. Arnold spent 10 years as a player and manager in the St. Louis Cardinals and Boston Red Sox minor league systems. Later, he coached the Tucson Cactus Little League in the 1960s. (Courtesy of Mary Alyce Riesgo Carrasco.)

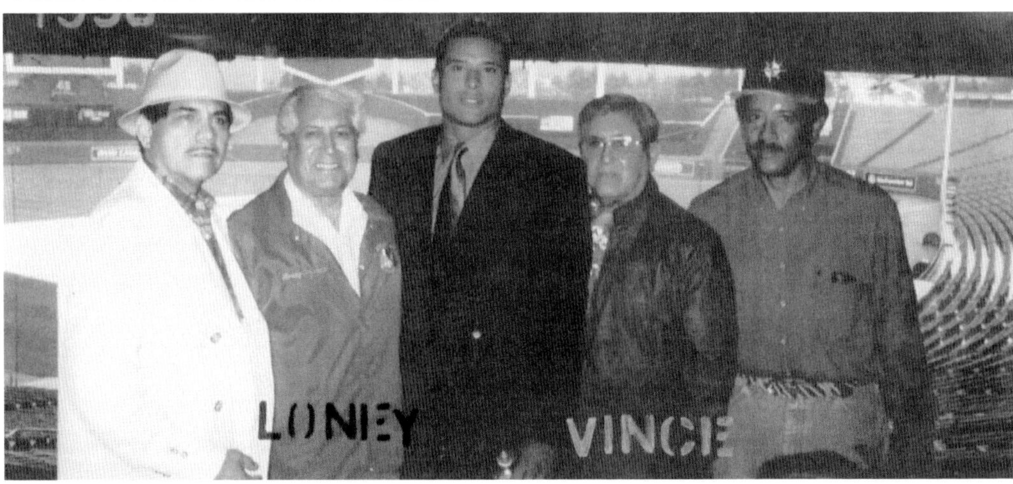

This picture of members of the Sauceda and Segui families demonstrates the connection between the Spanish-speaking Kansas City community to baseball and fast pitch softball. From left to right are Rick Sauceda, Loney Sauceda, David Segui, Vince Sauceda, and Diego Segui at Kauffman Stadium, home of the World Series champion Kansas City Royals in 1985 and 2015. Diego Segui, a Cuban immigrant, pitched for the Royals in 1962 and several other teams until his retirement in 1977. Segui married Emily Sauceda, whose family has Mexican roots. They had three children, including David who made his Major League debut in 1990. (Courtesy of Rick Sauceda.)

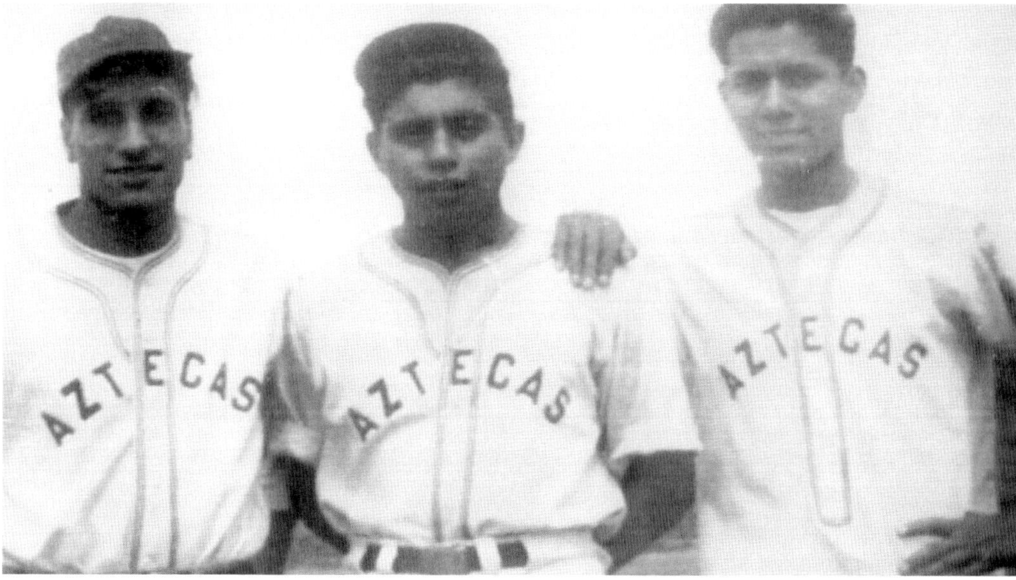

From left to right, Benny Terronez, Ray Alonzo, and Joe Muños are pictured around 1948 playing for the Silvis, Illinois, Aztecas. The most celebrated memorial of Mexican American patriotism is represented by this small town, where nearly 130 of its men fought in World War II, Korea, and Vietnam. A street in the heart of this close-knit community has been renamed Hero Street in memory of these men, including the eight who lost their lives. Hero Street was dedicated on October 31, 1971, after a long struggle with local city officials. (Courtesy of Tony Solíz.)

The Silvis, Illinois, community formed many teams including the Aztecas, Charros, and Rebels. Over the years, these teams produced outstanding players, including Raymond Alonzo, Tony Solíz, Benny Terronez, Tony Sandoval, Jesse Montéz, Pete Medina, Joe Muños, Charlie Guerrero, Joe Segura, Charlie Sandoval, Benny Montéz, Lupe Cruz, Jesse Bellman, Ángel Reyes, Manuel Hernández, Paul Solíz, Steve Terronez, Maugy Solíz, Bob Muños, Julián García, Emideo Sandoval, Vincent Medina, and Pete Hernández. Seen here is Louis Montéz in 1948, who cannot wait to play for the Aztecas. (Courtesy of Tony Solíz.)

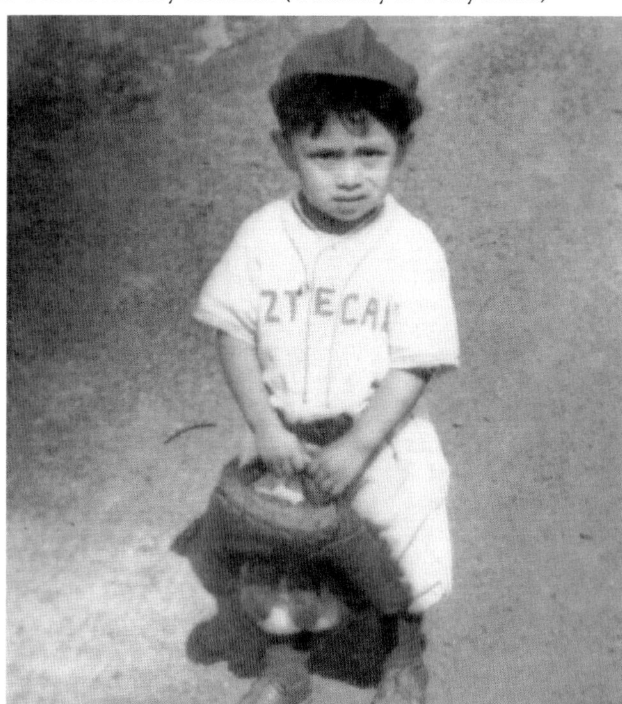

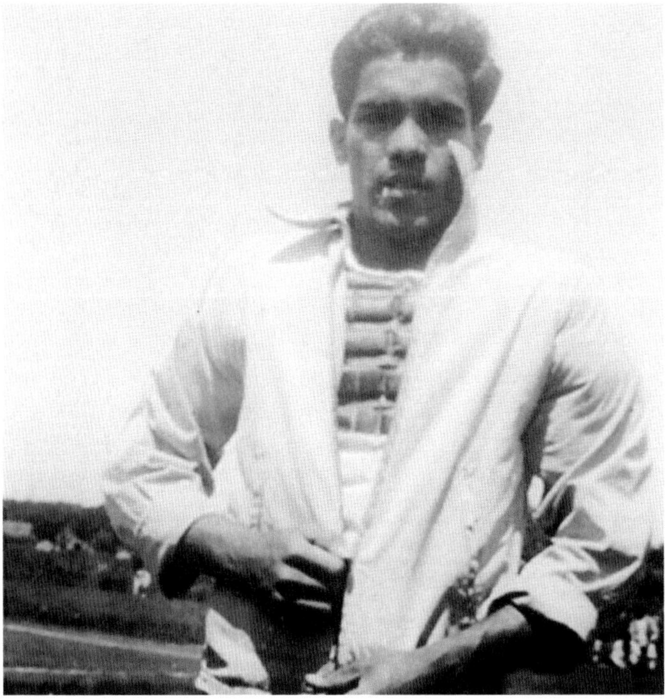

Ed Sandoval umpired games for the Aztecas. Their home field was between Ninth and Tenth Streets in Silvis, Illinois, about where the railroad park is now. The right-field line moved toward the Silvis railroad shops. (Courtesy of Tony Solíz.)

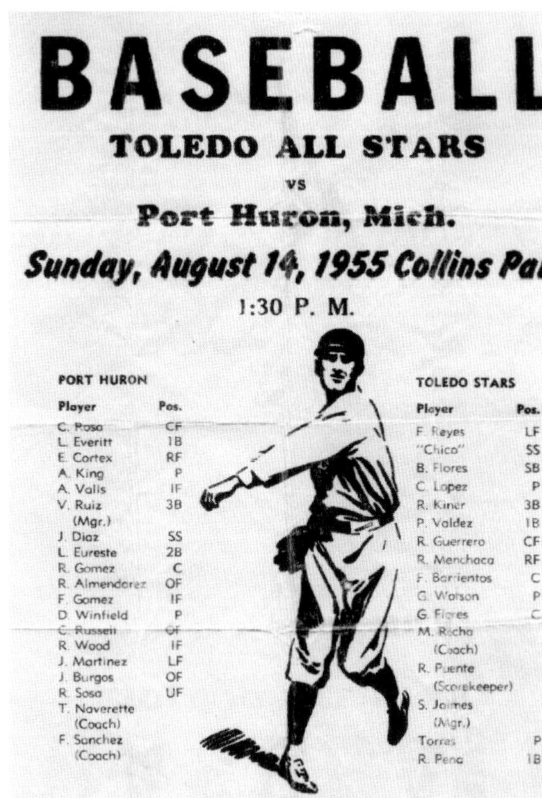

This 1955 poster announces a game between the Toledo, Ohio, All-Stars against the Port Huron, Michigan, team at Collins Park. The majority of the Toledo club were Mexican Americans with more on the Michigan team. Baseball and softball were and still are popular in Michigan. The city of Pontiac had the Mayans and Aztecs, Adrian had the Pirates, Saginaw had its Gallitos, and in 1958, Flint formed the Spanish American League. Other Mexican American teams could be found in Detroit, Ecorse, Lansing, Emily City, and Alma. (Courtesy of Dr. Cruz Torrez.)

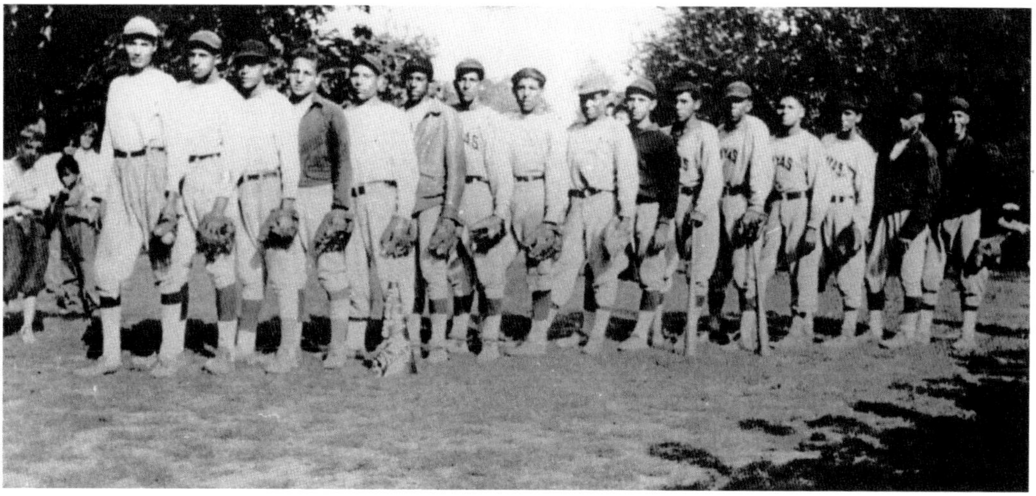

Despite the rigors and drudgery of workplace and home labor, leisure time activities played a central role in the lives of Mexicans in South Chicago. Chicago's extensive public park system played a fundamental role in providing them with organized and supervised activities for the youth. Under local Mexican leadership, men's organizations that began as baseball and basketball teams quickly grew into multifaceted associations with influence and importance far beyond the diamonds and courts. One of the early teams was the Mayas. (Courtesy of the Southwest Chicago Project and Michael D. Innis-Jiménez.)

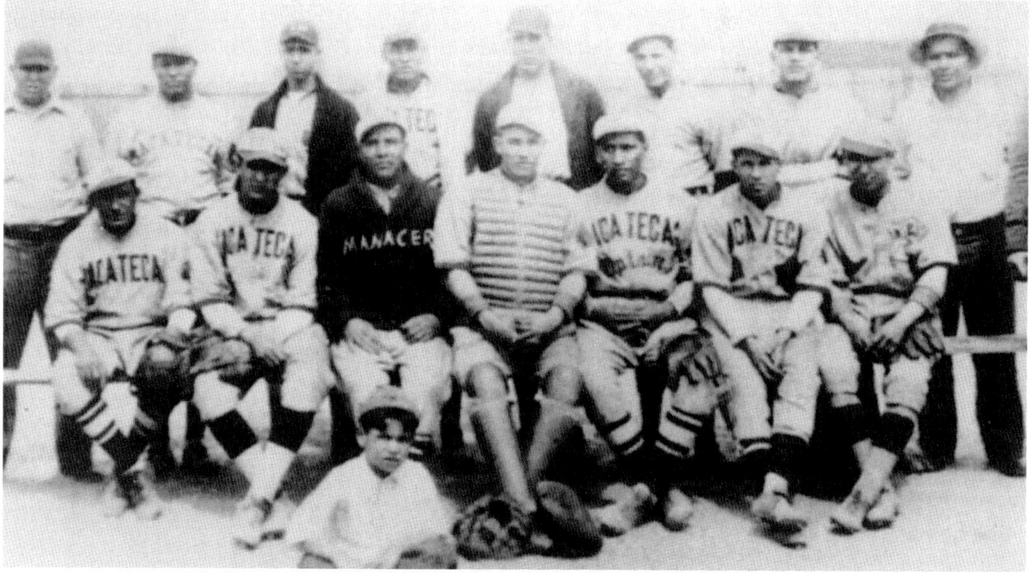

The East Chicago Zacatecas were one of the "harbor's" first baseball teams. The first Mexican baseball field was located on the corner of 142nd and Euclid Streets. Later, it was changed to north of Block Avenue near Field School. The players cleared the field. An enclosed baseball field was built around 1923 and named El Parque Anahuac. It seated nearly 500 fans. All the teams wore attractive uniforms, and the players wore them proudly. The local merchants donated funds for the uniforms and equipment. (Courtesy of Las Señoras of Yesteryear.)

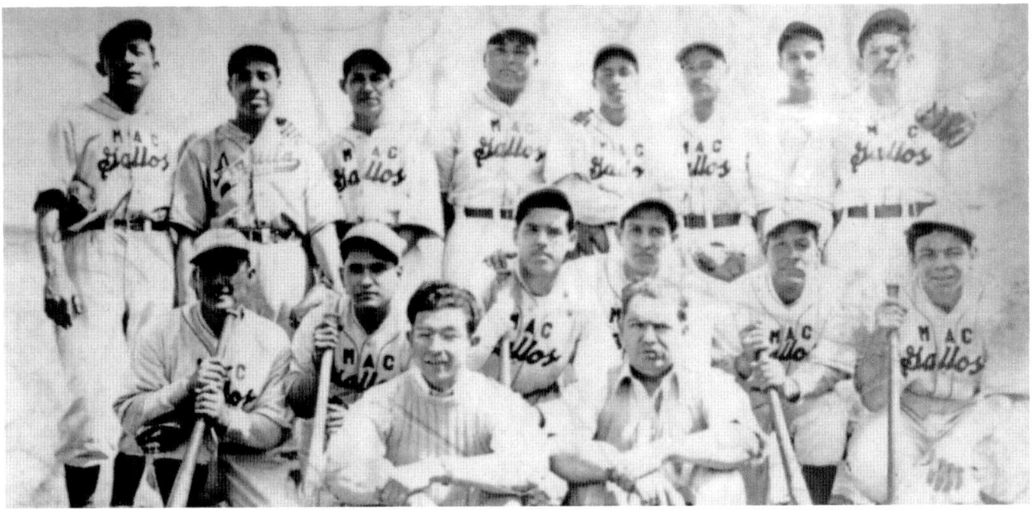

Los Gallos of East Chicago, Indiana, were an outstanding versatile team established in the 1930s. Every Sunday game was a special event when the Colonia Mexicana was there to morally support them. Hundreds of men and women and entire families followed them. Over the years, outstanding players included Joe González, Joe Sosa Alamillo, Robert Segovia, Art Morales, Al Sosa, Benny Ortega, Leno Garza, Nacho Valencia, Ángel Machuca, Fred Luna, Cipriano Hernández, Trini Castillo, Hank López, Andy Roque, Santos Godoy, Santos Torres, "Lefty" Padilla, Jesse Torres, and many more. (Courtesy of Las Señoras of Yesteryear.)

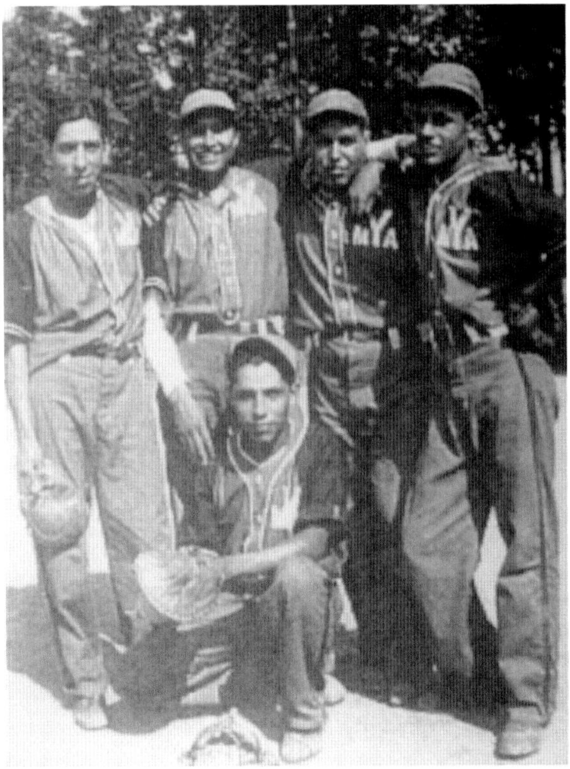

The first Mexicans in Lorain, Ohio, consisted of two or three families around 1921. The men may have been workers coming through with the Baltimore & Ohio Railroad Company. Two years later, the steel mill in Lorain began recruiting workers from Mexico. Other Mexican workers were recruited for the steel mills in Gary, Indiana, and Chicago, Illinois. By 1924, nearly 1,300 workers were in Lorain. In 1926, a baseball team was organized to play in the city Sunday league. Later, there were two teams, the Aztecas and Mayas. During the Great Depression, the US Repatriation Program nearly wiped out the Mexican community in Lorain. (Courtesy of Frank Jacinto.)

7

Field of Dreams

In the movie *Field of Dreams*, Iowa farmer Ray Kinsella, played by Kevin Costner, hears a voice in his cornfield tell him, "If you build it, he will come." After Ray constructs a ballfield on his farm, deceased players come to life and play the game they loved when they were young. In 2006, the Mexican American Baseball History Project was established because, like Ray Kinsella, the group wanted to build a project that would bring Mexican American players and their families to relive once again the fun and glory that these men and women enjoyed in the first innings of their lives. And like in the film, where Ray has an opportunity to play catch with his father, the Mexican American Baseball History Project has allowed children, grandchildren, and even great-grandchildren to connect with their family elders through stories and tributes.

Over the years, the Mexican American Baseball History Project (now the Latino Baseball History Project) has sponsored countless first pitch ceremonies, giving senior players a chance to play catch with their children, grandchildren, and great-grandchildren. Needless to say, these events are often quite emotional for everyone involved, as players don a glove and throw a ball for the first time in years. Even more touching is when the ballplayers sign baseballs on the sweet spot for family members, especially their children, now in their 60s, who did not know the entire story of their parents' remarkable playing and coaching careers in the United States and throughout the world, while playing minor league ball and military baseball.

Yet, despite their age, many of these players continue to compete in senior leagues throughout the country. Every Tuesday, for example, in Chino, California, players in their 80s and some in their 90s meet at Rubén Ayala Park to bat, run bases, and show the same passion that they displayed so long ago in a different world than today. Other former players still coach Little League or give their young family members tips on fielding, batting, running, and catching. At the end of *Field of Dreams*, when Ray's father asks him if this is heaven, Ray could have easily responded, "Yes, this is the Mexican American Baseball History Project."

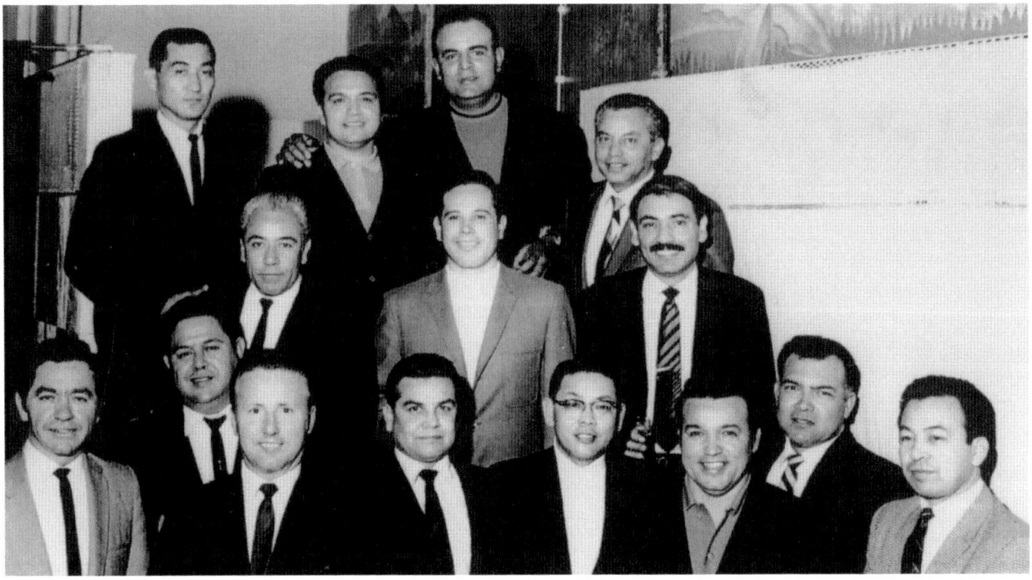

This photograph was taken around 1960 at Patriotic Hall in downtown Los Angeles. The retirement event was for longtime East Los Angeles coach Louis Lunetta (not pictured), who had coached these men as youngsters at Fresno, State, Hazard, and many other playgrounds. From left to right are (first row) Simón Trujillo, Frank Oblea, Jim Miller, Louis Gomes, Wally Poon, Richard and Johnny Peña, and Joe Gaitan; (second row) Phil Beltran, Bobby Recendez, and Percy Recendez; (third row) James Yoshishtake, Gabriel Peña, Henry García, and Charlie Sierra. (Courtesy of Bobby Recendez.)

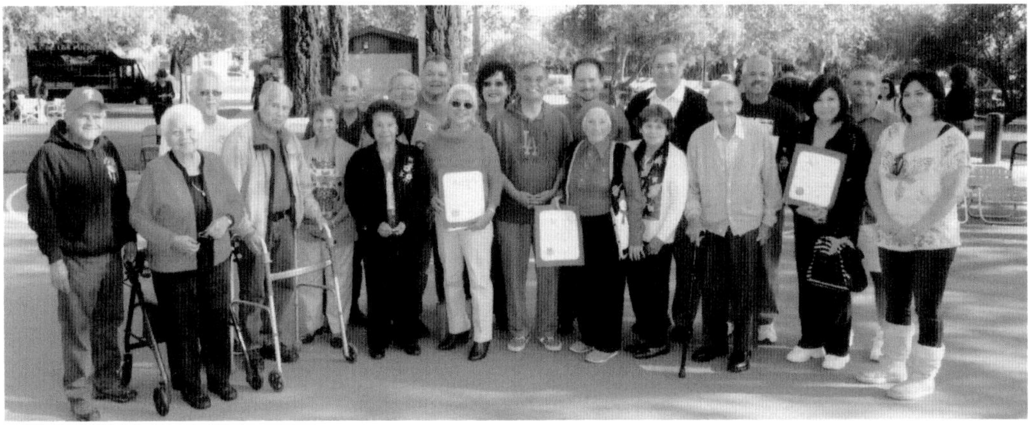

Pictured from left to right in Claremont, California, in 2015 are Al Villanueva of Claremont, Annie Belmúdez of Pomona, Ronnie Reynoso of Claremont, David Salazar of Claremont, Lupe Salazar of Claremont, Rey León of Upland, Anita Salazar of Chino, Arthur Gutiérrez of Claremont, David Ramírez of Pomona, Estella Elías Acosta of Pomona, Delia Sevilla Warrior of Claremont, Richard A. Santillán of Alhambra, Enrique López of Ontario, Mary Gutiérrez Ruiz of Ontario, Ray Sevilla of Walnut, Nellie Villanueva of Claremont, Chevy López of Ontario, Rudy Gomes of Montclair, Lorraine López Morales of Ontario, Richard Morales of Upland, and Veronica Morales San Miguel of Ontario. (Courtesy of Al Villanueva.)

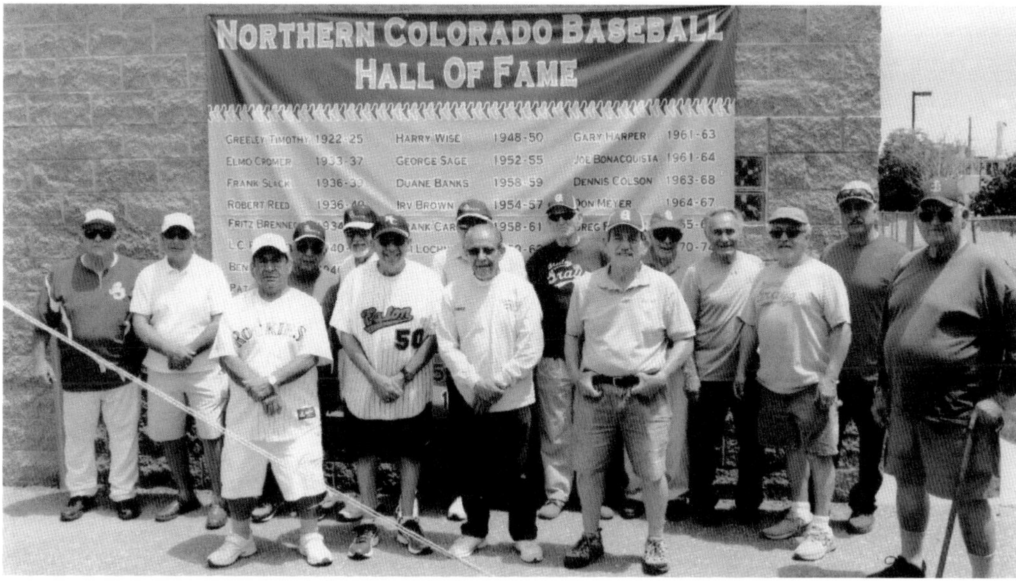

The Rocky Mountain League existed from the 1950s until 1969. On June 14, 2015, several players were honored at the Original Grays Day. Most of these men played for the Greeley Grays during the 1950s and 1960s. A handful played for other league teams. From left to right are (first row) Nick Hernández (Cheyenne Lobos), Tom Chagolla, Palmer López, Bill Crosier, and Bob Ferguson (Fort Collins Legionaries); (second row) coach John Barnes, Ed Dyer (Monfort Packers), Robert Hernández, Ricardo "Rico" López, Arnulfo "Nudy" López, Charles Smith, Tito "Butter" García Jr., Gil Carbajal, Abraham "Abe" García, and unidentified. (Courtesy of Gabriel and Jody López.)

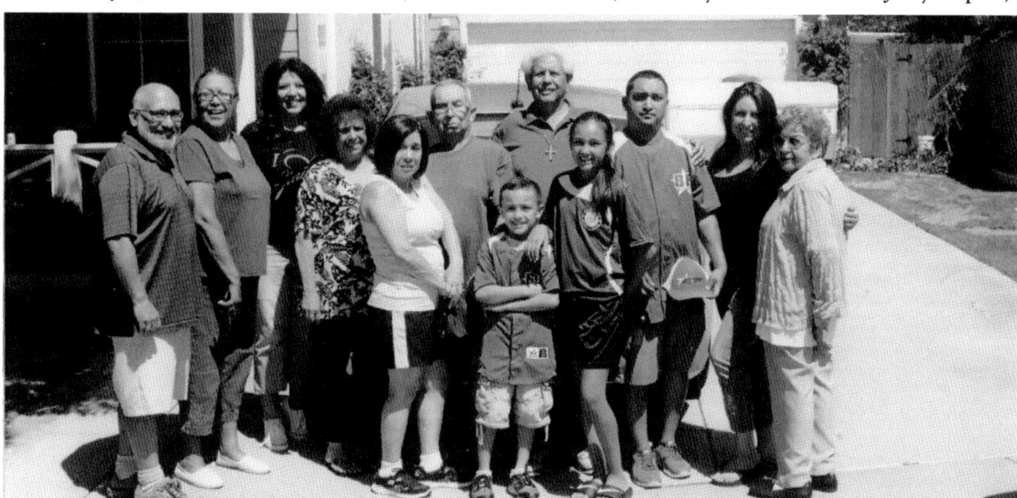

Phyllis Pérez has been a longtime supporter of the Latino Baseball History Project and has hosted a series of book signings in Modesto, California, including this one in August 2015. From left to right are Lázaro and Margarita Santiago, Patricia Amesquita, Loretta Marcele, Karen Ulloa, Jesse Ulloa, Danny Ramos, Julia Pérez, Rachel Pérez, Richard Pérez, Lezet ?, and Phyllis Pérez. (Courtesy of Richard A. Santillán.)

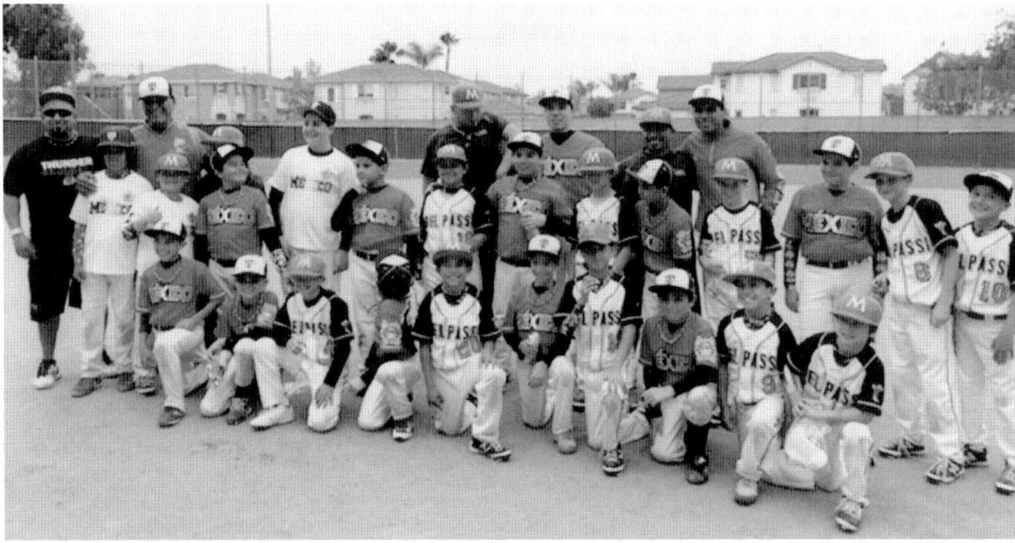

An annual tournament is played in Irvine, California, bringing youth teams from Mexico to play California teams. The Bel Passi team from Modesto, California, played a team from Los Mochis, Mexico. One of the coaches for Bel Passi is Francisco J. Pérez (third row, second from right), who played youth, high school, and community college ball. His son, Marcus (first row, fifth from left) is the catcher on the team. His favorite player is Josh Donaldson. Marcus won the Lew Hays Award for sportsmanship in a tournament in Walnut, California. (Courtesy of Francisco J. Pérez.)

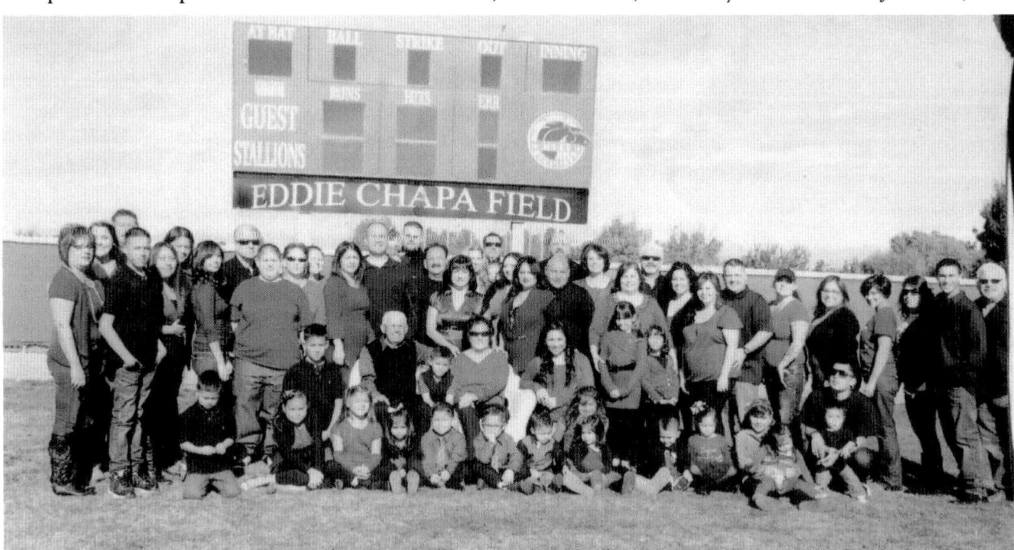

Eddie Chapa was born in Laredo in 1930. He played ball in Laredo in 1945 with an American Legion team. He made the all-star team the following year, the only Mexican American on the team. Eddie moved to Madera, California, where he started working at Merced High School in 1950; he devoted over 60 years to youth sports. The baseball field is named in his honor. He is seated in the black vest surrounded by his children, grandchildren, great-grandchildren, and other family members. (Courtesy of Eddie Chapa.)

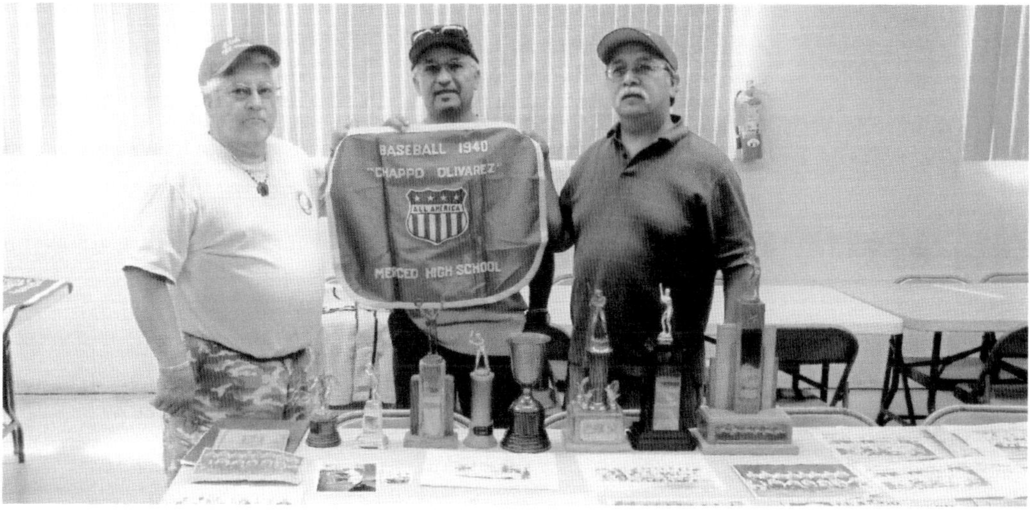

This photograph was taken in July 2015 at Club Mercedes Hall in Merced, California. From left to right are Raymond Olivares, Les Contreras, and David Contreras Jr. They are holding up their uncle Salvador "Chappo" Olivares's blanket he earned in baseball in 1940. Salvador Olivares played multiple sports but was best known as a great knuckleball pitcher. If not for World War II, he would have signed a contract to play professional ball in the Class A league. He was one of the founders of Club Mercedes in 1947. (Courtesy of Richard A. Santillán.)

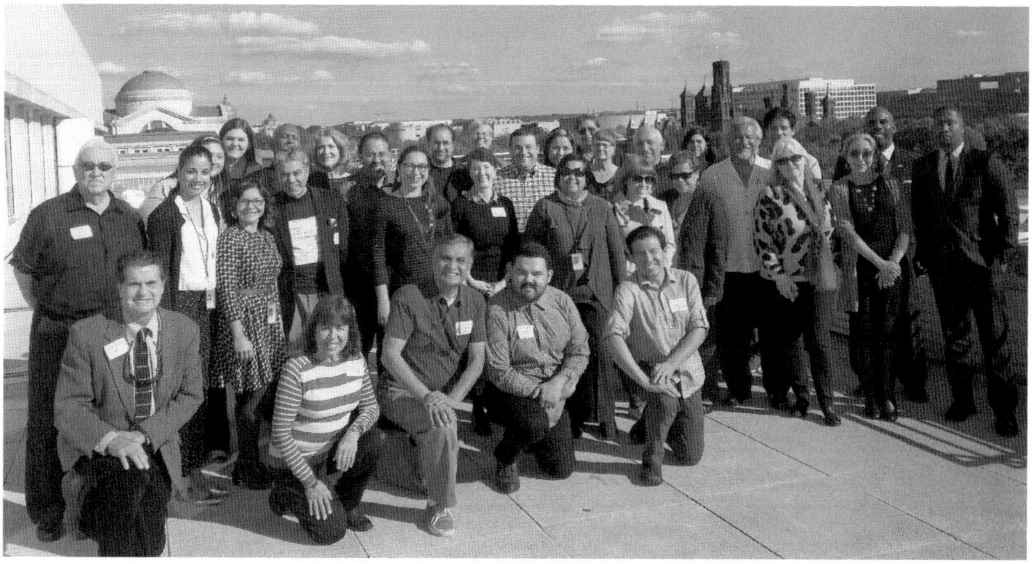

In October 2015, the Smithsonian's National Museum of American History in collaboration with the Smithsonian Latino Center hosted a two-day event in Washington, DC, titled Latinos and Baseball: In the BarRíos and the Big Leagues. The project is a multiyear community collecting initiative that focuses on the historic role that baseball and softball have played as a cultural and social force within the Latino communities and currently includes eight partner organizations, including the Latino Baseball History Project at California State University in San Bernardino. Some of the participants are seen here. (Courtesy of the Smithsonian.)

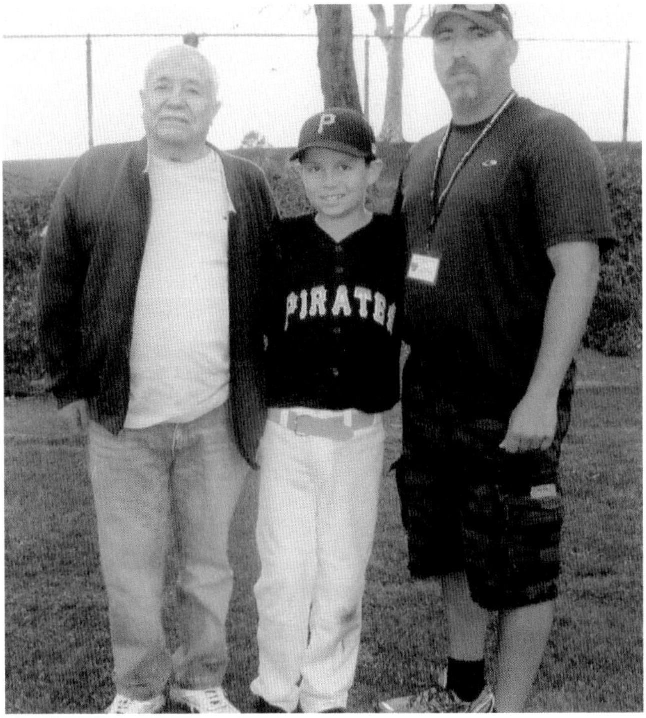

Joe Romero (left) is seen here with his nephew Eddie Roof (right) and great-nephew David Roof. Joe Romero was an outstanding player in the Inland Empire and Pomona Valley, playing for the Claremont Barons, Cucamonga Mets, and the Upland Angels. Eddie played outfield and pitched in Little and Pony League in Upland and has coached Little League for five years. David played Little League for the Angels and Pirates and made the all-star team. Because of his outstanding skills, he was selected to play for a traveling team as an outfielder and pitcher. (Courtesy of Joe Romero.)

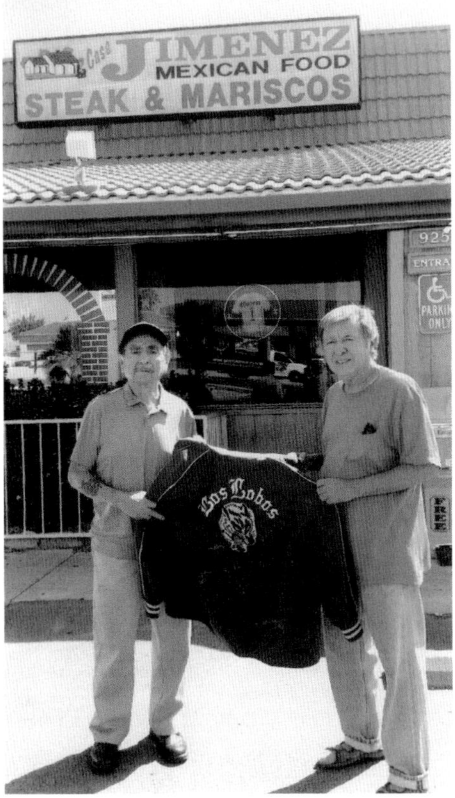

Aristeo Vargas (left) and his nephew David Vargas (right) were born in Barstow, California. Aristeo played ball as a youth along with his brother Mike (David's dad), who was an outstanding catcher. Both were drafted into the military, with Mike receiving the Purple Heart during the Korean War. After the war, the brothers formed, coached, and played for Los Lobos for many seasons. The team played hard and with passion, drawing hundreds of fans. David also played for Los Lobos and with youth, high school, and community college teams. He was an excellent third baseman and played in the 1969 all-star game in Winston Salem, North Carolina. David's sister Loretta played for the Loboettes. (Courtesy of David Vargas.)

Pedro "Lefty" López-Torres was born in 1924. Forever a genuine student and aficionado of professional baseball, he always wears one of his many Major League baseball caps. To this day, now 92 years of age, he still lives the life of a ballplayer. As he sees it, baseball is the best game ever played and served as a metaphor for life. He is now in the ninth inning of his life, bases loaded, full count, and batting a thousand. He would have made a great baseball manager, and for his sons, he has been. The children of Lefty would like to say, "Dad, we salute you and everything you have taught us in life through baseball." (Courtesy of the children of "Lefty.")

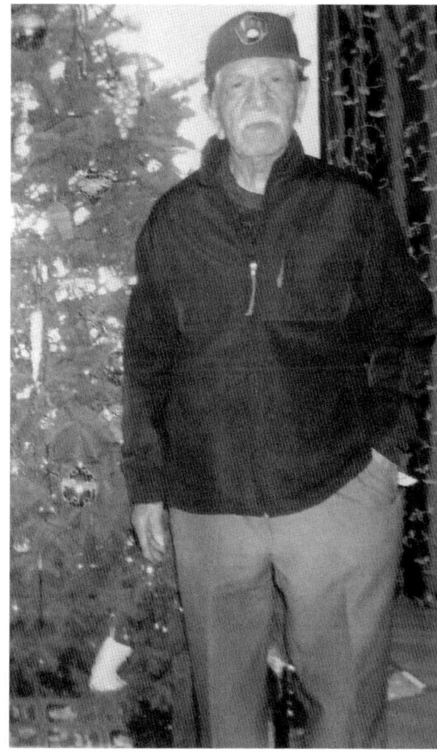

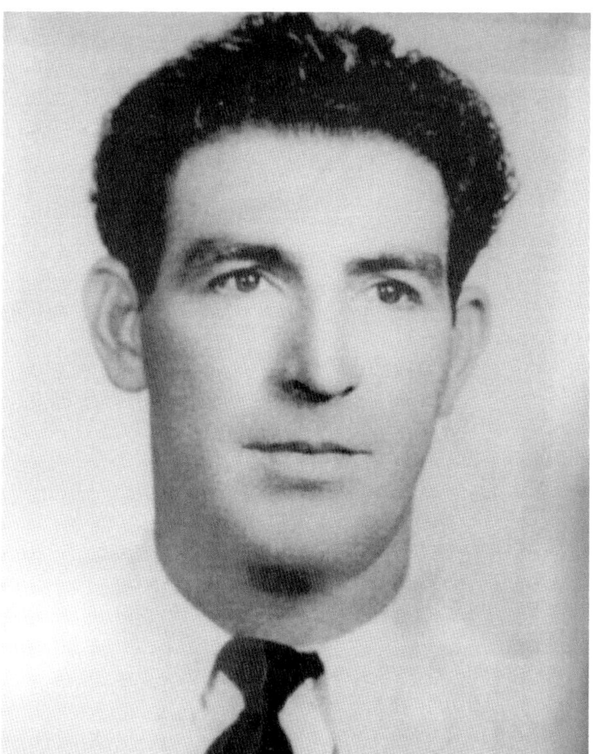

Rodolfo Martínez and his wife, Maria, were born in Monterey, Mexico. During the 1940s and 1950s, Martínez was an outstanding player. Little did he know that 35 years later, his son Fred would also play on the same field with the Monterrey Sultanes in the Mexican League in 1984. Fred has three brothers, Rudy, Oscar, and Sergio, who also played ball. All four went on to play college ball, with Fred and Rudy signing professional contracts. Fred was an outstanding pitcher for the California Angels. Rudy's two sons, Rudy Jr. and Adrián, played college ball. Adrián is currently pursuing a baseball career. (Courtesy of Fred Martínez.)

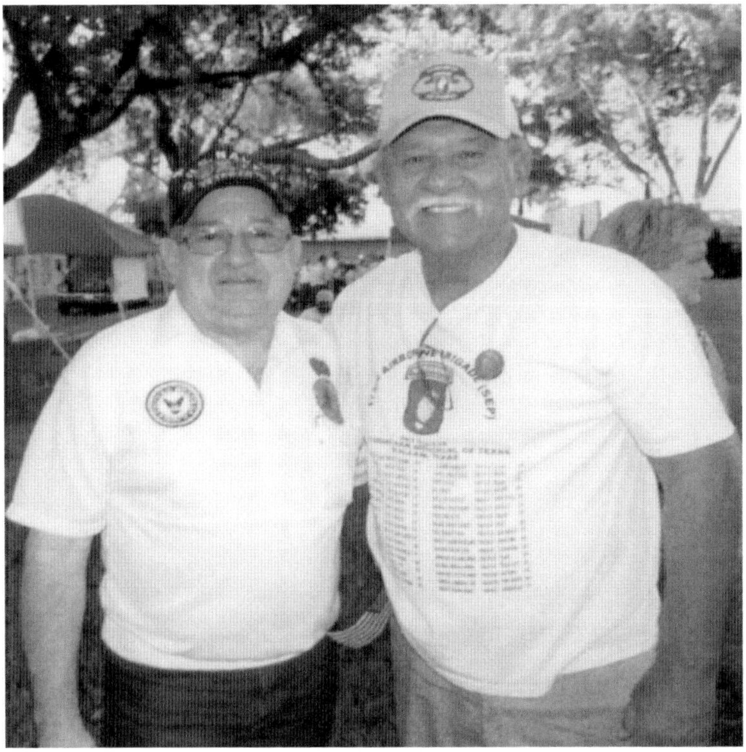

Old friends Charlie Calderón (left) and Val Estrello are seen here. Both played youth and high school baseball and were outstanding players, fast on the base paths. They are pictured at an appreciation ceremony for Vietnam veterans. (Courtesy of Charlie Calderón.)

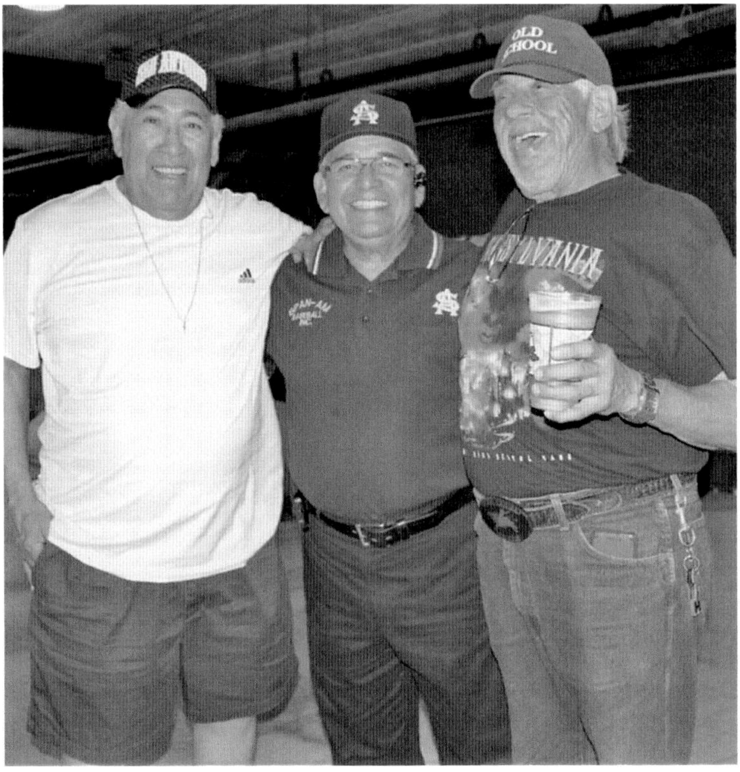

These are three very good friends who played in the Spanish American League years ago, (from left to right) Félix Uriegas, Joe Sánchez, and Izzy Garibay. Uriegas and Garibay were Spanish American players, while Sánchez and his family, including his father Sandy and brother Alfredo, were the handlers of the league through its long tenure in San Antonio. (Courtesy of Joe Sánchez.)

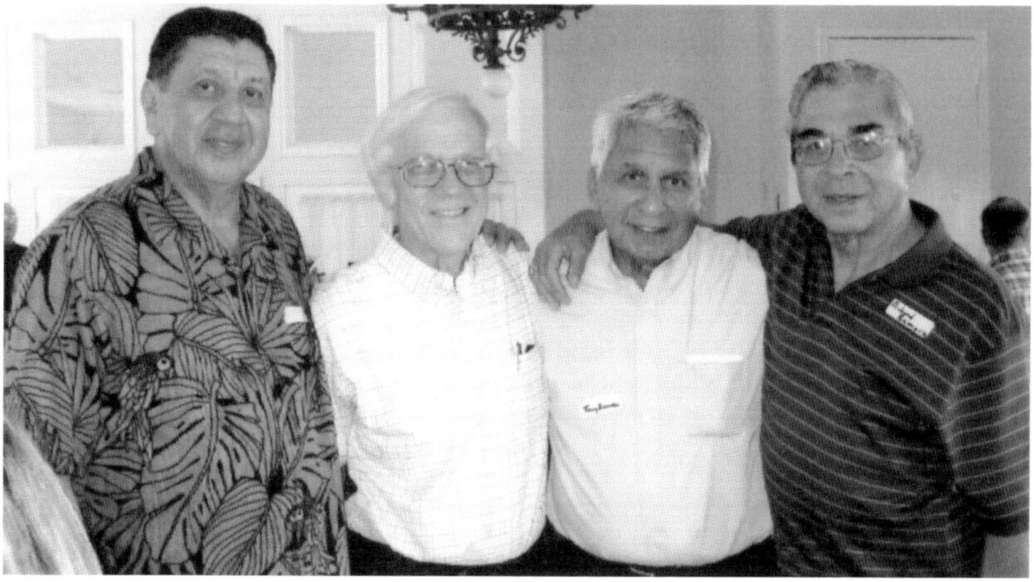

The Zamora family, especially the brothers, were one of South San Antonio's most prolific baseball families and community caretakers. Standing from left to right are Robert Zamora, unidentified, Tony Zamora, and Richard Zamora. (Courtesy of Richard Zamora.)

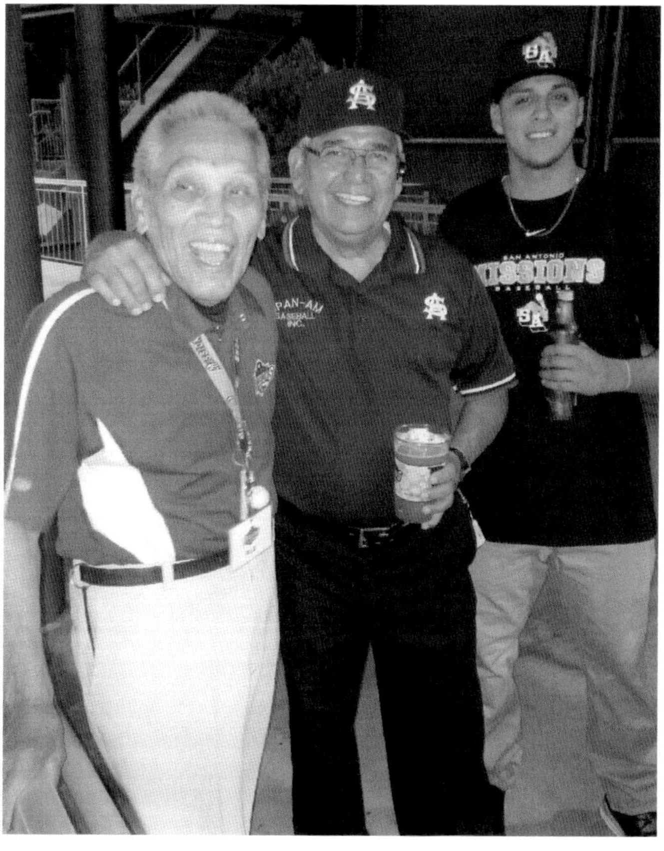

Willie Doria (left) stands with his grandson and Joe Sánchez. Willie was one of Sandy Sánchez's best players in the 1950s and 1960s for the Spanish American League. They are seen here at a San Antonio Missions game. Willie has worked with the Missions as an usher for the past 20 years. (Courtesy of Joe Sánchez.)

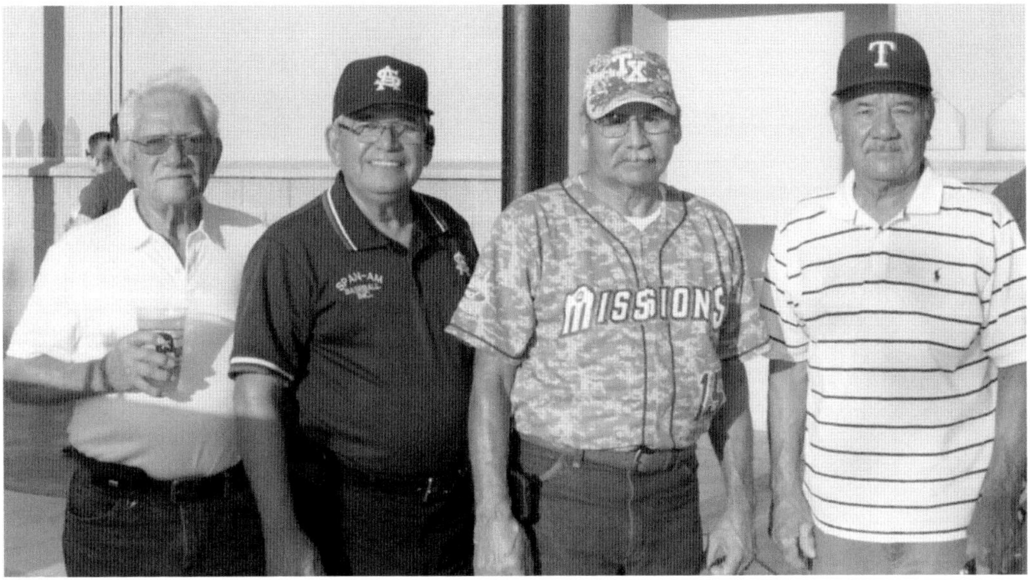

These four remarkable players were part of the Garza Finance Spanish American team. From left to right are Red Cervera, Joe Sánchez, Val Castillo, and Ray Lara. They are seen here at a Spanish American League Appreciation Night, sponsored by the San Antonio Missions. (Courtesy of Joe Sánchez.)

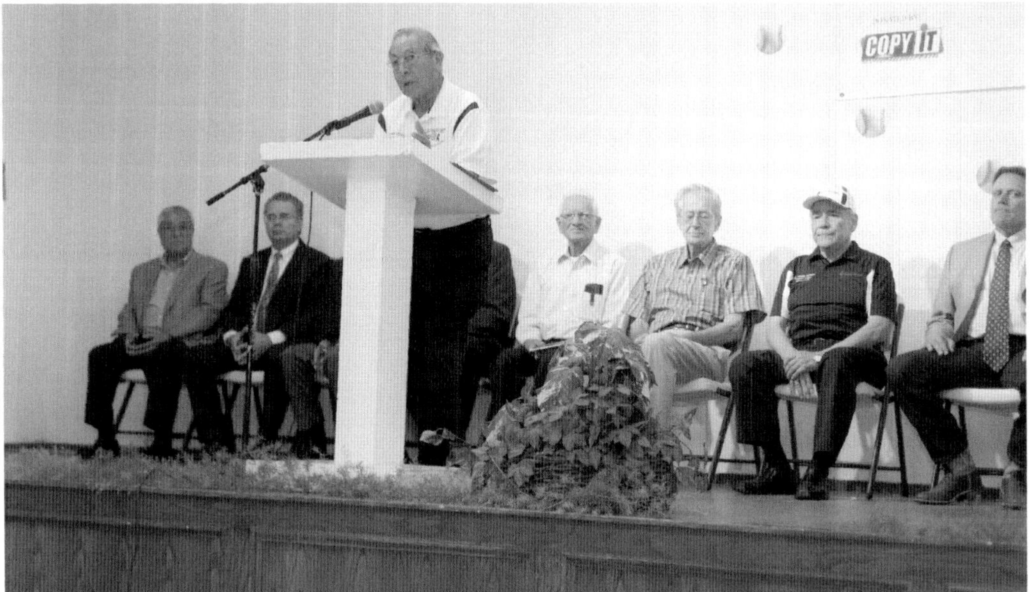

Vicente Estévis is the president of the Leo Najo Hall of Fame Baseball Committee. The group has an annual barbecue and a hall of fame induction ceremony. On October 3, 2015, the 44th annual ceremony was held at the Mission Community Center in Mission. The committee is comprised of former baseball players who consider local athletes for induction who have excelled in baseball. (Courtesy of Bert Lozano.)

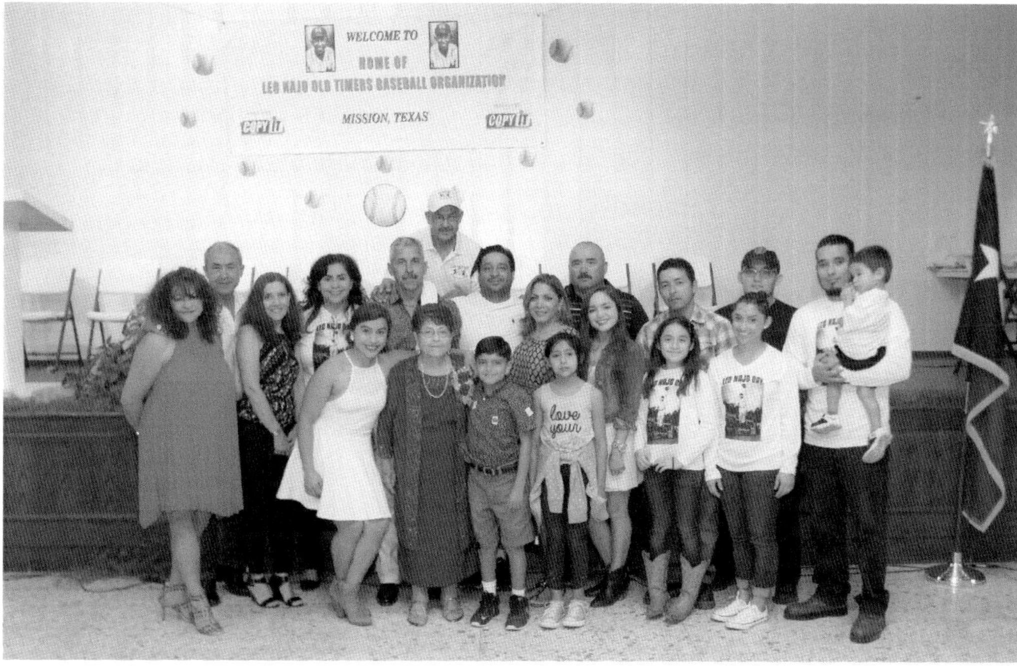

Jesús "Jesse" Alañiz (wearing white cap) is the son of the late Leo Najo. Alañiz serves on the Leo Najo Oldtimers Baseball Committee and presents his family at the event. He and other members of the Alañiz family have worked very closely with the committee to preserve both the memory of the legendary Leo Najo and the well-deserving athletes from the Rio Grande Valley. (Courtesy of Bert Lozano.)

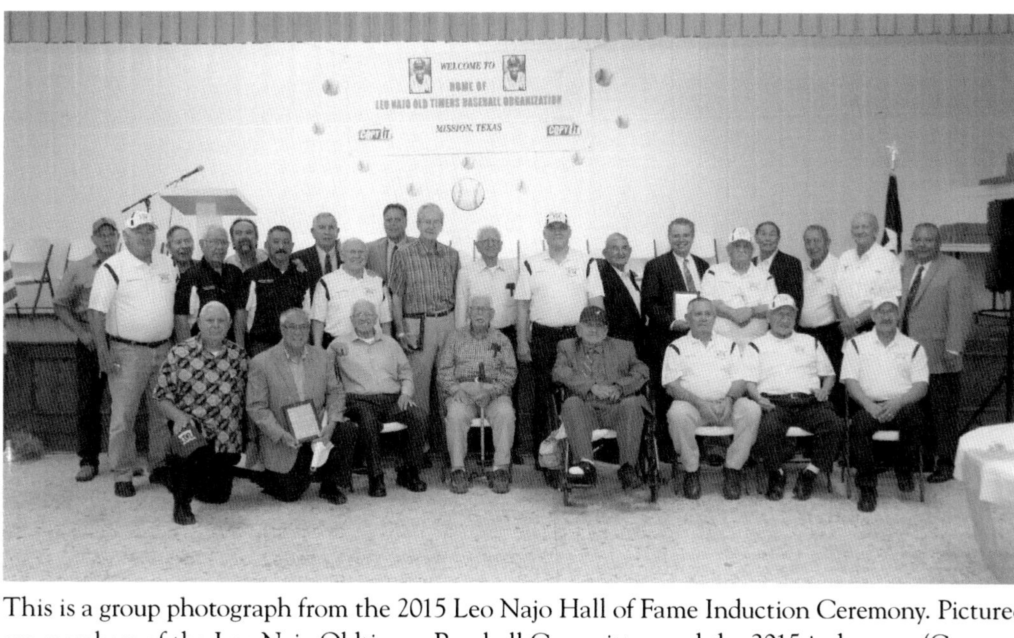

This is a group photograph from the 2015 Leo Najo Hall of Fame Induction Ceremony. Pictured are members of the Leo Najo Oldtimers Baseball Committee and the 2015 inductees. (Courtesy of Bert Lozano.)

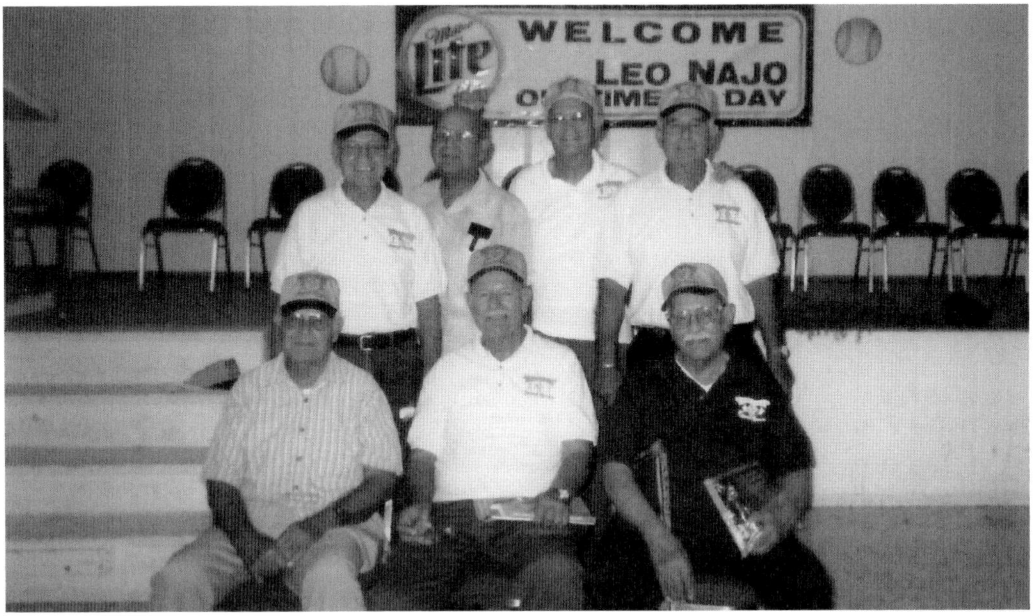

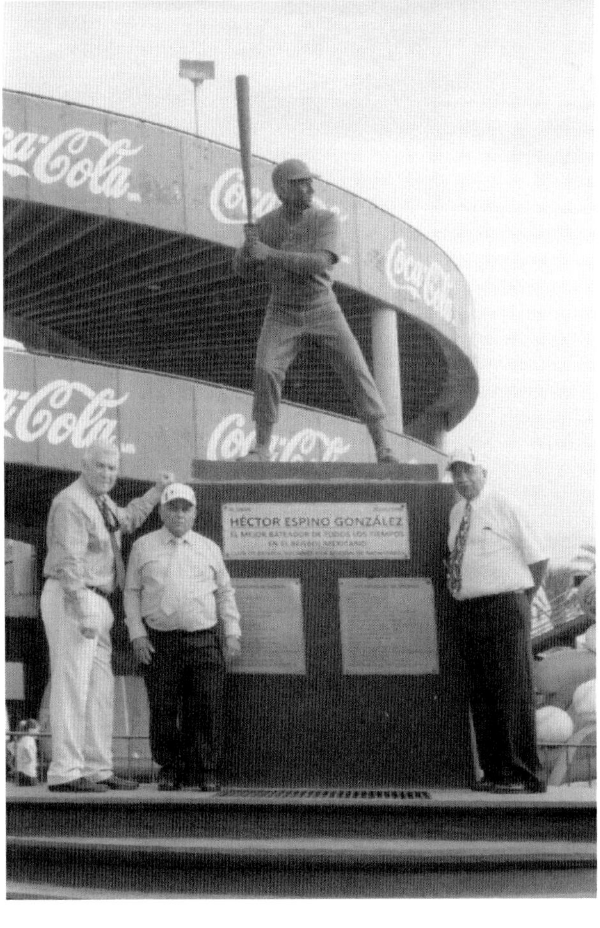

Pictured are the Cavazos brothers who were honored at a Leo Najo Hall of Fame induction ceremony. All seven brothers played ball at different levels. From left to right are (first row) Mateo, Francisco, and Héctor; (second row) Manuel, José Ángel, José Mario, and Faustino. (Courtesy of José Mario Cavazos.)

Bert Lozano (far left), who was honored at the Monterrey celebration, is seen here alongside the statue of legendary player Héctor Espino González. González, who is known as the "Babe Ruth of Mexico," often brought his Mexican teams to compete in South Texas. (Courtesy of Bert Lozano.)

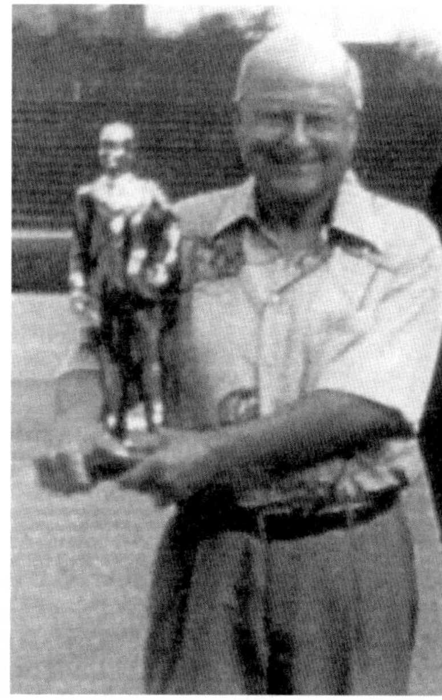

Nick Cantu from Edinburg, Texas, is the brother-in-law of Ramón Cantu. Ramón played semiprofessional baseball and umpired; Nick umpired high school, college, and semiprofessional ball. His son continued the family tradition by coaching the Edinburg North High School Cougars varsity baseball team. (Courtesy of Juan de la Rosa.)

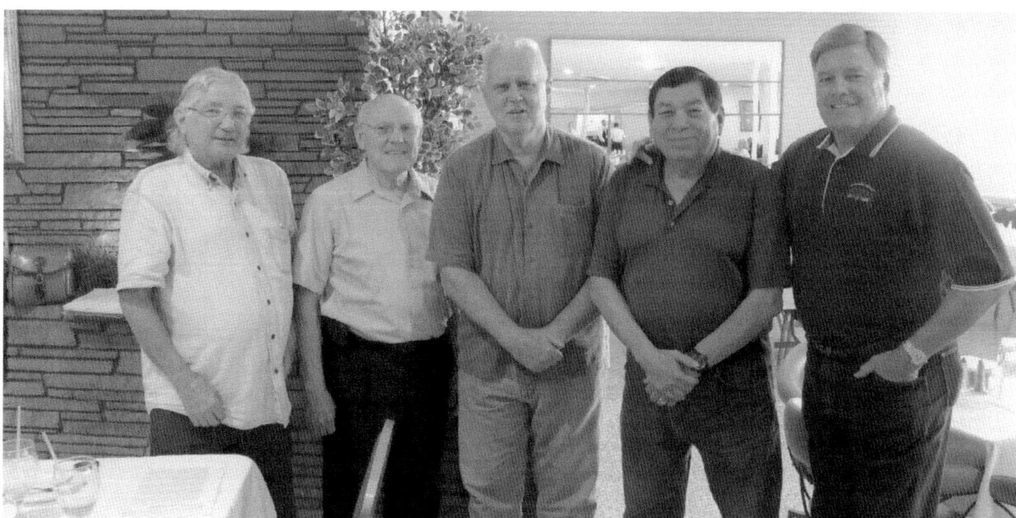

Seen here are the members of the Leo Najo Oldtimers Baseball Committee and the Rio Grande Sports Hall of Fame. From left to right are longtime sportswriter and member of both committees Pikey Rodríguez; Dr. Roberto Zamora, a member of the Leo Najo Oldtimers Baseball Committee; Jim Caldwell, the current treasurer for the Rio Grande Valley Sports Hall of Fame; Mo Molina, the current president of the Rio Grande Valley Sports Hall of Fame; and Charlie Vaughn, who has worked with the Rio Grande Valley Sports Hall of Fame in numerous capacities. After serving in Vietnam, Rodríguez dedicated his career to covering local sports and preserving the sports history of South Texas. Zamora was a member of the 1962 Hidalgo County Colt League world champions. Former collegiate football player Caldwell is the son of former Major League player Earl Caldwell. Molina is a longtime basketball coach. Vaughn pitched professionally for the Atlanta Braves. (Courtesy of Juan D. Coronado.)

LATINO BASEBALL HISTORY PROJECT ADVISORY BOARD

José M. Alamillo
Eduardo B. Almada T.
Richard Arroyo
Gabriel "Tito" Ávila Jr.
Francisco E. Balderrama
Tomas Benítez
Anna Bermúdez
Terry A. Cannon
Gene Chávez
Juan Conchola
David Contreras Jr.
Raúl J. Córdova
Juan D. Coronado
Christopher Docter
Peter Drier
Robert Elias
Luís F. Fernández
Maria García
Gregory Garrett
Jorge Iber
Rumaldo Z. Juárez
Bob Lagunas
Alfonso Ledesma
Enrique M. López
Jody L. López
Gabriel A. López
Susan C. Luévano
Amanda Magdalena
Rod Martínez
Douglas Monroy
Carlos Muñoz Jr.
Eddie Navarro
Victoria C. Norton
Mark A. Ocegueda
Alan O'Connor
Monica Ortez
Al Padilla
Richard Peña
Al Ramos
Samuel O. Regalado
Vicki L. Ruiz
Anthony Salazar
Richard A. Santillán
Teresa Santillán
Marcelino Saucedo
Ray P. Serra
Alicia S. Stevens
Joe Talaugon
Carlos Tortolero
Sandra L. Uribe
Alejo L. Vásquez
Angelina F. Veyna
David Vargas
Alfonso Villanueva Jr.
Roberto Zamora

BIBLIOGRAPHY

Alamillo, José. "Peloteros in Paradise: Mexican American Baseball and Oppositional Politics in Southern California, 1930–1950." *Western Historical Quarterly* 34.2, 191–212.

García, Gilberto. "Louis 'Count' Castro: The Story of a Forgotten Latino Major Leaguer." *Nine: A Journal of Baseball History and Culture* 16.2 (Spring 2008).

Iber, Jorge. *Mike Torrez: A Baseball Biography*. Jefferson, NC: McFarland Publishing, 2016.

———. "Introduction: Latinos/as and Sport in the American West." *Journal of the West* 54.4 (Fall 2015): 8–11.

———, ed. *More Than Just Peloteros: Sport and US Latino Communities*. Lubbock, TX: Texas Tech University Press, 2014.

———. "The Early Life and Career of Topeka's Mike Torrez, 1946–1978: Sport as a Means for Studying Latino/a Life in Kansas." *Kansas History: A Journal of the Central Plains* 37 (Fall 2014).

Marshall, Floyd Leslie. "History and Present Status of Latin American Education in Melvin, Texas." Master's thesis, Hardin-Simmons University, May 1950.

Regalado, Samuel O. *Viva Baseball: Latin Major Leaguers and Their Special Hunger*. Chicago, IL: University of Illinois Press, 1998.

———. "Dodgers Beisbol Is on the Air: The Development and Impact of the Dodgers' Spanish-Language Broadcasts, 1958–1994." *California History* 74.3 (Fall 1995): 280–289.

Santillán, Richard A., et al. *Mexican American Baseball in the Alamo Region*. Charleston, SC: Arcadia Publishing, 2015.

———, et al. *Mexican American Baseball in the San Fernando Valley*. Charleston, SC: Arcadia Publishing, 2015.

Torres, Noe. *Ghost Leagues: A History of Minor League Baseball in South Texas*. Coral Springs, FL: Lumina Press, 2015.

Winegardner, Mark. *The Vera Cruz Blues*. New York, NY: Penguin Books, 1996.

Discover Thousands of Local History Books Featuring Millions of Vintage Images

Arcadia Publishing, the leading local history publisher in the United States, is committed to making history accessible and meaningful through publishing books that celebrate and preserve the heritage of America's people and places.

Find more books like this at
www.arcadiapublishing.com

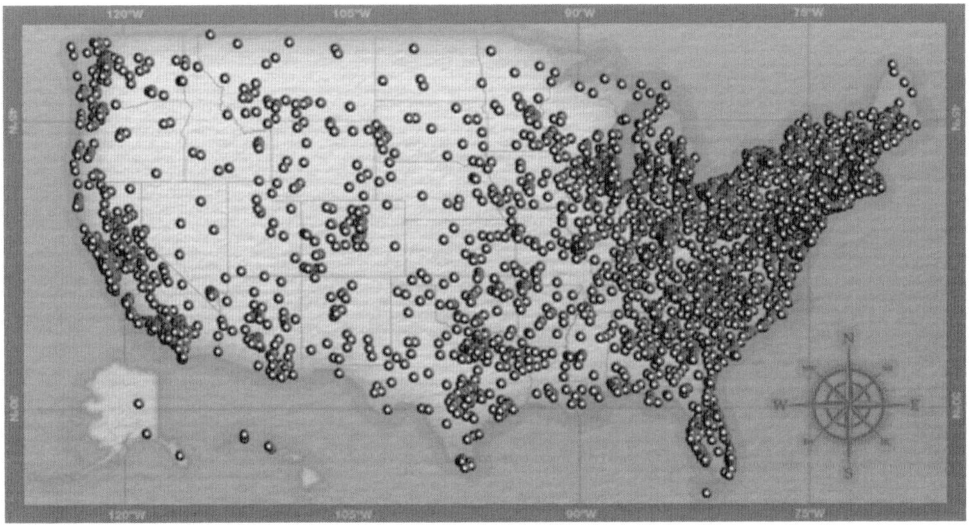

Search for your hometown history, your old stomping grounds, and even your favorite sports team.

Consistent with our mission to preserve history on a local level, this book was printed in South Carolina on American-made paper and manufactured entirely in the United States. Products carrying the accredited Forest Stewardship Council (FSC) label are printed on 100 percent FSC-certified paper.

MADE IN THE USA